Rituals and Magic to Celebrate the Reawakening Earth

IMBOLC

BY ROBIN GINTHER VENNERI

KIPS Publishing
Rochester, Pennsylvania

Imbolc: Rituals and Magic to Celebrate The Awakening Earth
© 2023 by Robin Ginther Venneri

Print ISBN 13: 979-8-218-12612-4
Second Edition, 2024
10 9 8 7 6 5 4 3 2
KIPS Publishing LLC
Rochester, PA
All rights reserved.
www.kipspublishingllc.com

LEGAL DISCLAIMER

We, KIPS Publishing, and the author, Robin Ginther-Venneri, are not herbal experts by any means and are not medical professionals. The products available, along with statements, opinions, views expressed, ideas, notes, procedures, and suggestions in this book, on the blog, on the website, in e-books, on Facebook, Pinterest, and Twitter pages, and any follow-up comments on-site or by email, are opinions and are meant for informational purposes only. They are not meant to be used to diagnose, treat, prescribe, prevent, or cure any disease or to administer in any manner to any physical ailments. They are not intended as a substitute for the medical advice of a trained health professional. We cannot be held liable for your decisions and choices and the outcome of those decisions and choices. You are encouraged to do your own research and consult your healthcare professional before treating yourself or anyone else.

The information in this book, on the blog, on the website, in e-books, on Facebook, Pinterest, and Twitter pages, and any follow-up comments on-site or by email are general and not specific to individuals and their circumstances. You must study herbs thoroughly and talk with a healthcare practitioner before you treat yourself or anyone else. I would like you to know that all matters regarding your health require medical supervision. Please consult your health care professional before adopting the statements, opinions, views expressed, ideas, notes, procedures, and suggestions in this book, on the website, in e-books, on Facebook, Pinterest, and Twitter pages, and any follow-up comments on-site or by email, as well as about any condition that may require diagnosis or medical attention.

Herbs are very powerful, and if they are misused, they can be harmful. Herbs can also cause allergic reactions and interfere with traditional medications by blocking their effectiveness, increasing their effectiveness, or reacting with them harmfully. Always check with your health care professional before using herbs or herbal products!

Do not use herbal products of any kind if you are nursing, pregnant, taking medications, or undergoing treatment for any medical condition without consulting your health care professional.

Any plant substance, whether used as food or medicine, externally or internally, can cause an allergic reaction in some people. Neither KIPS Publishing nor the author Robin Ginther-Venneri can be held responsible for claims arising from the mistaken identity of any herbs or the use of any remedy or healing regime or because you did not first seek the advice of a trained healthcare professional as recommended. Do not try self-diagnosis or self-treatment for serious or long-term problems without consulting a healthcare professional. Do not undertake self-treatment while undergoing a prescribed course of medical treatment without seeking professional advice. Always seek medical advice if symptoms persist.

We, KIPS Publishing, and Robin Ginther-Venneri disclaim any liability arising directly or indirectly from using this book, on the website, on the blog, in e-books, a class, class notes, follow-up email contacts, or of any products available or mentioned herein.

Additionally, the FDA has not evaluated the statements on the website, blog, e-books, Facebook, Pinterest, and/or Twitter pages, and any follow-up comments on these sites or by email. The information on this site is not intended to diagnose, treat, or cure any disease.

Thank you,
KIPS Publishing LLC

"As a human being, I understand that errors are a natural part of the learning process. These mistakes have taught me valuable lessons and have reminded me of the infinite knowledge that awaits us."

"As you read my work, I ask that you see it as a result of my hard work and imperfect nature. I am excited to share both the polished outcomes of my research and the raw, unrefined process that led to them. Together, we can appreciate the evolution of ideas and the remarkable journey of seeking knowledge."

With gratitude and humility,
Robin

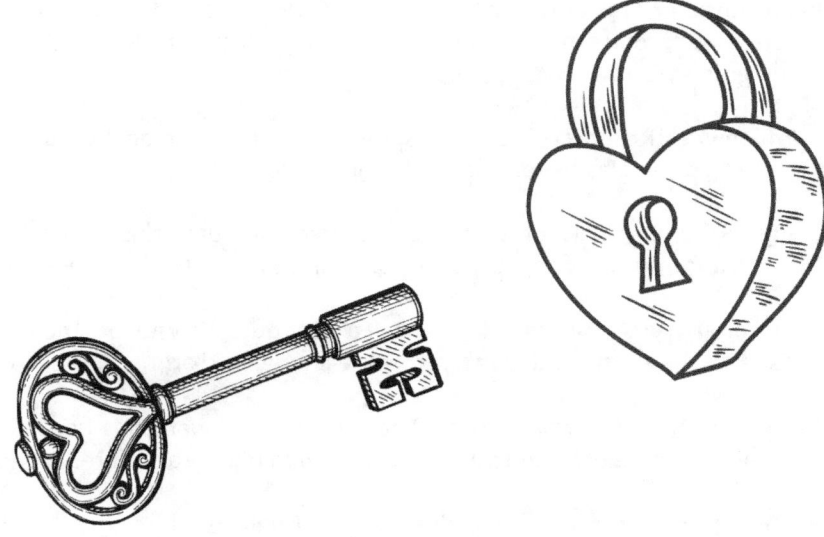

Book Blessing and Protection Spell

Supplies:
The book you wish to bless and protect
A small white candle
A sprig of Rosemary
Clear quartz crystal or amethyst (optional)
A quiet and sacred space

Preparation: Choose a time when you can be undisturbed and when you feel calm and focused. Place the book, the candle, the Rosemary, and any optional crystals on a clean and sacred surface.

Cleanse the Space: Light the white candle. As it flickers, visualize its flame clearing and purifying the energy around you. Pass the book and the Rosemary through the candle flame, visualizing any negative or stagnant energies being cleansed.

Invoke Divine Energy: Close your eyes and take a few deep breaths to center yourself.
If you work with specific deities, call upon them for blessings. Otherwise, you can invoke the universal energies of light, wisdom, and protection.

Blessing the Book: Hold the book in your hands and visualize a warm, golden light surrounding it.

Say aloud or in your mind: "By the light of this flame and the wisdom it contains,
I bless and protect this book and its knowledge to sustain. May it be a source of insight, growth, and grace, Guarded by the energies of this sacred space."

Infuse with Rosemary: Take the sprig of Rosemary and gently wave it over the book. Feel the protective energies of Rosemary infusing the book.

Say: "Rosemary, herb of wisdom and protection. Guard this book with your magical reflection. Shield it from harm, keep its pages pure, Infuse it with the knowledge that will endure."

Optional Crystal Blessing: If you have a clear quartz crystal or amethyst, hold it in your hands. Visualize the crystal radiating a protective energy field around the book.

Say: "Crystal clear, amplify this protective sphere, Guard this book, keep it ever dear. May its energies be enhanced and pure, Infusing it with magic to endure."

Closing: Thank the divine energies, deities, or universal forces you invoked. Blow out the candle, visualizing the protection lingering around the book.

Placement: Keep the book in a safe and sacred space. You may choose to keep the rosemary sprig with the book for continued protection.

Remember to perform this spell with respect, intention, and a focused mind. The energies you infuse into the book will contribute to its positive atmosphere and long-lasting protection.

Acknowledgments

Expressing Gratitude to Mentors,
I owe a great deal of thanks to my mentors for their invaluable wisdom and experience. Without them, I wouldn't have made it this far. It's hard to believe that it's already been a year since I began this journey – it's been quite a ride. Some might call it a spiritual awakening, but I think it's more of a reawakening. Regardless, I want to take a moment to express my love and gratitude to all those who have come into my life and helped me along the way. I couldn't have made it this far without you, and for that, I am forever grateful.

To my Hubby and Daughter,
My heart is overflowing with gratitude as I look back on our journey. Jeff, you're my knight in shining armor, always pushing me to strive for greatness. And Caitlan, your helping hand has given me the energy to tackle the day and make more time to make books. We did it together! This success is as much yours as it is mine. I'm the luckiest to have a family as amazing as you both.

Appreciating the hard work of My Editor,
I want to express my sincere gratitude to my editor, who diligently reviewed my notes and made this book the best it could be. Your dedication and expertise were crucial in bringing my vision to life. Any errors are solely mine.

Grateful Acknowledgment to My Friends
I want to express my gratitude to my friends for their unwavering support and friendship. Your encouragement has given me the strength to write these books and pursue my passion. Thank you!

To Lylah and Beau, my beloved grandchildren,

I am profoundly grateful to Lylah and Beau, my cherished grandchildren, whose joyous spirits and love have filled my life with warmth and inspiration. This book is dedicated to you as a token of appreciation for the happiness you bring and the boundless love that fuels my creativity. Thank you for being the brightest chapters in my story.

Love, Mimi

Map to Start Your Spiritual Journey

Get Organized

Start by making space
Make lists (shopping, to-do, bills, home repair, etc.)
Create a schedule
Create a budget
Organize your living space
Get rid of stuff (less stuff - less anxiety)

Self-Reflection

Know yourself, Ask yourself.
Who am I, really?
Am I living authentically?
Are my beliefs supporting my spiritual growth?
Am I spending my time wisely?

Be Still

Quiet your mind. Hear your soul.
Commit 15 min a day
to sitting in silence and solitude.
Allow your thoughts to pass w/out
judgment, bring your attention back to your breath, and slowly see your mind clear.

Grounding

Repeat after me:

I am firmly grounded in the Earth.

I am calm, strong, and centered, with a peaceful mind.

I deserve all the beauty in the world.

Cleansing Chant
I rid this sacred space of negative
thoughts, energies, and intentions.
Any negativity that resides here, I banish you away using the light
within me. I clear the path for positive thoughts, energies, and
intentions to enter in my sacred space. I only allow love and light
to enter here.

CHAPTER 1

Wheel of the
Year

The Wheel of the Year Explained

The Wheel of the Year, also known as the Wheel of Life, symbolizes the Earth's cycles and the cycle of life itself. Our ancestors used it to mark the turning of the seasons and years, for farmers to plan their work, and for modern pagans to reconnect with nature's rhythms.

The Wheel of the Year consists of eight holidays or festivals, also known as holy days. These festivals follow the cyclical calendar of the sun and moon and the natural world's rhythms. Four of them are solar festivals or lesser Sabbats, which are associated with the sun and God. The other four are season-change festivals, or Grand Sabbats, related to the Earth and Goddess.

The Wheel of the Year has two halves: a dark half marking Autumn/Winter and a light half marking Spring/Summer. Each half has two lesser Sabbats and two Grand Sabbats. The lesser Sabbats are Yule, the Winter Solstice; Ostara, the Spring Equinox; Litha, the Midsummer Solstice and Equinox; Litha, the Midsummer Solstice, and Mabon, the Autumn Equinox. The two annual equinox solstices are the solar festivals or lesser Sabbats. The equinoxes occur when we have a day and night of almost equal length because the sun is directly over the equator. The solstices occur when we have the shortest day (June) and the longest day (December), related to the Earth's tilt. The exact date varies each year by a few days due to the Earth's rotation around the sun in 365.25 days, while our calendar is set for 365 days. Hence, we have a leap year every four years to balance the calendar.

Wheel of the Year

Pagan Sabbats

A pagan sabbat is a seasonal festival celebrated by some pagan and Wiccan traditions. There are eight sabbats in a year, marking key points in the solar cycle. These include Samhain, Yule, Imbolc, Ostara, Beltane, Litha, Lammas, and Mabon. Each sabbat has its own significance, rituals, and traditions. For example, Samhain is often associated with honoring ancestors and the thinning of the veil between worlds, while Beltane is a celebration of fertility and the coming of summer. These festivals are a way for practitioners to connect with nature, celebrate the changing seasons, and honor spiritual beliefs.

Light and Dark

Sabbat Dates

Sabbat	Northern Hemisphere Date	Southern Hemisphere Date
Imbolc	February 1-2	August 1-2
Ostara	March 19-21	September 20-23
Beltane	May 1	October 31
Litha	June 20-22	December 20-23
Lammas	August 1-2	February 1-2
Mabon	September 21-24	March 20-22
Samhain	October 31	April 30
Yule	December 20-23	June 20-22

CHAPTER 2

Imbolc

Imbolc

Imbolc is a Celtic festival that marks the halfway point between the winter solstice and the spring equinox. The name "Imbolc" is derived from the Old Irish word "Imbolg," which means "in the belly." It is traditionally celebrated on February 1st or 2nd, representing the early signs of spring and the awakening of the Earth from its winter slumber.

Origins: Imbolc has ancient roots and is associated with the goddess Brigid, who was honored as a fire, poetry, and fertility deity. Brigid was a triple goddess, often depicted as three sisters, and she played a significant role in Celtic mythology. Imbolc is thought to have originated as a pagan festival in honor of Brigid, and later, it was incorporated into the Christian calendar as the feast day of St. Brigid.

Ancient Celtic Origins: Imbolc has ancient roots in Celtic mythology and the agricultural calendar. It was a time to celebrate the goddess Brigid, associated with fertility, healing, poetry, and craftsmanship.

Celebration: Imbolc is a time to celebrate the increasing daylight, the first signs of spring, and the promise of new life. Traditionally, people would gather to perform rituals, light bonfires, and make offerings to Brigid. The lighting of candles and fires symbolizes the returning warmth and the increasing power of the sun.

One of the central customs associated with Imbolc is the weaving of Brigid's crosses, which are typically made from rushes or straw. These crosses are believed to protect homes from harm and evil spirits. Another common tradition is the creation of Brigid's Bed, where a small bed is made for Brigid and adorned with flowers and greenery as a symbol of fertility.

Christian Influence: With the spread of Christianity, many pagan festivals were adapted into the Christian calendar to facilitate the conversion of the Celtic peoples. Imbolc became associated with the feast day of St. Brigid, who, like the pagan goddess, was associated with healing and fertility. St. Brigid became one of the most venerated saints in Ireland.

Modern Celebrations: In contemporary times, Imbolc is still celebrated by modern pagans and practitioners of Wicca. Many ancient traditions, such as candle lighting, bonfires, and the weaving of Brigid's crosses, are still observed. Some people also use this time for introspection, setting intentions for the coming year, and welcoming the renewal of life.

Imbolc bridges the gap between winter and spring, symbolizing hope, new beginnings, and the eternal life cycle. While its origins are rooted in ancient Celtic traditions, its spirit endures in various forms in the celebrations of diverse communities worldwide.

Goddess Brigid: Brigid was a triple goddess, embodying three aspects: Brigid the healer, Brigid the poet, and Brigid the smith. She was revered as a guardian of the hearth and home and was considered a powerful and benevolent deity.

Goddess of Healing. Brighid is renowned for her healing abilities. Springs and wells dedicated to her were believed to possess transformative and curative powers. Pilgrims would visit these sacred sites seeking physical healing, and Brighid's presence was invoked in healing rituals.

Goddess of Poetry and Inspiration:

Brighid is also associated with the arts, particularly poetry and inspiration. Bards and poets would seek her blessings for eloquence and creativity. Her connection to the spoken and written word highlights her role in fostering intellectual and artistic endeavors.

Goddess of Smithcraft:

As a goddess of Smithcraft, Brighid is linked to the transformative power of fire. Smiths and craftsmen would invoke her before forging tools and weapons. As a symbol of creation through fire, the forge became a sacred space dedicated to Brighid's influence.

Goddess of Fertility and the Hearth

Brighid's association with fertility is reflected in traditions like the Brideog dolls crafted during Imbolc. These dolls, placed in special beds, symbolize the fertile aspects of the goddess. As a hearth goddess, Brighid is honored in the heart of the home, and her presence ensures warmth, protection, and sustenance.

Brighid's significance transcends ancient Celtic mythology; she has endured through the centuries, adapting to different cultural and religious contexts. In the Christian era, St. Brigid of Kildare became associated with the earlier pagan goddess, a testament to the enduring spiritual importance of this revered figure. Whether venerated as a goddess or a saint, Brighid continues to inspire those seeking healing, creativity, and the nurturing forces of the divine.

Agricultural Significance:

Imbolc was a period of preparation for the upcoming agricultural season. Seeds and tools were blessed, and the focus was on seeking the goddess's blessings for a fruitful year.
Dairy-based foods, such as butter and cheese were central to feasting, symbolizing the lactating ewes and the return of fertility.

In modern times, Imbolc celebrations often reflect a blend of pagan and contemporary spirituality, accommodating diverse beliefs and practices.

Neo-Pagan and Wiccan Practices:
Many contemporary celebrations maintain traditional elements, such as crafting Brighid's crosses, lighting candles, and honoring the goddess in rituals. Altars may be adorned with symbols of Brighid, candles, and seasonal items, creating a sacred space for reflection and connection.

Personalized and Inclusive Celebrations:
Imbolc is now celebrated by people of various spiritual paths, including those who identify as Neo-Pagan, Wiccan, and even those with Christian or eclectic beliefs. Modern celebrations may include individual or community activities like candle-making, planting seeds, or engaging in creative pursuits to honor the themes of renewal and growth.

Adaptation to Urban Lifestyles:
In contemporary settings, where many may not have access to open fires or agricultural practices, celebrations are adapted to urban lifestyles, emphasizing the symbolic aspects and spiritual connections.

While the core themes of Imbolc remain consistent – renewal, purification, and the anticipation of spring – the expressions of these celebrations have evolved, incorporating a diverse range of practices that resonate with individuals in the present day.

Cross-Quarter Day: Imbolc is one of the four Gaelic seasonal festivals considered "cross-quarter days," falling between solstices and equinoxes. It is positioned between the winter solstice and the spring equinox.

Fire and Light Rituals: Imbolc was traditionally associated with fire and light. Bonfires were lit as a symbol of the increasing power of the sun and to welcome the returning warmth. Candles were also important in rituals, symbolizing the growing light.

Brigid's Mantle: A common tradition during Imbolc involved creating a "Brigid's Mantle" or "Brat Bríde." This was a piece of cloth left outside overnight for Brigid to bless. The fabric was believed to have healing properties and could be used for protection.

Purification and Cleansing: Imbolc was a time for purification and cleansing. Homes were cleaned, and rituals were performed to invite positivity and fertility for the coming season.

Seasonal Transition: Imbolc marked the transition from the dormancy of winter to the awakening of spring. It was a time to celebrate the first signs of life in the natural world, such as snowdrops' emergence and ewes' lactation.

Christian Adaptation: With the spread of Christianity, Imbolc was adapted into the feast of St. Brigid, the Christianized version of the goddess Brigid—the date of St. Brigid's feast day is February 1st, aligning with the traditional timing of Imbolc.

Modern Celebrations: In contemporary times, Imbolc is still celebrated by modern pagan and Wiccan communities, often incorporating traditional rituals, feasts, and symbolism associated with the season.

Cultural and Regional Variations: Imbolc traditions may vary across regions and communities, but the central theme of celebrating the shift from winter to spring and honoring the goddess Brigid persists.

Imbolc continues to be observed by various communities today, often focusing on connecting with nature, expressing gratitude for the changing seasons, and celebrating light, fertility, and renewal themes.

CHAPTER 3

Imbolc at a
Glance

Imbolc at a Glance

Imbolc - February 2nd
Pronounced: Imbolc or Imbolg (Irish pronunciation: [ɪˈmˠɔlˠg]), also called Saint Brigid's Day (Irish: Lá Fhéile Bríde; Scottish Gaelic: Là Fhèill Brìghde; Manx: Laa'l Breeshey), is a traditional Gaelic festival. It marks the beginning of spring; for Christians, it is the feast day of Saint Brigid, Ireland's patron saint. It is held on February 1st, about halfway between the winter solstice and the spring equinox. Historically, its traditions were widely observed throughout Ireland, Scotland, and the Isle of Man. It is one of the four Gaelic seasonal festivals, along with Bealtaine, Lughnasadh, and Samhain.

As we emerge from the dark winter months, it's time to start making plans for the spring. This is a time to connect with our animal guides and ask for their help in removing any obstacles standing in the way of our lives blossoming. Let's clear out any negative energy that's no longer serving our highest good and make room for all the fantastic possibilities coming our way.

See Also: Mid-Winter, Goddess Brigid, Feast of Saint Brigid, Feast of Saint Mary, Candlemas, Little Candlemas, The Dionysia, The Festival of Saint Trifon, Lupercalia, Cross Quarter Days, Juno Februa, The Festival of Juno Sospita, The Feralia, Parentalia, Oya, Saint Agatha, The Feast Day of Saint Agatha, Anthestheria, Lunar New Year, Groundhog Day, Fat Tuesday, Ash Wednesday, Mardi Gras, Valentine's Day, Presidents Day, Leap Day, and National Time Refund Day.

There is no right or wrong way to celebrate any of the Sabbats. Pagans base their celebrations on cultural traditions, historical practices, and inclinations.

So live and let live!

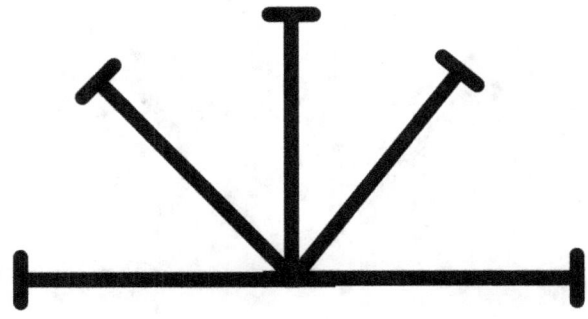

Quicky Imbolc Correspondences

Heroes, Deities and Goddesses
Brigid (Trish)
Aphrodite/Venus (Greco-Roman)
Diana (Etruscan/Roman)
Arianrhod (Welsh)
Artio (Swiss)
Athena (Greek)
Danu (Irish)
Gaia (Greek)
Inanna (Sumerian, Babylonian, Assyrian)
Juno (Roman)
Selene (Greek)
Vesta (Roman)
Selu (Cherokee)

Gods
Februus (Roman)
Bragi (Norse)
Cupid (Roman)
Dian Cecht (Irish)
Dumuzi (Sumarian)
Eros (Greek)

Archaeoastronomical Timing
The astronomical midpoint between the Winter Solstice and the Vernal Equinox; the Sun at 15° of Aquarius in the Northern Hemisphere, Sun at 15° of Leo in the Southern Hemisphere; some Pagans celebrate Imbolc on the astronomical date, while others stick to February 2nd out of tradition.

Archetypes
FEMALE
The Goddess transforming from Crone to Maiden; the Goddess in the form of young mother tending to her growing child.

MALE
God in the form of a child exploring the world; the innocence of the masculine.

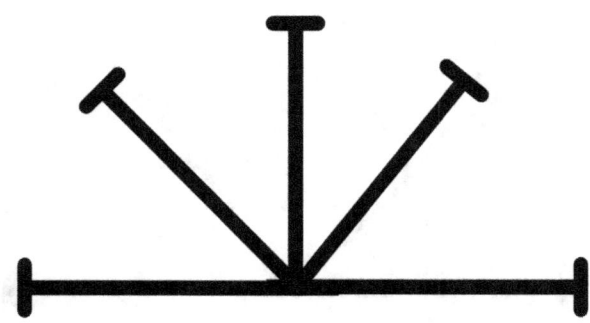

Flowers
Crocus and daffodil

Trees
Blackthorn, cedar, rowan, and sycamore

Crystals
Amethyst and turquoise

Metals
Antimony, brass, and gold

Incense
Cedar, peppermint, styrax, basil and cinnamon

Herbs
Angelica, basil, blackberry/ bramble, cinnamon, grain, reed, and wormwood

Animals, Totems, and Mythical Creatures
Cow, dragon, groundhog, lark, robin, sheep, snake and swan

Symbols and Tools
Brid's Cross/ Brigid's Cross, corn dollies, Brid's bed, candles, Saint Brighid, Saint Mary, the cauldron, broom/besom, and whistle

Food
Dried fruits, grains, potatoes, cornmeal, dried/salted meats, cheese, pickled or canned foods, nuts, and eggs

Drinks
All dairy products, ale, mead, and cider

Colors
Light green, pink, white, and yellow

Activities and Traditions of Practice
Making a corn dolly or Brigid's Cross, candle making and/ or blessing, making fortune cookies, dedicating new magical tools, blessing animals, blessing new projects, divination, and fireworks.

Acts of Service
Clear snow /ice from public walkways, gather blankets for the needy, clear and prepare a community garden or flower bed for planting, clean the home of a physically limited person

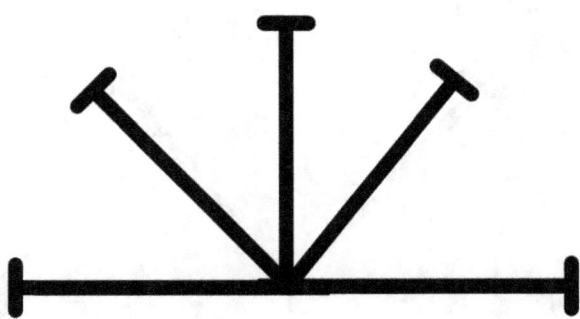

Alternate Names for Imbolc in Other Pagan Traditions

Imbolc or Imbolg (Gaelic for "in the belly,"
referring to the ewes' first milk of the year) Oimelc (Saxon for "ewe's milk")
Feast of Brighid Lá Fhéile Bríde (Irish)
Laa'l Breeshey (Manx)
Feast of Mary of the Candles (Welsh)

Holidays or Traditions Occurring During Imbolc in the Northern Hemisphere:

RELIGIOUS

Feast Day of Saint Brigit of Kildare (Catholic, February 1st)
Presentation of Jesus at the Temple or Candlemas (Christian, February 2nd, also called "Feast of the Purification of the Virgin " and "The Meeting of the Lord") The Feast of St. Valentine (February 14th)
Lupercalia/Pan's Day (February 15th)
Milk/Nursing Moon (varies but usually during Imbolc)
Pre-Lenten festivals and the start of Lent (Catholic, moveable dates; between February 4th and March 10th)
Parinirvana/Nirvana Day (Mahayana Buddhist, February 8th or February 15th)

SECULAR

Groundhog Day (February 2nd)
Valentine's Day (February 14th)
Chinese New Year (varies)
Mardi Gras (varies)

Holidays or Traditions Occurring During Imbolc in the Southern Hemisphere:

RELIGIOUS

Festival of the Dryads (Grecian, August 1st-3rd)
Nemoralia (Roman, August 13th-15th)
Tisha B'Av (Jewish, July or August, variable dates according to the lunar calendar)
Assumption Day (Christian, August 15th)

SECULAR

Picnic Day (Australia's Northern Territory, first Monday of August)
National Women's Day (South Africa, August 9th)
Various independence days in South America (July 9th, Argentina; July 28th, Peru; August 6th, Bolivia; August 10th, Ecuador; Aug. 25th, Uruguay)
Birth of Simon Bolivar, liberator of Venezuela, Colombia, Ecuador, Peru, and Bolivia(July 24th)
Heroes' Day (various African countries, July/ August)
Farmers Day (various African countries, July / August)

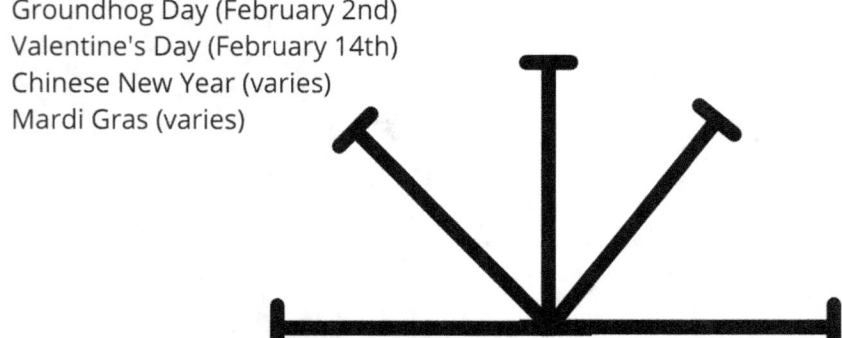

Celebration Ideas

Candle Lighting: Lighting candles is a central theme in Imbolc celebrations, symbolizing the increasing light and the returning warmth of the sun. Some practitioners may light candles in every room of their homes or create a central altar with candles representing the four directions.

Bonfires: The tradition of lighting bonfires harks back to the ancient practice of lighting fires in honor of the returning sun. Bonfires may be lit in modern celebrations, and people gather around them for ritual, reflection, and socializing.

Rituals and Ceremonies: Imbolc rituals often involve invocations to the goddess Brigid, acknowledging her various aspects—goddess of fire, poetry, healing, and fertility. These rituals may include prayers, meditations, and activities that honor the symbolism of the season.

Crafting: Creating crafts associated with Imbolc is a common practice. This may include making Brigid's crosses, which are woven from straw or rushes and symbolize protection and blessings for the home. Other crafts may consist of creating a Brigid's Bed or crafting candles.

Feasting: Sharing a meal with family and friends is a way to celebrate community and the season's blessings. Traditional foods associated with Imbolc include dairy products (as this is a time when ewes begin to lactate), grains, and early spring vegetables.

Planting Seeds: Imbolc is a time associated with the first signs of spring, and some individuals celebrate by planting seeds or bulbs as a symbolic act of welcoming new growth and fertility.

Spring Cleaning: Many people use Imbolc as a time for symbolic or literal spring cleaning, clearing away the old to make space for the new. This can extend to both physical spaces and emotional or spiritual aspects of one's life.

Divination: Some practitioners engage in divination or seek guidance for the coming year during Imbolc. This can involve various methods such as tarot readings, scrying, or other forms of divination.

It's important to note that Imbolc is a flexible and personal celebration, and individuals or groups may incorporate different elements based on their own spiritual beliefs and practices. As with many pagan and Wiccan festivals, the emphasis is often on connection with nature, the changing seasons, and life cycles.

CHAPTER 4

Imbolc
Activities

Imbolc Activities

Get some winter blooms for your home.
You can add Imbolc touches to your altar.
Write a journal entry about what.
Imbolc means to you.
Craft an abundance jar.
Plan your spring garden.
Craft a St. Brigid's Cross.
Prepare a special Imbolc meal.
Do an Imbolc Oracle or Tarot card reading.
Light a candle to welcome back the light.
Bake seed cakes.
Wake with the sun.
Perform a sunrise meditation.
Burn incense of Vanilla, Lavender, or Basil.
Perform a house blessing.
Craft a simmer pot for hope.
Start your spring cleaning.
Craft a St. Brigid's doll.
Enjoy an Imbolc tea blend.
Honor Goddess Brigid.
Practice fire scrying.
Craft an Imbolc oil or herb blend.
Make blackberry jam.
Perform a cleansing ritual bath.
Give an offering to Brigid.
Write out 3 affirmations that you will focus on this month.
Bake fresh bread.
Mix up an energy-boosting magical mist.
Craft an intention-setting jar.
Perform a releasing ritual.
Write out an Imbolc blessing of your own.
Take a walk outside and appreciate the fresh, crisp air.
Perform a sunrise ritual.
Cleanse and charge your crystals.
Purge what no longer serves you.
Give thanks and leave out an offering to the earth.

Spring Cleansing

I like to cleanse and bless my home each spring .
Embrace the Season by Blessing Your Home and Honoring the Goddess Brigid
Imbolc, a Gaelic festival that celebrates the goddess Brigid and marks the start of spring, is a great time to bless your home and invite positive energy into your space. Here are some ways to get started: Smudge your home with sage, cedar, or sweetgrass for cleansing and protection. Offer a prayer or affirmation to Brigid for added protection.
Set up a small altar with candles and images of Brigid to welcome her energy into your home. Light the candles on Imbolc to honor the goddess.
Create a physical representation of your intention for the season. Consider making a charm bag filled with dried herbs, crystals, and symbols associated with Brigid or a small goddess sculpture. Place your creation on your altar and set an intention for the year.
Fill your home with symbols of prosperity, fertility, and abundance, such as a bowl of fruit or a corn dolly. Create a spell or blessing to ask Brigid to bring those things into your home.
Show gratitude to Brigid and the season by offering foods associated with Imbolc, like apples, honey, and dairy products. Share the food and drink with your loved ones as an offering to the goddess.
These are just a few ideas for blessing your home on Imbolc and welcoming Brigid. Remember to stay mindful and intentional as you honor this special time of year.

A Home Blessing for Imbolc
Imbolc is an ancient Celtic celebration to welcome spring's arrival and the land's awakening from its wintry slumber. It is customary to bless the home and all those who reside in it on this day.
May this home be a place of tranquility and bliss, where all inhabitants are secure, well, and content. May love and laughter fill the walls, and may the doors always welcome friendship and hospitality.
May this home be a place of knowledge and enlightenment where everyone can achieve their greatest potential. May everyone be able to express their creativity and develop their skills.
May this home be a place of spiritual harmony where all can find inspiration in the divine. May the house be a haven of warmth and comfort, illuminated by the light of compassion and understanding.
May this home be gifted with abundance, health, and success. May the love and joy within it be shared and spread worldwide.
May blessings be bestowed upon this home and everyone who dwells in it. So mote it be.

CHAPTER 5

Imbolc
Tidbits

Imbolc Tidbits

Imbolc is the day the Cailleach gathers her firewood for the rest of the winter. Legend has it that if she intends to make the winter last a good while longer, she will make sure the weather in Imbolc is bright and sunny so she can gather plenty of firewood to keep herself warm in the coming months. As a result, people are generally relieved if it is a day of foul weather, as it means the Cailleach is asleep, she will soon run out of firewood, and therefore winter is almost over.

Imbolc Incense
6 parts Frankincense
4 parts Dragon's Blood
2 parts Red Sandaterood
I part Cinnamon

Imbolc Essential Oils
8 drops Frankincense
6 Srops Rosemary
2 drops Cinnamon
1/2 cup Base Oil

Out With The Old To Make Room For The New

As the dawn of Imbolc approaches, let the warmth of the flame light your way. May it ignite your inner fire, fill your heart with hope, and deepen your faith.

Imbolc Cleansing Spray
Rosemary is Used for protection against evil spirits, clearing negative energy, and cleansing.
Lemon Essential Oil is used for clarity, purification, and aura
Thyme is used to dispel melancholy, hopelessness, and negative vibrations, used in spring festivals to leave the old behind and bring in the new
Cinnamon is used for purification, great for prosperity, and cleansing, rejuvenating, uplifting, represents the Sun
Water Distilled is best, universal, acts as a binder to bring everything together, and represents Brigid's Well
Clear Quartz amplifies
Citrine invites prosperity and good vibrations

Imbolc Simmer Pot
Lemon for love, purification, longevity, and friendship
Lavender for calm and peace
Chamomile happiness, peace, protection, purification
Rosemary protection
Vanilla for healing, love, protection, and purification

Imbolc Mini Altar

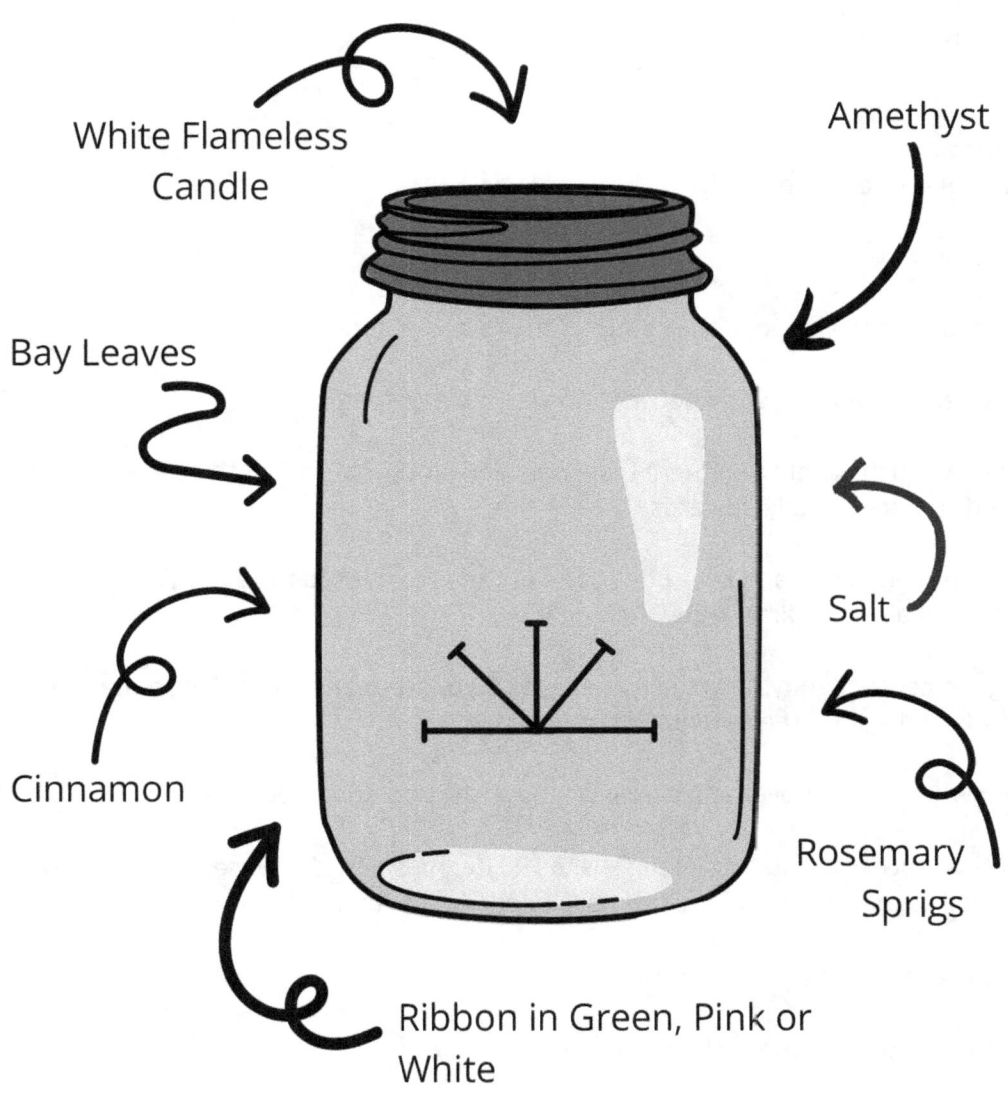

White Flameless Candle

Amethyst

Bay Leaves

Salt

Cinnamon

Rosemary Sprigs

Ribbon in Green, Pink or White

DIY Brigid Cross

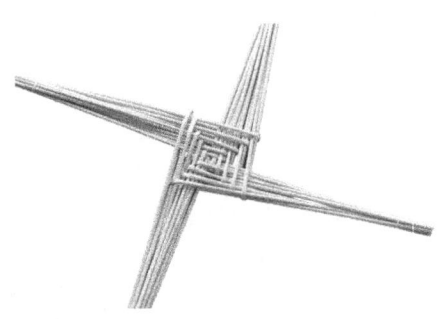

Ingredients:
16 reeds (or straws)
4 small rubber bands
Scissors

Directions:
Hold one of the reeds vertically.

Fold a second reed in half.

Place the first vertical reed in the center of the folded second reed.

Hold the center overlap tightly between the thumb and forefinger.

Turn the two rushes held together 90 degrees anti-clockwise so that the second reed's open ends point vertically upwards.

Fold a third reed in half and over both parts of the second reed to lie horizontally from left to right against the first straw. Hold tight.

Holding the center tightly, turn the three reeds 90 degrees anti-clockwise so that the open ends of the third reed are pointing upwards.

Fold a new reed in half over and across all the rushes pointing upwards.

Repeat the process of rotating all the rushes 90 degrees anti-clockwise, adding a new folded reed each time until all rushes have been used to make the cross.

Secure the arms of the cross with elastic bands.

Trim the ends to make them all the same length.

DIY Brideog

Ingredients:
Raffia (paper ribbon) or burlap ribbon
A cork
Feathers
Lace ribbon

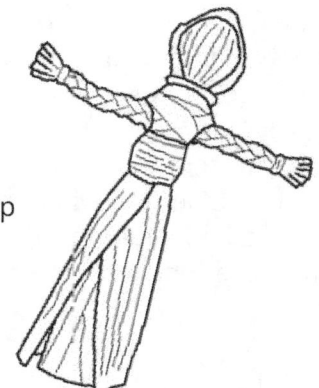

Directions:
Add a line of hot glue along one side of your cork. Wrap your raffia or ribbon around the cork until it is fully covered.

Use a small book to wrap your raffia or burlap ribbon around it several times.

Pull the ribbon off of the book and cut the bottom loops.

Find the middle of the ribbon (where your top loops still are) and glue it to the top of your cork.

An additional strand of ribbon is wrapped underneath the cork until space is no longer visible.

With six stands of ribbon about six inches long, tape down the top of the strands with a space between each two (creating three strands). Braid the three strands together. Add hot glue to the ends, and once done, try to trim them down.

Creating a teardrop shape, glue the two ends of the "arms" together at the top. Glue to the back of the doll and add an embellishment to the "hands" if you'd like!

Fan out your choice of feathers and either glue or tie them onto your doll.

Cut ribbon and glue around the "skirt" of your doll. Change up the lengths and textures to make her unique!

Never Forget a Petition Again

Have you ever had a great idea for a petition but forgotten about it when the timing was right? Try this easy trick: place a bowl, dish, or basket with some notecards nearby. When you think of a request, jot it down and put it in the container. When the "perfect" time arises, you won't have to rely on your memory to remember what to do.

Corn Dolly

Brigid's Corn Husk Dolls: A Celebration of the Arrival of Springtime

Corn dollies have been a part of springtime celebrations for centuries. These handcrafted figures, made of corn husks or straw, mark the end of winter and the rebirth of the land. Traditionally, they were created around the time of Imbolc, a pagan festival that celebrates the first signs of spring.

The history of corn dollies dates back to ancient times when people saw the changing seasons as a time of spiritual renewal and rebirth. Small bundles of harvested corn were shaped into figures and animals to represent the cycle of life. These corn dollies were then used in festivals and religious ceremonies associated with changing the season.

The symbolism of corn dollies has deep roots in folklore, with each region having its own unique meaning. Some cultures believed corn dollies represented goddesses, while others believed they brought good luck or warded off evil spirits. In some regions, corn dollies were even thought to bring fertility to the land.

Today, corn dollies are still used to celebrate the arrival of springtime, but the focus has shifted from a spiritual tradition to a more decorative one. People create colorful corn dollies to decorate their homes and gardens during Imbolc and help mark the season's change.

Creating a corn dolly is a simple and rewarding craft project. All you need is some dried corn husks or straw, tools, and imagination. You can shape the husks or straw into an animal, person, or symbol of your choice. Then, add ribbon, fabric, beads, or other decorations to make it more personal.

Corn dollies serve as a great reminder of the cycle of life and the power of nature.

CHAPTER 6

Recipes
for
Imbolc

Traditional Mardi Gras King Cake

Ingredients
For the Dough:
1 cup of warm milk (110°F/43°C)
2 packages of (1/4 ounce each) active dry yeast
1/2 cup of granulated sugar
4 cups of all-purpose flour
1 teaspoon of salt
1/2 teaspoon of ground nutmeg
1/2 cup of melted butter
5 large egg yolks

For the Filling:
1/2 cup of softened butter
1 cup of packed brown sugar
2 1/2 teaspoons of ground cinnamon

For the Icing:
2 cups of powdered sugar
2 to 3 tablespoons of milk
1/2 teaspoon of vanilla extract
Purple, green, and gold-colored sugars (for decoration)

Directions
Prepare the Dough:
Combine warm milk, yeast, and a pinch of sugar in a bowl. Let it sit for about 5 minutes until it becomes frothy.
Combine flour, remaining sugar, salt, and nutmeg in a large mixing bowl.
Make a well in the center and pour the yeast mixture, melted butter, and egg yolks.
Mix until a dough forms. Knead the dough on a floured surface until smooth and elastic.
Place the dough in a greased bowl, cover it with a clean cloth, and let it rise in a warm place for about 1 to 1.5 hours or until it doubles in size.

Prepare the Filling:
Mix the softened butter, brown sugar, and ground cinnamon in a bowl until well combined.

Assemble the King Cake:
Punch down the risen dough and roll it out into a rectangle.
Spread the filling evenly over the dough, leaving a border around the edges.
Roll up the dough from the long side to form a log.
Shape the log into a ring, sealing the edges.
Place the ring on a baking sheet lined with parchment paper.

Second Rise
Cover the ring with a cloth and let it rise for another 30-45 minutes.

Bake:
Preheat the oven to 350°F (175°C).
Bake the King Cake for 25-30 minutes or until golden brown.
Allow the cake to cool completely.

Prepare the Icing:
Mix powdered sugar, milk, and vanilla extract in a bowl to make a smooth icing. Adjust the consistency with more milk if needed.

Decorate:
Once the cake is cool, drizzle the icing over the top.
Sprinkle colored sugars in alternating sections of purple, green, and gold.

Enjoy:
Slice and enjoy your homemade King Cake! Remember to hide a small plastic baby or figurine in the cake before serving.

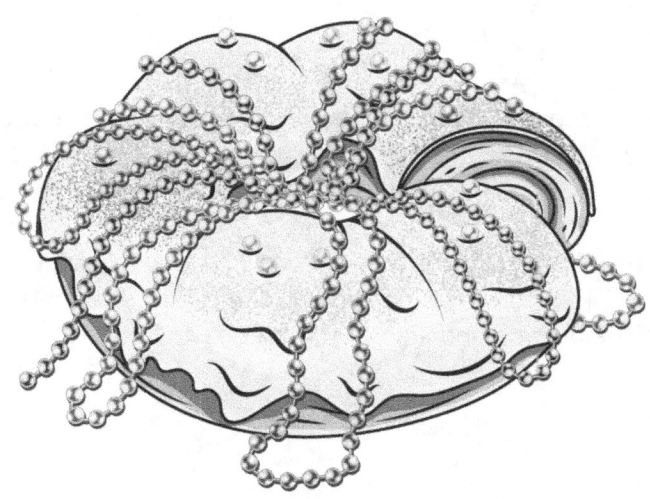

Pavlova

Pavlova is a popular dessert with New Zealand and Australian origins. It consists of a crisp meringue shell with a soft, marshmallow-like interior, typically topped with whipped cream and fresh fruits.

Ingredients
For the Pavlova:
4 large egg whites at room temperature
1 cup of granulated sugar
1 teaspoon of white vinegar or lemon juice
1 teaspoon of cornstarch (cornflour)
1 teaspoon of vanilla extract

For Topping:
1 cup of whipped cream
Fresh fruits (such as berries, kiwi, passion fruit, etc.)

Directions:
Preheat the Oven
Preheat your oven to 300°F (150°C). Line a baking sheet with parchment paper.

Prepare the Meringue
In a clean, dry bowl, beat the egg whites with an electric mixer until soft peaks form. Gradually add the sugar, one tablespoon at a time, while continuing to beat until the meringue is glossy and stiff peaks form.
Sprinkle in the vinegar or lemon juice, cornstarch, and vanilla extract. Gently fold them into the meringue.

Shape the Pavlova:
Spoon the meringue onto the prepared baking sheet, forming a round mound. You can shape it with a slight indentation in the center.

Bake
Place the baking sheet in the preheated oven and immediately reduce the temperature to 250°F (120°C). Bake for about 1 hour and 15 minutes or until the pavlova is crisp on the outside and soft on the inside.

Cool
Allow the pavlova to cool completely on the baking sheet.

Assemble

Once cooled, transfer the pavlova to a serving plate.
Whip the cream until it forms soft peaks and spread it over the pavlova.
Top with fresh fruits of your choice.

Serve

Slice and serve your pavlova immediately.

IYKYK

Pavlova is a delightful and visually appealing dessert, perfect for special occasions or whenever you crave a sweet treat.

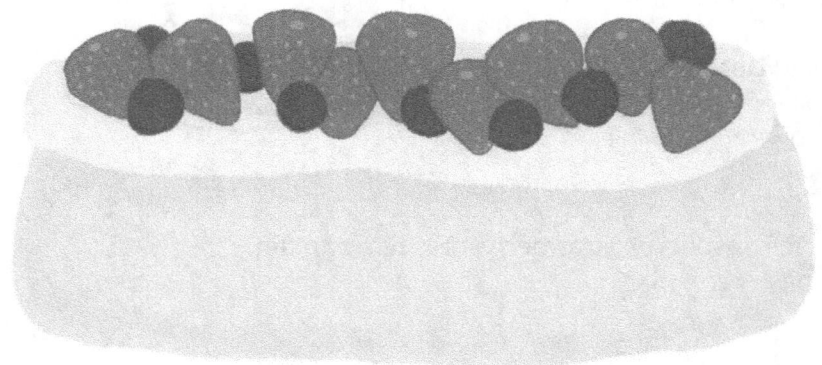

Paczki

Pączki (pronounced "ponch-key") are Polish doughnuts traditionally enjoyed on Fat Thursday, the last Thursday before Lent. These delightful pastries are filled with various sweet fillings and then deep-fried to perfection.

Ingredients
For the Dough:
4 cups of all-purpose flour
1/2 cup of granulated sugar
1 packet of (2 1/4 teaspoons) active dry yeast
1 cup of whole milk, lukewarm
4 large egg yolks
1/2 cup of unsalted butter, softened
1 teaspoon of vanilla extract
1/2 teaspoon of salt
Zest of 1 lemon or orange

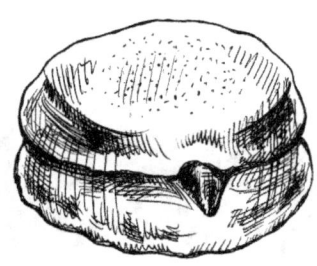

For Frying and Dusting:
Vegetable oil for frying
Powdered sugar for dusting

For Filling:
Fruit preserves (raspberry, strawberry, rose hip, or plum)
Custard or pastry cream

Directions
Prepare the Dough:
Combine the lukewarm milk and a pinch of sugar in a small bowl. Sprinkle the yeast over the milk, stir gently, and let it sit for about 5-10 minutes until it becomes frothy.
Combine the flour, sugar, salt, and citrus zest in a large mixing bowl.
Add the yeast mixture, egg yolks, softened butter, and vanilla extract to the dry ingredients. Mix until a dough forms.
Knead the dough on a floured surface for about 5-8 minutes until it becomes smooth and elastic.

Place the dough in a greased bowl, cover it with a clean kitchen towel, and let it rise in a warm place for about 1-2 hours or until it doubles in size.

Shape and Fry the Pączki:

Punch down the risen dough and roll it out on a floured surface to about 1/2 inch thickness.

Use a round cutter or glass to cut out circles from the dough.

Place the dough circles on a baking sheet lined with parchment paper, cover them with a kitchen towel, and let them rise for another 30 minutes.

Heat the vegetable oil in a deep fryer or a heavy pot to 350°F (175°C).

Carefully place a few dough circles into the hot oil and fry until golden brown on both sides (about 2-3 minutes per side).

Remove the fried Pączki and drain them on paper towels.

Fill and Dust:

Once the Pączki is cool enough to handle, use a pastry bag or injector to fill them with your choice of fruit preserves or custard.

Dust the filled Pączki with powdered sugar.

Serve and enjoy!

Pączki are best when fresh, so try to enjoy them on the day they are made. They are a delightful treat perfect for celebrating special occasions or enjoying coffee.

Brighid's Bannocks

Ingredients:
1 cup of oats
1 cup of whole wheat flour
1/2 teaspoon of baking soda
1/2 teaspoon of salt
1 tablespoon of honey
1 cup of buttermilk

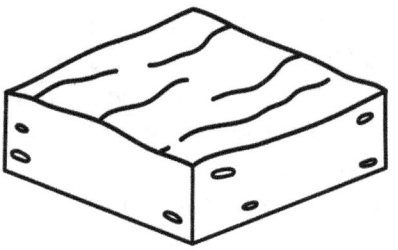

Directions:
Mix dry ingredients in a bowl.
Add honey and buttermilk, stirring until just mixed.
Drop spoonfuls onto a hot griddle, cooking until golden on each side.

Imbolc Honey Cake

Ingredients:
1 cup of flour
1 teaspoon of baking powder
1/4 teaspoon of salt
1/2 teaspoon of cinnamon
1/2 cup of butter
1/2 cup of honey
2 eggs
1/4 cup of milk

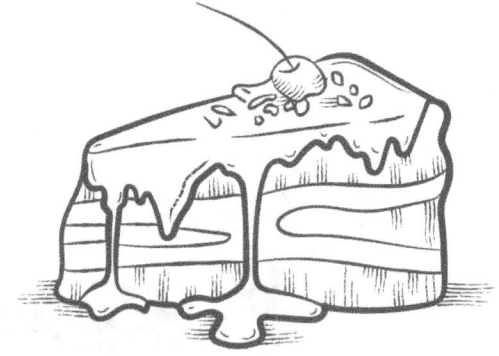

Directions:
Preheat oven to 350°F (175°C).
Cream together butter and honey. Add eggs one at a time, beating well after each.
In a separate bowl, mix dry ingredients. Add dry ingredients to wet ingredients, alternating with milk.
Pour into a greased cake pan and bake for 30-35 minutes or until a toothpick comes out clean.

Lavender Shortbread Cookies

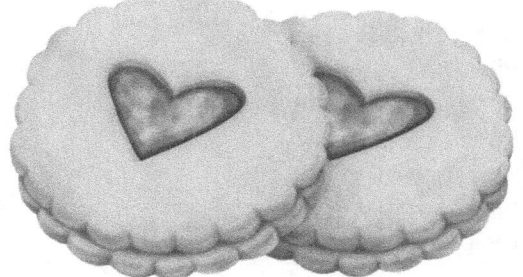

Ingredients:
1 cup of butter, softened
1/2 cup of powdered sugar
2 cups of all-purpose flour
1 tablespoon of dried lavender buds

Directions:
Cream together butter and powdered sugar.
Mix in flour until a dough forms.
Stir in dried lavender.
Roll into small balls and flatten with a fork on a baking sheet.
Bake at 325°F (163°C) for 15-20 minutes or until the edges are golden.

A Toast for Health and Prosperity

As the Wheel turns on this blessed Imbolc day,
We invoke the protection and healing of the Goddess Brigid.
May the light of the God Lugh guide us on our way,
As we strive to grow in spirit and sight.
Emerging from the darkness of winter's days,
We seek blessings for our new paths in life,
And ask for guidance to fulfill our plans,
For all people, in all lands.
With the colors of green and white,
And candles burning through the night,
We call upon Brigid's sacred flame,
To bring healing, protection, and peace in Her name.
In this chalice of milk and honey,
We bless our heads, hearts, minds, and money,
And pray for abundance and health in the year ahead,
By the power of Brigid, our spirits are fed.

Love Bath

Ingredients:
Pink or red candle
Rose or Jasmine incense
Rose essential oil
Rose petals
Pink Himalayan bath salts
Rose quartz

Directions:
Clear an evening for a self-pampering ritual to draw in love to you. Prepare your bathroom with fluffy towels, something to sip on, soft background music, and anything you love to bathe with.
Draw a warm bath and pour in pink Himalayan bath salts.
Add 9 drops of rose essential oil and 27 rose petals to the bath, Place your rose quartz crystal in the bath.
Light your Cleansing bubble bath Ritual candle and light your incense. Say the following prayer to your higher self as you immerse yourself in the bath water.

"May my heart resonate with the melody of self-love. May I embrace every facet of my being, cultivating confidence and self-worth. May joy, prosperity, and peace blossom abundantly in the garden of self-love. I am my own greatest supporter, finding solace and strength within. With gratitude, I affirm my commitment to letting love in—thank you, thank you, thank you."

Milk and Honey Bath

2 cups of milk
4 tablespoons of honey
2 teaspoons of coconut oil
5 drops of jasmine essential oil (*or another white flower oil such as gardenia, heliotrope, lily, or frangipani)
5 drops of lavender essential oil
Blend in a warm bath.

Blackberry Jam

Ingredients:
up to 4-6 cups of mashed fresh blackberries; they must be fresh
up to 4-6 cups of sugar to equal the measurement of the mashed blackberries

Directions:
Prepare the jars and lids by sterilizing them. Jars can be sterilized by running them through the dishwasher and drying them in high heat. Place the lids in a saucepan with water covering them. Put them on to boil while you are doing all the rest. {Keep an eye on them so they don't boil dry.}Rinse and mash the fresh blackberries. Rinse the fresh berries by running them underwater in a colander. {You MUST use fresh berries for this method.} Mash the berries with a vegetable or potato masher until there are no big seeds. Measure out the sugar. Measure out an equal part of sugar to match the exact amount of mashed berries. (**NOTE: Use only between 4-6 cups of mashed berries per batch.)
Cook the berries. Pour mashed berries into a large saucepan and put over high heat. Stir constantly with a large spoon until it boils. Boil for 3 minutes.
Add sugar to the boiling blackberries. Once the berries have boiled for 3 minutes, slowly add all the sugar while stirring constantly.
Cook the berries and sugar together. Bring the mixture to a boil again while continuing to stir constantly. Boil for 3 minutes more.
Bring out the natural pectin by whisking together. Remove from heat and beat with a whisk for 3 minutes. {The "beating" forces the natural pectin out of the berries.}
Pour into jars and place lids on tightly. Pour into sterilized jars. {Don't overfill. Just pour up to the narrow part of the jar.}
Using tongs, place a hot lid on each jar. Screw the rings on tightly. {Yep, it's a little hot on your hands!}
Each batch makes approximately 8 jam jars full.

Imbolc Essential Oil

5 drops of Jasmine EO
5 drops of Rose EO
5 drops of Chamomile EO
5 drops of Lemon EO
5 drops of Lavender EO

Use a 1/4 oz bottle. Add essential oils, then fill with grapeseed, avocado, or almond oil.

Lavender Tea

Ingredients:
1 cup of milk per serving.
1 tsp honey
¼ tsp of vanilla extract
½ a cup of brewed lavender tea, Lavender buds, or cinnamon

Directions:
Steep lavender buds or any lavender tea in ½ a cup of hot water. The more tea leaves or buds you use, the stronger the lavender taste will be.
Warm a cup of milk on the stove; be careful not to boil, or else it'll froth up and make a mess.
Once warmed, pour in the tea, honey, and vanilla extract.
Serve in a teacup and sprinkle lavender buds or cinnamon on top.

Imbolc Seed Blessing

Blessed seeds of Imbol's embrace, Your potential, a sacred space. Sprout and grow with vigor and might, Nurtured 'neath the sun and moon's soft light.
As roots delve deep and branches unfurl, May your bounty sustain a precious pearl. In the dance of seasons, your journey unfolds, A tapestry of life as ancient tales are told.

So mote it be, in nature's grand decree, Imbolc seeds, blessed be thee.

CHAPTER 7

all About
The Love

DIY Self Love

Practice Self-Compassion:
Be kind to yourself during difficult times, acknowledging that everyone makes mistakes and faces challenges.

Prioritize Self-Care:
Establish a routine including activities you enjoy, whether reading, baths, or spending time in nature.

Set Boundaries:
Learn to say no when necessary and establish healthy boundaries to protect your mental and emotional well-being.

Positive Affirmations:
Incorporate positive affirmations into your daily routine to boost self-esteem and cultivate a positive mindset.

Celebrate Achievements:
Acknowledge and celebrate your accomplishments, both big and small, to reinforce a sense of achievement and self-worth.

Mindful Practices:
Engage in mindfulness activities such as meditation or deep breathing to stay present and reduce stress.

Healthy Lifestyle Choices:
Nourish your body with nutritious foods, exercise regularly, and prioritize sufficient sleep for overall well-being.

Learn and Grow:
Pursue personal development and learning opportunities to foster a sense of accomplishment and growth.

Surround Yourself with Positivity:
Build a supportive network of friends and loved ones who uplift and encourage you.

Gratitude Journaling:
Keep a journal where you regularly write down things you're grateful for, fostering a positive perspective.

Treat Yourself:
Occasionally, indulge in small treats or activities that bring you joy, whether a favorite meal or a leisurely day off.

Forgive Yourself:
Let go of past mistakes and forgive yourself, recognizing that growth comes from learning and evolving.

Connect with Nature:
Spend time outdoors to rejuvenate your mind and body, benefiting from the therapeutic effects of nature.

Creative Expression:
Explore creative outlets like art, writing, or music to express yourself and tap into your inner passions.

Therapeutic Support:
Seek professional help, such as therapy or counseling, to address and navigate complex emotions when needed.

Remember, self-love is an ongoing process, and finding what works best for you may involve combining these practices. It's about nurturing a positive and compassionate relationship with yourself.

It's All About the Love

Rose Uses

Make Rose Water.
Burn Rose incense.
Wash your body with rose water.
Rub rose petals on your skin.
Add rose petals to bath water.
Wash your hair with rose water.
Place next to your bed at night for fragrant sleep.
Make your own magical oils and perfumes to anoint yourself,
candles, or add to baths.
Correspond your nail polish and lipstick colors with your intentions.
Add self-love affirmations and mirror magic to your routine.
Create a self-love and cleansing bath or shower ritual.
Use a rose quartz roller for self-love, improve circulation,
and uplift mood.
Draw sigils or runes with your foundation or creams.
Decorate with roses to raise loving vibrations in your home.
Celebrate your self-love and practice self-care with a relaxing
bubble bath.
Leave out offerings for a love goddess such as Aphrodite.
Burn pink or red candles to encourage self-love and passion.
Cook a romantic meal to honor your self-worth.
Indulge in chocolate to welcome sensuality to your life.
Cleanse your Oracle cards with dried rose buds and place one
inside your bag to keep it cleansed.
Burn rose buds to clear the air after a fight and to make amends.
Dress candles with the ash of dried rose petals for return-to-sender spells.

It's All About the Love

Rose Water

Ingredients:
Fresh, organic rose petals (about 2 cups)
Distilled water (enough to cover the petals)

Directions:
Prepare Rose Petals:
Rinse rose petals to remove any impurities.
Harvest petals in the morning for the best fragrance.

Simmering:
Put rose petals in a pot.
Pour enough distilled water to cover the petals.
Cover and simmer on low heat; don't boil.

Collect Steam:
Place a heat-safe bowl in the pot's center.
Invert the lid over the bowl to collect steam.

Condensation:
Add ice cubes to the lid to speed up condensation.
Simmer for 20-30 mins until enough rose water collects.

Strain:
Remove from heat and strain through cheesecloth or a strainer.

Store:
Let it cool, then transfer to a glass container.
Store in the fridge; it lasts a few weeks.

Tips:
Use as a facial toner or in cooking.
Label and keep refrigerated for a longer shelf life.

It's All About the Love

Rose Incense

Ingredients:

2 tablespoons dried rose petals
1 tablespoon ground cinnamon
1 tablespoon ground cloves
1 tablespoon ground benzoin resin (a natural binding agent)
1 tablespoon ground sandalwood
1 tablespoon makko powder (an incense-making binder available online or at specialty stores)
5-10 drops of rose essential oil (optional for enhanced fragrance)
Distilled water (as needed)

Directions: Prepare Ingredients. Ensure all ingredients are finely ground. If using whole cloves or cinnamon sticks, grind them into a powder using a spice grinder.

Mixing: In a mixing bowl, combine the dried rose petals, ground cinnamon, ground cloves, ground benzoin resin, ground sandalwood, and makko powder.

If desired, add a few drops of rose essential oil for more pronounced fragrance.

Adding Water: Gradually add distilled water to the mixture, a few drops at a time, until you achieve a dough-like consistency. Be cautious not to make it too wet.

Kneading: Knead the mixture thoroughly to ensure an even distribution of water. The consistency should be similar to cookie dough.

Molding: Place the dough on a parchment paper or a silicone mat.

Use incense molds or a small cookie cutter to shape the incense. Alternatively, roll the dough into thin sticks.

Drying: Dry the shaped incense for at least 24-48 hours. Ensure they are completely dry before use.

Curing (Optional): For a more refined scent, allow the dried incense to cure in a cool, dark place for an additional week.

Usage: Once dried and cured (if chosen), your homemade rose incense is ready to use. Burn the incense on a heat-resistant surface using bamboo skewers or incense sticks.

Note: Experiment with proportions to adjust the fragrance according to personal preferences. Always burn incense in a well-ventilated area and follow safety precautions.

It's All About the Love
Love Herbs and Crystals

Spell Bag Starter
Rose Petals
Few Drops of Rose Oil
Lavender
Lemon Balm
Rose Quartz
Himalayan Salt

Self Love Spell Jar Starter
Rose Petals
Lavender
Amethyst
Sugar
Orange Essential Oil
RoseQuartz
Rosemary
Pink Salt

Give it a little pizzazz by tossing in some of these other ingredients you have lying around.

Herbs
Lemon Verbena
Rose
Hibiscus
Mullein
Jasmine
Violet
Magnolia
Primrose
Thyme
Vanilla
Garden Sage
Cinnamon
Cherry Blossom
Lady's Bedstraw
Apple Blossom
Calendula
Hawthorn
Meadowsweet
Ginger
Damiana
Nutmeg
Dragon's Blood (resin)
Mistletoe

Crystals
Kunzite - Facilitates Love
Malachite - Opens Up For Love
Rose Quartz - Unconventional Love, Peace and Harmony
Rutilated Quartz - Stabilizes Love
Chrysoprase - Love, Healing, Joy
Emerald - Love, Compassion, and Abundance
Garnet - Manifesting, Self-worth, and Healing
Jade - Abundance and Wellbeing
Rhodochrosite Emotional Healing, Nurturing, and Joy
Rhodonite - Purpose, Generosity, and Self Acceptance
Rose Quartz - Love, Trust, and Emotional Healing
Watermelon Tourmaline - Serenity and Joy
Citrine - Joy and Optimism
Clear Quartz - Healing and Amplifies Other Crystals
Turquoise - Honor Who You Are
Smoky Quartz - Mindfulness
Pink Calcite - Inner Peace and Emotional Balance
Red Jasper - Self Love and Self Acceptance
Lapis Lazuli - Self Awareness and Self-Expression
Green Adventurine - Heart Chakra

It's All About the Love
Self Love Altar

Building your Self-Love Altar

Rose Quartz
Selenite
Clear Quartz
Rhodochrosite
Meaningful Items
Pink and Red Candles
Oracle Cards
Self Love Sigils
Self Love Spell Jar
Rose Petals, Jasmine Flowers Lavender Chamomile or/and Lilies
Personal Mantra, Affirmation, or Love Letter

Suggested Mantras:
I am deserving of happiness.
I love the person I am becoming.
I have beautiful qualities to offer this world.
I am enough.

It's All About the Love
Self Love Box

Creating a self-love box can be a wonderful and personal way to cultivate self-care and positivity. Here's a suggested guide my mentor told me on making a box with paints, crystals, petitions, and more.

Credit: Jamie Wareham

Materials Needed:
Wooden box
Acrylic paints, brushes
Crystals (rose quartz, amethyst, selenite)
Petitions or affirmations on paper
Candles (LED or real in safe holders)
Essential oils (lavender, chamomile)
Small mirror

Directions
Paint box with self-love colors.
Decorate the exterior with symbols or words.
Arrange crystals inside.
Place folded petitions in a dedicated section.
Add candles, ensuring safety.
Anoint items with essential oils.
Include the mirror for self-reflection.
Personalize with meaningful items.
Use regularly for self-love rituals.
Create a sacred space that resonates with positive energy and intentions, fostering self-love and reflection.

Remember, the key to a self-love box is personalization and intention. Feel free to adapt the steps and materials based on your preferences and spiritual beliefs. Enjoy the process of creating a sacred space dedicated to nurturing self-love and positivity.

She suggested one for every important intention, holiday, and moon.

It's All About the Love
Self Love Spell Jar

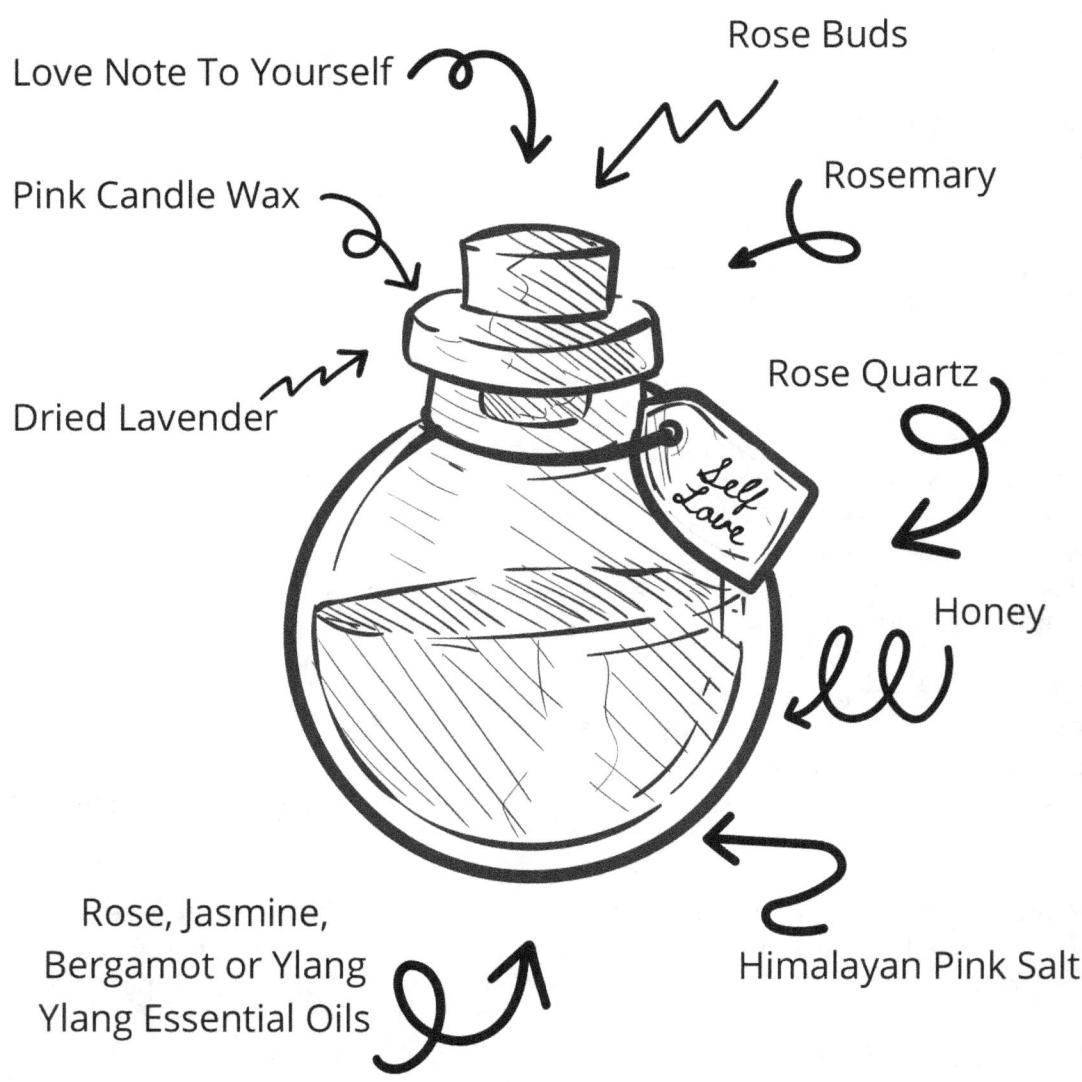

Love Note To Yourself

Rose Buds

Rosemary

Pink Candle Wax

Dried Lavender

Rose Quartz

Self Love

Honey

Rose, Jasmine,
Bergamot or Ylang
Ylang Essential Oils

Himalayan Pink Salt

It's All About the Love

Rose Petal Bath Recipe

Ingredients:
1 cup dried rose petals (or fresh petals if available)
1 cup Epsom salts
1/2 cup baking soda
1/4 cup dried lavender buds (optional for added relaxation)
5-10 drops of rose essential oil
Petals from 1-2 fresh roses (optional, for a luxurious touch)
Warm running water

Directions:
Prepare the Rose Petals: If using fresh roses, carefully pluck the petals. If using dried rose petals, measure out 1 cup.
Combine Dry Ingredients: In a mixing bowl, combine the dried rose petals, Epsom salts, baking soda, and dried lavender buds (if using).
Add Rose Essential Oil: Add 5-10 drops of rose essential oil to the dry mixture. Adjust the quantity based on your preference for fragrance.
Mix Thoroughly: Stir the ingredients well to distribute the essential oil evenly throughout the mixture.
Prepare Fresh Rose Petals (Optional): If you have fresh roses, delicately pluck them and set them aside for a decorative touch.
Run a Warm Bath: Fill your bathtub with warm water. Ensure the temperature is comfortable for you.
Add the mixture to the Bath: Sprinkle it into the running water, allowing it to dissolve.
Scatter Fresh Rose Petals (Optional): Add the fresh rose petals to the bathwater or scatter them on the surface for a visually stunning and aromatic experience.
Mix Well: Gently mix the water to disperse the ingredients evenly.
Enjoy Your Rose Petal Bath: Step into the soothing bath and relax. Allow the aromatic properties of roses and the soothing effects of Epsom salts to rejuvenate your senses.
Relaxation Time: Soak in the bath for at least 20-30 minutes to fully enjoy the benefits. Close your eyes, breathe deeply, and let the calming scent of roses envelop you.
Rinse Off: After your relaxing soak, rinse off in a warm shower to remove any residue.
Moisturize (Optional): Pat your skin dry and follow up with your favorite moisturizer for an extra touch of self-care.

Understanding the Practice of Holding Space

"Holding space" is a term used in therapeutic or supportive contexts, which refers to providing a supportive, compassionate, and non-judgmental environment for someone to express themselves freely. This means being fully present and attentive without imposing judgments, solutions, or opinions.

Here's an explanation of what holding space entails:

Presence and Attention: Holding space involves being fully present and attentive to the person you support. This means setting aside distractions, actively listening, and offering undivided attention, which creates a safe and focused environment for individuals to share their thoughts and feelings.

Non-Judgmental Attitude: It requires maintaining a non-judgmental and open-minded attitude. When holding space for someone, you refrain from criticizing, evaluating, or imposing your beliefs onto their experiences. This allows them to express themselves authentically without fear of judgment.

Empathy and Compassion: Holding space is infused with empathy and compassion. It involves acknowledging and validating the other person's emotions, even if you may not fully understand their perspective. Demonstrating empathy fosters a sense of trust and understanding.

Suspending Ego and Solutions: Holding space requires suspending the need to fix or solve the person's problems. It's about acknowledging that each individual has the wisdom and capacity to navigate their challenges and may simply need a supportive presence.

Creating a Safe Emotional Container: Holding space is often likened to creating a metaphorical container for someone's emotions. This container is a safe space where individuals can explore and express their feelings without fear of rejection or invalidation.

Respecting Boundaries: Holding space involves respecting the other person's boundaries and pacing. It means allowing them to share as much or as little as they are comfortable with and not pressuring them to disclose more than they are ready to express.

Facilitating Self-Reflection: By holding space, you encourage self-reflection and self-discovery. The focus is on allowing the individual to explore their thoughts and feelings, facilitating a process of understanding and insight.

In essence, holding space is a practice that honors and supports another person's autonomy and individual journey. It's about creating a nurturing and accepting environment for authentic expression and emotional exploration. Whether in personal relationships, counseling, or supportive friendships, holding space can be a powerful way to provide comfort and encouragement to those going through challenging times.

Stop Giving Your Power Away

Emotional Intelligence

Take responsibility for your emotions with self-regulation practices. Don't let an emotional reaction to a situation become you. Pause. Welcome it as a teacher to help you respond. Don't see the emotion as an enemy that causes you to react, drain your energy, or give your power away.

Discernment

Ask yourself before you invest energy into an interaction, comment, or judgment from another if it's worth your time & energy. How meaningful is this relationship to you? Is the person able to hold space for other perspectives? Stop trying to prove people wrong- this will drain you.

Embody Your Values

Everyone has different values, perceptions, & thoughts about life. There is no one "right way" or "right path." You're not for everyone and that's okay. Identify the most important things to you, live accordingly, and let others do the same. We don't want to "force" our reality on anyone.

Self Image

What are limiting beliefs causing you to seek or depend on others' approval? Your self-image was mainly formed between the ages of 1-7. Take your power back by digging deep into what weakened your self-image. Regulate your nervous system to feel safe & confident in your body. You can build yourself back up.

Protect Your Power

Visualize - Visualization can be done anywhere, anytime: Walking, on a train, during meditation, or even during a conversation. First, powerfully state your intention and visualize key elements integral to your prayer. Then, let yourself be guided by your higher Self.

De-cording - A cleansing technique is like removing energetic knots from the field. "The cord" is a connection to feelings/beliefs/ people and acts like a conduit that allows that particular energy to come in and out of our space. So be aware of cords that save you and don't, and start by consciously weeding out those that aren't sustainable for you.

Clear and Protect your field - With closed eyes, visualize a healing light teaming from your hands. Powerfully sweep your hands across your body with a strong exhale. Complete sealing your aura with protective oils such as Copal, Rue, St John's Wort, Yarrow, Cedarwood, and Juniper.
Sandalwood, Myth, and more.

Floral or medicinal water to seal the aura - Medicinal baths, or floral water, can significantly assist in protection and flushing toxicity. Use native plants local to your home, protective crystals, and infuse them directly in water or both. Then, apply the blessed water to your body or take a bath.

Clear your physical space - Call upon the cardinal directions while praying to harmonize the energetics within your space using the power of archetypes.
North: Wisdom, Ancestral Guidance
South: Growth, Self Discovery
East: New Beginnings, Transmissions
West: Death, Ending, Self-worth

Use your grounding cord - Upon beginning or ending your practice, it is important to locate your grounding cord. Imagine luminous energy that runs through you, in-between your legs + through your crown. Maintaining its health by upgrading or replacing your old grounding cord with a fresh one is vital, which helps anchor you into the present.

Hot Mess

Ways to keep your crap together, aka grounding

Crystals protect and ground an empath.

Eating healthy food and having a nutritious diet.

Sea salt can dissolve negative and toxic energies.

Balancing masculine and feminine energy.

Smudging clears unwanted and negative energy.

Regular exercise helps with grounding.

Meditation helps with stress.

Being creative has an uplifting effect on the psyche.

Balancing the chakras help with mental peace.

Practicing yoga helps in grounding.

Being outdoors in nature is healing.

Laughing a lot and staying childlike.

Drinking a lot of water.

Essential oils help in relaxation.

Earthing helps to stay grounded.

CHAPTER 8

Other Holidays

In addition to Imbolc, several other holidays are celebrated at the beginning of February, representing various cultural, religious, and secular traditions.

Here are a few examples:

Chinese New Year (Date Varies):
Also known as the Spring Festival, Chinese New Year marks the beginning of the lunar new year in the Chinese calendar. The date varies yearly but is usually between January 21 and February 20. It is a time of family gatherings, feasts, and various traditional customs.

Groundhog Day (February 2):
A North American tradition, Groundhog Day involves a groundhog emerging from its burrow, and its behavior is believed to predict the coming weather. If the groundhog sees its shadow, there will be six more weeks of winter.

Valentine's Day (February 14): Celebrated globally, Valentine's Day is dedicated to expressing love and affection. People often exchange cards, flowers, and gifts with their loved ones. It is associated with the Feast of Saint Valentine in Christian traditions.

Maha Shivaratri (Date Varies):
Maha Shivaratri is a Hindu festival dedicated to Lord Shiva. It is observed on the 13th night and 14th day of the lunar month of Phalguna (February or March). Devotees often fast, visit temples and perform prayers and rituals.

Purim (Begins at Sunset on February 26):
Purim is a Jewish holiday commemorating the saving of the Jewish people from Haman, as told in the Book of Esther. It is marked by festive celebrations, reading the Megillah (Book of Esther), and exchanging gifts and charity.

Carnival / Mardi Gras (Date Varies):
Carnival is a festive season that occurs before Lent in many cultures. Mardi Gras, or Fat Tuesday, is the culmination of Carnival, marked by colorful parades, costumes, music, and revelry. It is celebrated in various locations around the world.

Ash Wednesday (Date Varies):
Ash Wednesday marks the beginning of Lent in many Christian traditions. It is a day of repentance and reflection, often observed with church services where ashes are applied to the foreheads of participants.

These holidays represent a mix of cultural, religious, and secular observances, showcasing the diversity of celebrations in February. The specific dates of some holidays, like Chinese New Year and Mardi Gras, vary each year based on lunar or traditional calendars.

Candlemas

Candlemas, also known as the Feast of the Presentation of Jesus Christ, is a Christian holiday celebrated annually on February 2nd. It marks the presentation of the infant Jesus in the Temple and the purification of the Virgin Mary according to Jewish tradition. The name "Candlemas" is derived from the practice of blessing candles on this day.

Biblical Background:
The celebration is based on the biblical account found in the Gospel of Luke (Luke 2:22-40), where Mary and Joseph present the baby Jesus at the Temple in Jerusalem 40 days after his birth. This event is based on Jewish customs outlined in the Old Testament.

Purification of Mary:
According to Jewish law, a woman who gave birth was considered ritually unclean for a certain period. After this time, she was required to present an offering for purification. In the case of Mary, this was a pair of turtledoves or pigeons.

Recognition by Simeon and Anna:
Two individuals in the Temple, Simeon, and the prophetess Anna, recognized Jesus as the words known as the "Nunc Dimittis," which are often recited or sung during Candlemas services.

Blessing of Candles:
One of the distinctive customs of Candlemas is the blessing of candles during a church service. The candles may be used in the church or taken home by parishioners. This practice symbolizes the light of Christ coming into the world.

Symbolism of Light:
The blessing and lighting of candles symbolize some traditions; there is a procession with candles, emphasizing the theme of Jesus as the "light to lighten the Gentiles."

Seasonal Marker:
Candlemas falls 40 days after Christmas, marking the end of the Christmas season. Some cultural and meteorological traditions also consider it a transitional point between winter and spring.

Groundhog Day Connection:
In some regions, Candlemas is associated with weather prediction. The saying goes that if the weather is clear on Candlemas Day, there will be six more weeks of winter. This folklore is sometimes connected to the American tradition of Groundhog Day.

Chinese New Year

The Chinese New Year, the Spring Festival, or Lunar New Year, is the most important traditional festival in Chinese culture. It marks the beginning of the lunar new year and is celebrated by Chinese communities worldwide. The date of the Chinese New Year varies each year based on the lunar calendar, but it generally falls between January 21st and February 20th on the Gregorian calendar.

Animal Zodiac Cycle
Each Chinese New Year is associated with one of the twelve animals of the Chinese zodiac. The cycle includes the Rat, Ox, Tiger, Rabbit, Dragon, Snake, Horse, Goat (or Sheep), Monkey, Rooster, Dog, and Pig. Each animal is believed to influence the personality traits of individuals born in that year.

Spring Festival Celebrations
The Chinese New Year festivities traditionally last for 15 days, starting from the first day of the lunar new year and culminating with the Lantern Festival on the 15th day. The Spring Festival is a time for family reunions, feasts, and cultural activities.

Reunion Dinners
The eve of the Chinese New Year is marked by a reunion dinner, where family members gather to share a festive meal. This dinner is considered one of the most important family events of the year.

Red Decorations
Red is a prominent color during the Chinese New Year, associated with good luck and prosperity. Homes are often adorned with red decorations, and people exchange red envelopes (hongbao) containing money as a symbol of good fortune.

Fireworks and Dragon Dances
Fireworks, firecrackers, and dragon dances are traditional elements of Chinese New Year celebrations. The loud noises and vibrant performances are believed to ward off evil spirits.

Cleaning and Decorating
In the days leading up to the Chinese New Year, families thoroughly clean their homes to sweep away bad luck. Decorations featuring symbols of good fortune, prosperity, and happiness are then put up.

Lantern Festival
The Lantern Festival, which marks the end of the Chinese New Year celebrations, involves lighting lanterns, parades, and various activities. It usually takes place on the 15th day of the lunar new year.

Feast of the Purification of the Virgin ~ Candlemas

The Feast of the Purification of the Virgin, also known as Candlemas, is a Christian liturgical celebration observed on February 2nd. It commemorates the presentation of Jesus at the Temple in Jerusalem and the purification of the Virgin Mary according to Jewish law. This feast is also known as the Presentation of Jesus in the Temple.

Biblical Basis
The origins of this feast are found in the Gospel of Luke (Luke 2:22–40), which describes how Mary and Joseph brought the infant Jesus to the Temple in Jerusalem 40 days after his birth. According to Jewish law, a woman who had given birth was considered ritually unclean for 40 days and needed to undergo a purification ceremony.

Simeon's Prophecy
The Gospel narrative recounts the encounter between the Holy Family and Simeon, a devout and righteous man, who, upon seeing the baby Jesus, proclaimed the Nunc Dimittis, a prayer expressing readiness for death, as he recognized the fulfillment of God's promise in the arrival of the Messiah.

Candlemas Traditions
The feast is also associated with the blessing of candles, a practice symbolizing Jesus as the "Light of the World." In some Christian traditions, candles are blessed during a liturgical ceremony for various religious observances throughout the year.

Symbolic Significance
The Feast of the Purification emphasizes themes of ritual purification, the presentation of the divine in human form, and the acknowledgment of Jesus as the long-awaited Messiah.

Liturgical Observances
In Christian liturgy, the celebration includes reading relevant biblical passages, prayers, and hymns. Some denominations may also conduct a procession with candles, reflecting the theme of Christ as the Light.

It's important to note that the exact practices and emphasis on this feast can vary among different Christian denominations. The Feast of the Purification of the Virgin is a significant event in the liturgical calendar, drawing attention to key moments in the early life of Jesus and the religious customs of the time.

Feast of Saint Valentine ~ St. Valentine's Day

The Feast of Saint Valentine, commonly known as Valentine's Day, is a Christian liturgical celebration that honors Saint Valentine, a Christian martyr of the Roman Empire. While the exact origins and details of Saint Valentine's life are somewhat unclear, he is traditionally associated with acts of love and compassion.

Date
Valentine's Day is observed annually on February 14th.

Historical Background
Saint Valentine is believed to have been a Christian priest or bishop who lived during the Roman Empire in the 3rd century. Historical uncertainties and varying accounts somewhat obscure the details of his life.

Association with Love
The connection between Saint Valentine and love is primarily based on the legend that he performed weddings for soldiers forbidden to marry. Additionally, some stories suggest that he helped Christians persecuted under the Roman Empire.

Martyrdom
Saint Valentine was said to have been martyred for his Christian faith. One common narrative suggests that he was executed on February 14th, around the year 269 AD.

Cultural Traditions
Over the centuries, Valentine's Day evolved beyond its religious origins and became a cultural celebration of romantic love and affection. The exchange of love notes, cards, flowers, and gifts has become a widespread tradition associated with the holiday.

Symbols
The heart shape, Cupid (the Roman god of love), and the colors red and pink are common symbols associated with Valentine's Day. These symbols represent love, romance, and affection.

Modern Celebrations
In contemporary times, Valentine's Day is widely celebrated around the world. Couples have to express their love for each other through various gestures, such as exchanging gifts, sharing romantic meals, and sending greeting cards.

Religious Observance
While Valentine's Day has primarily secularized, some Christian denominations may still observe the Feast of Saint Valentine liturgically, remembering the saint's life and contributions.

It's important to note that while Valentine's Day's romantic and commercial aspects are well-known today, the holiday has Christian roots that trace back to the veneration of Saint Valentine. However, the specifics of Saint Valentine's life and actions remain the subject of historical ambiguity and legend.

Groundhog Day

Groundhog Day, celebrated annually on February 2nd, is rooted in ancient weather lore. The tradition is linked to Candlemas Day, a Christian festival marking the midpoint between the winter solstice and the spring equinox. On this day, clergy would bless candles, and superstition held that clear weather on Candlemas meant a prolonged winter.

The connection to groundhogs emerged in the 19th century, notably in Punxsutawney, Pennsylvania. German immigrants brought the tradition of using a hedgehog to predict the weather, and in the absence of hedgehogs in the United States, groundhogs became the chosen animal. Punxsutawney Phil, the most famous groundhog, emerged as the central figure in the annual ritual.

The magical significance lies in the belief that the groundhog's behavior on this day predicts the duration of winter. Tradition suggests six more weeks of winter if the groundhog sees its shadow and retreats to its burrow. If no shadow is seen, an early spring is anticipated.

While the accuracy of this weather forecasting method is questionable, Groundhog Day has evolved into a widely celebrated and quirky tradition, popularized by the 1993 film "Groundhog Day," starring Bill Murray. The film's protagonist relives the same day repeatedly, highlighting personal growth and self-improvement themes, adding a layer of cultural significance beyond weather predictions.

I am from Pennsylvania, and I still find this custom to be weird.

Lupercalia

Lupercalia was an ancient Roman festival celebrated annually on February 15th. It was dedicated to Faunus, the Roman god of fertility, as well as to the founders of Rome, Romulus and Remus. The festival had a unique blend of fertility rituals, purification ceremonies, and activities believed to ward off evil spirits.

Lustratio:
The festival began with a purification ritual called "lustratio," during which priests known as the Luperci would sacrifice a goat and a dog. The blood of these animals was then used to purify and anoint the foreheads of two to purify and anoint the foreheads of two young priests.

Feast and Celebration:
After the purification ritual, the Luperci would partake in a feast. This was a time of revelry, where participants would indulge in food and wine. It was considered a festive occasion, and the atmosphere was one of merriment.

Running of the Luperci:
The most well-known and distinctive aspect of Lupercalia was the "Running of the Luperci." The young priests, having been anointed with sacrificial blood, would run around the Palatine Hill in Rome, striking onlookers, especially women, with thongs made from the goat's hide.

Fertility Symbolism:
The act of striking women with the thongs was seen as a symbol of fertility. It was believed that this ritual could enhance women's fertility and bring about easy childbirth. Women often willingly participated in this practice, as they considered it a means of promoting fertility and ensuring the well-being of their future children.

Connection to the Founding of Rome:
Lupercalia had a connection to the mythical founding of Rome by Romulus and Remus. The Luperci were said to reenact aspects of the twins' story during the festival, emphasizing themes of fertility and the nurturing of the city.

Transformation into Valentine's Day:
Over time, Lupercalia underwent transformations and reinterpretations. As Christianity spread and traditions evolved, Lupercalia was eventually replaced by the St. Valentine's Day Christian feast, celebrated on February 14th.

While Lupercalia was a significant Roman festival in ancient times, many aspects of its rituals and practices have faded over the centuries. The festival is often cited as an example of ancient Roman society's complex interweaving of religious, cultural, and agricultural themes.

Mardi Gras

Mardi Gras, which translates to "Fat Tuesday" in French, is a festive celebration that takes place before the Christian season of Lent. It is known for its vibrant and exuberant festivities, including parades, costumes, music, and indulgent feasting. Mardi Gras is particularly associated with the city of New Orleans, Louisiana, in the United States, where it has become a major cultural event.

Date
Mardi Gras is celebrated on the Tuesday before Ash Wednesday, which marks the beginning of the 40-day Lenten period leading up to Easter. The date varies yearly but usually falls between February 3rd and March 9th.

Carnival Season
Mardi Gras is part of the broader Carnival season, which begins on January 6th (Twelfth Night or Epiphany) and extends until Fat Tuesday. During this period, various regions around the world host festive events.

Parades and Floats
One of the central features of Mardi Gras is the elaborate parades featuring colorful floats, marching bands, and performers. These parades often depict themes, and participants throw strings of beads, doubloons, and other trinkets to the crowd.

Costumes and Masks
 Costumes and masks are common during Mardi Gras celebrations. Whether on floats or in the streets, participants often dress in vibrant outfits, masks, and accessories. It is a time for creativity and self-expression.

King Cake
King Cake is a traditional Mardi Gras dessert. It is a sweet, circular pastry decorated in the colors of Mardi Gras—purple, green, and gold. Hidden within the cake is a small plastic baby figurine, and tradition holds that the person who finds it must host the next gathering.

Beads and Throws
The tradition of throwing beads and other items to the crowd during parades is a hallmark of Mardi Gras. Spectators eagerly collect these "throws" as part of the festive atmosphere.

Masks and Krewes
 Social clubs known as krewes organize many Mardi Gras events. These krewes plan and fund the parades, balls, and other festivities. Masks are often worn during the various events to enhance the celebratory atmosphere.

Nirvana ~ Parinirvana Day

Nirvana Day, also known as Parinirvana Day, is a Buddhist observance commemorating Siddhartha Gautama's death, the historical Buddha. The term "Nirvana" refers to the state of liberation from the cycle of birth, death, and rebirth in Buddhism. It is believed that upon his physical death, the Buddha achieved the final Nirvana, also known as Parinirvana, on Nirvana Day.

Date
Nirvana Day is typically observed on February 15th in Mahayana traditions, while Theravada traditions may observe it on a different date, often in March.

Significance
The day marks the Buddha's death and his attainment of complete Nirvana, signifying the end of his earthly existence and the release from the cycle of samsara (the cycle of birth, death, and rebirth).

Observances
Buddhists observe Nirvana Day with reflective and meditative practices. Many visit temples to participate in ceremonies and listen to teachings on impermanence, the nature of existence, and the path to Nirvana.

Cultural Practices
Customs may vary across Buddhist traditions, but common practices include making offerings, reciting sutras, and engaging in acts of kindness and compassion.

Reflection on Impermanence
Nirvana Day emphasizes the Buddhist concept of impermanence and the transient nature of life. It serves as a reminder of the impermanence of all things and the importance of the Buddhist path toward liberation.

It's important to note that the exact practices and significance of Nirvana Day can vary among different Buddhist communities and schools of thought. The observance holds deep spiritual and philosophical meaning for Buddhists, underscoring the ultimate goal of attaining Nirvana and breaking free from the cycle of suffering.

CHAPTER 9

Dedication
to
Dieties

Dedication

Imbolc is celebrated in February and marks the halfway point between the winter solstice and the spring equinox. It is a time to celebrate the return of light and Brigid, the Celtic goddess of poetry, healing, and fire.

As the wheel of the year turns to Imbolc, a sacred time marking the earth's awakening, many choose to embark on a journey of dedication to a deity. This pivotal moment, when the promise of spring begins to stir, invites individuals to forge a connection with their chosen deity and carry that devotion throughout the cycles of the year. In this dedication, seekers embrace the energies of Imbolc and commit to a year-long exploration of spiritual growth guided by the divine presence they invoke.

A Guide to Dedicating to a Deity for Imbolc

Choosing a Deity:
Select a deity for your observance. During Imbolc, many practitioners choose to honor Brigid, a Celtic goddess associated with poetry, fire, healing, and the arrival of spring.

Research and Understanding:
Gain knowledge about the deity you wish to dedicate yourself to. Understand their attributes, mythology, and cultural significance. This forms the foundation for a meaningful connection.

Personal Connection:
Reflect on why you feel drawn to this particular deity. Consider personal experiences, feelings, or intuitions that lead you to make this dedication.

Create a Sacred Space:
Create a sacred space for your dedication. This can be a physical altar, a quiet corner, or a place in nature. Decorate it with symbols that represent the deity and items that embody the themes of Imbolc, such as fresh flowers, candles, and seeds.

Offerings and Intentions:
Prepare offerings for the deity, such as food, drink, or symbolic objects that are personally significant. In addition, set intentions for your dedication and express your commitment and purpose.

Ritual or Ceremony:
Formally dedicate your observance to the deity by performing a ritual or ceremony. This can involve prayers, invocations, and specific rituals associated with the deity or the themes of Imbolc.

Written Statement of Dedication:
Craft a sincere statement expressing your dedication to the deity. This can include your intentions, aspirations, and commitment to building a connection.

Meditative and Contemplative Tools:
Have tools for meditation or contemplation, such as crystals, beads, or a ritual knife. These can aid in focusing your thoughts and energy.

Time and Intentions:
Set aside dedicated time for the ritual. Clearly define your intentions and the purpose of your dedication.

Respect and Reverence:
Approach the dedication with respect and humility. Acknowledge the sacredness of the moment and the deity's presence.

Journal or Record:
Keep a journal or record of your dedication experience. Document your emotions, insights gained and the impact on your spiritual journey.

Ongoing Practices:
Plan for ongoing practices to maintain your connection, such as regular rituals, prayers, or acts of service related to the deity.

Remember, the process of dedicating to a deity is deeply personal. Tailor these essentials to align with your beliefs, preferences, and the unique nature of your spiritual journey.

Paganism Wicca Witchcraft

Pagan: A pagan worships Nature. They adhere to religious guidelines that follow things like the seasons, natural occurrences, the bodies,
The Sun, the Moon, and other celestial gods and goddesses correspond mostly to things in Nature and the universe.

Pagan is the umbrella term, and religions that fall under its perview are Wiccan, Hinduism, Shintoism, and many more. All these believe in both a god and goddess, light and dark. Everything is about balance.

Wicca: Wiccans are pagans who practice witchcraft in their religion. They also follow astronomy and astrology. The Moon is representative of the goddess, and the Sun is representative of the god figure. In some traditions of.

Wicca only believes in one god and goddess, but in many, they follow many deities; in Wicca, they also observe the Wheel of the Year, a seasonal and celestial event at different times of the year. These holidays celebrate the birth, ascension, and death of the Sun (god). Wiccan traditions have evolved from the paganism in varying cultures around the world.

Witchcraft: Anyone who practices witchcraft is a witch. Witchcraft includes performing rituals with chants, incantations, and tools. They also use herbalism, aromatherapy, and divination. There are many paths a witch can follow, deities or without. Many witches are secular and use their craft for more practical matters.

CHAPTER 10

Intro to
Deities

Introduction to Deities

Worshiping and dedicating to gods and goddesses is an important aspect of many pagan traditions, including those celebrating the Litha Sabbat. The honored and revered deities can vary greatly depending on the individual or group's beliefs and practices. Some may worship a pantheon of gods and goddesses, while others may focus their devotion on a single deity. Regardless of the approach, dedicating oneself to these powerful spiritual forces can be a significant and transformative experience.

Many pagans see their relationship with the divine as a two-way street. They believe they can receive blessings, guidance, and protection by offering devotion and reverence to the gods and goddesses. This energy exchange is often seen as a way to maintain balance in the world and one's life. Some also view the deities as archetypes or personifications of natural forces, such as the sun or the moon, and may seek to align themselves with these energies through worship.

There are many ways to worship and dedicate oneself to the gods and goddesses. Some may perform rituals or ceremonies, make food or drink offerings, or create sacred spaces in their homes or outdoor areas. Others may meditate, pray, or engage in personal acts of devotion. Whatever form it takes, this connection with the divine can be a source of inspiration, comfort, and spiritual growth for those who seek it.

Aphrodite / Venus (Greek/Roman)

Birth: Aphrodite is said to have been born from the sea foam that formed after the genitals of Uranus (the sky) were cast into the sea by his son Cronus. Alternatively, in Hesiod's account, she is born after the castration of Uranus.

Parentage: In most accounts, Aphrodite is considered the daughter of Uranus and sometimes Gaia (the Earth). In other versions, she is born solely from the sea.

Attributes: Aphrodite is the goddess of love, beauty, pleasure, and procreation. She is often depicted as a radiant and enchanting figure.

Symbols: The dove, myrtle, rose, and swan are often associated with Aphrodite. These symbols represent love, beauty, and fertility.

Marriage: In some myths, Aphrodite is married to Hephaestus, the god of blacksmiths and craftsmanship. Despite her marital ties, she is involved in various love affairs with gods and mortals.

Offspring: Aphrodite is the mother of several notable figures, including Eros (Cupid), the god of love, and Aeneas, a Trojan hero.

The Judgment of Paris: Aphrodite played a crucial role in the judgment of Paris, a mortal prince. She promised him the love of the most beautiful mortal woman, Helen of Troy, leading to Paris awarding her the golden apple in a contest among Hera, Athena, and Aphrodite.

Cult and Worship: Aphrodite had numerous temples and worshipers across ancient Greece. Her worship was often associated with fertility rites, love rituals, and celebrations.

Roman Equivalent: In Roman mythology, Aphrodite is identified with Venus. While the Greek and Roman myths share similarities, their respective traditions have distinct cultural and narrative differences.

Influence: Aphrodite's influence extends beyond mythology, as her image and themes related to love and beauty have permeated art, literature, and culture throughout history.

Arianrhod/Arianrod (Welsh)

Welsh Mythology: Arianrhod is a figure in Welsh mythology associated with the Mabinogion, a collection of Welsh tales.

Meaning of the Name: The name Arianrhod is often interpreted as "Silver Wheel" or "Silver Circle," with "arian" meaning silver and "rhod" meaning wheel or circle.

Parentage: Arianrhod is the daughter of the sea god Llyr (Lear in Irish mythology) in some accounts. In other versions, she is Beli Mawr's daughter and Gwydion and Gilfaethwy's sister.

Children: Arianrhod is the mother of two sons, Dylan ail Don and Lleu Llaw Gyffes. Dylan is associated with the sea, while Lleu becomes a central figure in the Fourth Branch of the Mabinogi.

Virginity Test: In one well-known myth, Arianrhod imposes a virginity test on her son, Lleu. He gains a name and arms only when he steps over a magical rod placed by his uncle Gwydion.

Celtic Astronomy: Arianrhod is sometimes associated with celestial phenomena. In some interpretations, she is linked to the northern constellation Corona Borealis, which is known as "Caer Arianrhod" or "Arianrhod's Castle."

Fate of Her Sons: Arianrhod plays a role in the tragic fate of her son Dylan, who meets his end in the sea. Her relationship with Lleu is complex and includes elements of deception, testing, and eventual reconciliation.

Symbolism: Arianrhod's association with silver and the celestial elements suggests connections to lunar and cosmic symbolism. Her role as a mother, particularly in testing her sons, contributes to the complex family dynamics within Welsh mythology.

Cultural Impact: The myths surrounding Arianrhod have left a mark on Welsh folklore and literature. Her stories contribute to the rich tapestry of Welsh mythology and continue to be studied and interpreted in modern times.

Artio (Celtic)

Celtic Goddess: Artio is a bear goddess worshipped in ancient Celtic religion, primarily among the Gaulish tribes.

Name Meaning: The name "Artio" is derived from the Celtic word for "bear." The name reflects her association with bears in the religious context.

Symbolism: Artio is often depicted with bear-related symbols and attributes, emphasizing her connection to these animals. She is sometimes shown accompanied by a bear or depicted in the company of bears.

Cult Centers: While the worship of Artio was not uniform across all Celtic regions, there is evidence of her cult being present in some Gaulish areas. Inscriptions and artifacts related to her have been found in regions such as modern-day Switzerland and France.

Offerings and Rituals: Little is known about the specific rituals and practices associated with the worship of Artio. However, offerings, votive inscriptions, and artifacts suggest that she was venerated in a religious context.

Associations with Other Deities: In some inscriptions, Artio is mentioned in connection with other deities, potentially indicating her role in a broader pantheon or divine network within Celtic belief systems.

Bronze Statue: One notable artifact associated with Artio is a bronze statue found in Switzerland. The statue depicts the goddess sitting on a throne or rock, holding a bowl of fruit in one hand and a small bear at her side.

Roman Influence: The worship of Artio was influenced by Roman interactions with Celtic cultures. The bronze statue mentioned above and other artifacts suggest a syncretic blending of Celtic and Roman religious elements.

Surviving Records: Much of what is known about Artio comes from archaeological findings, inscriptions, and depictions of artifacts. There are limited written records about her compared to other deities from Celtic mythology.

Decline: With the Romanization of Gaul and the spread of Christianity, the worship of Celtic deities, including Artio, gradually declined, and many aspects of their mythology were lost or transformed.

Athena / Athene (Greek)

Goddess of Wisdom and Warfare: Athena is one of the twelve Olympian deities in Greek mythology, and she is primarily associated with wisdom, strategic warfare, and crafts.

Parentage: According to the most common myth, Athena is the daughter of Zeus, the king of the gods, and Metis, a Titaness associated with wisdom. However, Zeus swallowed Metis while she was pregnant with Athena, and Athena then emerged fully grown and armored from Zeus's forehead.

Virgin Goddess: Athena is often referred to as a virgin goddess. She chose to remain unmarried and dedicated herself to intellectual pursuits and martial skills.

Attributes: Athena is typically depicted wearing a helmet and carrying a shield, spear, and sometimes an owl, a symbol of wisdom. The olive tree is also associated with her, as she is said to have created it as a gift to the city of Athens.

City of Athens: Athena is the patron goddess of the city of Athens, and she won this honor in a competition with Poseidon. According to the myth, she offered the olive tree, symbolizing peace and prosperity, while Poseidon provided a saltwater spring.

Warrior Goddess: Athena is a strategic and disciplined warrior, contrasting with the more chaotic aspects of war associated with Ares. She is often invoked by soldiers for her guidance and protection in battle.

Mythological Stories: Athena plays a significant role in various myths, including the Judgment of Paris, the story of Arachne, and the adventures of Odysseus in the "Odyssey."

Civic and Intellectual Contributions: Beyond warfare, Athena is the goddess of civilization, wisdom, and various crafts. She is associated with developing agriculture, the arts, and the sciences.

Parthenon: The Parthenon on the Acropolis in Athens is dedicated to Athena Parthenos, and it housed a massive chryselephantine (gold and ivory) statue of the goddess crafted by the renowned sculptor Phidias.

Roman Equivalent: Athena is equated with the goddess Minerva in Roman mythology. While their myths share similarities, there are differences in their cultural interpretations and associations.

Brigid (Celtic)

Celtic Goddess: Brigid is a prominent goddess in Celtic mythology, particularly in Irish mythology. She is associated with various aspects of life, including poetry, healing, smithcraft, and fertility.

Triple Aspect: Brigid is often depicted as a triple goddess, embodying three aspects or functions—Poetry (Filidh), Healing (Leighean), and Smithcraft (Gobhniu).

Parentage: In different myths, Brigid is described as the daughter of the Dagda, a major deity in Irish mythology, or as the daughter of a Tuatha Dé Danann chief named Brigid (possibly a later Christianized version).

Festival of Imbolc: Brigid is closely associated with the Celtic festival of Imbolc, celebrated around February 1st or 2nd, marking the beginning of spring. Imbolc is dedicated to Brigid as the goddess of fertility, purification, and the awakening of the land.

Sacred Flame: Brigid is often linked to a burning sacred flame at her sanctuary in Kildare, Ireland. This flame was tended by a group of priestesses known as the "Daughters of the Flame."

Symbolic Animals: Brigid is associated with several symbolic animals, including the swan, the serpent, and the cow. These animals are often linked to her various aspects and attributes.

Christian Saint: With the Christianization of Ireland, Brigid was adapted into Christian traditions as Saint Brigid. The Christian Saint Brigid is associated with miracles, hospitality, and acts of charity. Her feast day in the Christian calendar is celebrated on February 1st.

Cultural Influence: Brigid is a significant figure in Irish folklore and remains an important symbol in modern Irish culture. Many places, wells, and landmarks are named after her, reflecting the enduring impact of her mythology.

Imbolc Customs: Traditional customs associated with Imbolc involve making Brigid's crosses, which are woven from reeds or straw and symbolize protection and blessings. These crosses are often hung in homes.

Surviving Stories: While some of the original myths about Brigid may have been lost over time, references to her can be found in medieval Irish manuscripts and texts like the Lebor Gabála Érenn (The Book of Invasions) and the Dindsenchas (lore about place names).

Brigid's multifaceted nature as a goddess of poetry, healing, and smithcraft highlights her importance in Celtic mythology, and her enduring presence in Irish culture is reflected in both pagan and Christian traditions.

Brighid ~ Brigid ~ St. Brigid

The distinction between the Celtic goddess Brigid and St. Brigid of Kildare involves a fascinating blend of pagan and Christian traditions. Brigid, the Celtic goddess, was revered for her association with healing, poetry, and Smithcraft. Imbolc, celebrated around February 1st or 2nd, marked the halfway point between the winter solstice and the spring equinox and was dedicated to this goddess. Ancient traditions included creating Brigid's crosses, making Brideog dolls, and lighting bonfires to symbolize purification and the returning sun.

St. Brigid of Kildare, on the other hand, is a Christian saint associated with the same geographical region. Born in the 5th century, she founded a monastery in Kildare and became known for her compassion and miracles. The Christian Church eventually canonized her, and her feast day falls on February 1st, closely aligned with the pagan celebration of Imbolc. Interestingly, many of St. Brigid's attributes and miracles mirror those of the earlier pagan goddess, suggesting a deliberate effort to integrate pre-existing traditions into the Christian narrative.

Modern celebrations often intertwine both the pagan and Christian aspects of Brigid. Imbolc ceremonies may honor the goddess and the saint, recognizing the common themes of creativity, healing, and protection. Some individuals may participate in pagan and Christian rituals, highlighting the continuity of veneration across different belief systems.

Contemporary celebrations of Imbolc may involve a diverse range of practices. Pagans and Wiccans may focus on the goddess Brigid, engaging in traditional rituals or adapting them to suit personal beliefs. For those with Christian inclinations, St. Brigid's feast day may be marked with prayer, acts of charity, or attending church services. In essence, the celebration of Imbolc and Brigid has evolved into a dynamic and inclusive expression that accommodates various spiritual perspectives.

Brighid, often spelled Brigid, is a revered figure in Celtic mythology and spirituality, embodying a multifaceted and dynamic aspect of the divine. She is a goddess associated with various domains, including healing, poetry, Smithcraft, fertility, and the hearth. Brighid is often considered a tripartite goddess, with each facet representing different aspects of her character.

Dana (Irish)

Primordial Mother Goddess: Dana, often associated with Danu or Anu, is a primordial mother goddess in Celtic mythology. She is considered a mother figure and a source of life.

Matron of the Tuatha Dé Danann: Dana is revered as the ancestral mother and matron goddess of the Tuatha Dé Danann, a mythical race in Irish mythology known for their magical and supernatural qualities.

Etymology: The name "Dana" is often linked to the Old Irish word "dánu," meaning "knowledge" or "wisdom." In this context, Dana is associated with wisdom and divine knowledge.

Alternative Names: Dana is sometimes called Danu or Anu in different texts and traditions. These names may be used interchangeably to represent the same or similar goddess figures.

Mother of Deities: Dana is considered the mother of several prominent deities among the Tuatha Dé Danann, including gods like the Dagda, Lir, and Ogma.

Cultural Significance: Dana is an important Irish cultural and mythological heritage figure. The Tuatha Dé Danann are believed to have brought various skills and attributes to Ireland, including magic and craftsmanship.

Otherworldly Realm: Dana is often associated with an Otherworldly realm or divine homeland of the Tuatha Dé Danann, which some interpretations place beneath the earth's surface or in a parallel dimension.

Festivals and Celebrations: In some interpretations, the festival of Beltane, celebrated around May 1st, is considered a time when the veil between the mortal world and the Otherworld is thin, and Dana is honored along with other divine beings.

Linguistic Connections: Dana's name has linguistic connections to other Indo-European languages, and variations of her name appear in the mythologies of different cultures.

Surviving Texts: Much of what is known about Dana comes from medieval Irish texts such as the Lebor Gabála Érenn (The Book of Invasions), where the arrival of the Tuatha Dé Danann in Ireland is described.

While the specifics of Dana's mythology may vary across different texts and traditions, her role as a mother goddess and matron of the Tuatha Dé Danann underscores her significance in Celtic mythological narratives.

Gaia (Greek)

Primordial Goddess: Gaia is one of the primordial deities in Greek mythology, representing the Earth and the ancestral mother of all life.

Parentage: Gaia is born from Chaos, the primeval void that existed at the beginning of the cosmos. She is considered one of the first beings in the universe.

Progeny: Gaia is the mother of the Titans, the Cyclopes, and the Hecatoncheires (Hundred-Handed Ones) with her brother Uranus (the sky). She is also the mother of various other deities, including the Furies and the Giants.

Uranus and Cronus: Gaia played a significant role in the overthrow of Uranus by her son Cronus. She encouraged and aided Cronus in castrating Uranus, leading to the establishment of Cronus as the ruler of the cosmos.

Mother of Olympian Deities: After Cronus, Gaia became the grandmother of the Olympian gods, as Cronus and Rhea's children included Zeus, Hera, Poseidon, Hades, Demeter, and Hestia.

Revenge on Uranus: Gaia's support for Cronus was motivated by her resentment toward Uranus, who had imprisoned her other offspring, the Cyclopes and Hecatoncheires, in Tartarus. After Uranus's overthrow, these beings were released.

Deity of the Earth: Gaia is considered the personification of the Earth itself. She is often depicted as a maternal figure, and her union with Uranus represents the cosmic marriage that produced all life.

Gaia's Wrath: In some myths, Gaia is portrayed as a force to be reckoned with. She could be vengeful, particularly when angered or when witnessing the mistreatment of her children.

Cult and Worship: Gaia was not typically worshipped in structured cults like some other deities in the Greek pantheon. However, her importance in the cosmogony and her association with the Earth made her a concept that permeated Greek religious thought.

Modern Usage: The name Gaia has been adopted in modern times to represent the Earth as a living and interconnected entity, reflecting ecological and environmental concerns.

Gaia's role as the Earth itself and her involvement in the cosmic events of Greek mythology make her a foundational figure in Greek cosmogony and a symbol of the interconnectedness of all life on Earth.

Inanna (Sumerian, Babylonian, Assyrian)

Goddess of Love and War: Inanna is a prominent goddess in the ancient Mesopotamian pantheon, associated with love, fertility, sex, and war. She is often considered the Queen of Heaven.

Sumerian Origins: Inanna originated in Sumerian mythology as the daughter of the god Nanna (Sumerian) or Sin (Akkadian), the moon god. She was later associated with the Akkadian and Babylonian goddess Ishtar.

Descendant of An: Inanna is often described as the granddaughter of An, the sky god, and the daughter of Nanna/Sin and Ningal.

Symbols: Inanna is commonly associated with the planet Venus, which appears both in the morning and evening sky. Her symbols include the eight-pointed star and the rosette.

The Descent of Inanna: One of the most well-known myths about Inanna is the "Descent of Inanna" or "Inanna's Descent to the Underworld." In this myth, Inanna descends to the Underworld, but she is subjected to various trials and challenges. Her sister, Ereshkigal, queen of the Underworld, kills Inanna and hangs her on a hook. However, Inanna is eventually resurrected and returns to the world of the living.

Sacred Marriage Rite: Inanna was associated with the sacred marriage rite, a ritual that symbolized the union between the goddess and the king, enhancing fertility and prosperity.

Cultural Influence: Inanna's worship had a significant impact on the cultures of Sumer, Akkad, Babylon, and Assyria. She was one of the most venerated deities in the Mesopotamian region.

Ishtar in Babylonian and Assyrian Cultures: Inanna was later assimilated with the Babylonian and Assyrian goddess Ishtar. In these cultures, Ishtar continued to be associated with love, war, and fertility.

Epic of Gilgamesh: In the "Epic of Gilgamesh," Ishtar plays a prominent role. She is rejected by the hero Gilgamesh, leading to her seeking vengeance by sending the Bull of Heaven to destroy him.

Resurgence in Modern Spirituality: Inanna's mythology has gained renewed interest in modern times, particularly in feminist and neopagan circles, where she is celebrated as a symbol of feminine strength and empowerment.

Inanna's multifaceted character as a goddess of love, war, and fertility, as well as her journey to the Underworld and subsequent resurrection, makes her one of the most intriguing and enduring figures in ancient Mesopotamian mythology.

Juno (Roman)

Goddess of Marriage and Queen of the Gods: Juno is a major goddess in Roman mythology and is often considered the queen of the gods. She is associated with marriage, fertility, and the well-being of women.

Greek Equivalent: Juno's Greek equivalent is Hera, the wife and sister of Zeus in Greek mythology. However, Juno has distinct characteristics and roles in the Roman context.

Parentage: Juno is the daughter of Saturn (Cronus in Greek mythology) and Ops (Rhea in Greek mythology). She is also the sister and wife of Jupiter (Zeus in Greek mythology).

Matron Goddess: Juno is revered as a protective deity for women, particularly in the context of marriage and childbirth. She is often invoked as a matron goddess overseeing the well-being of married couples.

Cult and Festivals: Juno had several cults and festivals dedicated to her worship in ancient Rome. The most significant was the Matronalia, celebrated on March 1st, which honored Juno as the protector of married women.

Symbols: Juno is commonly depicted with various symbols, including the peacock, a symbol of immortality and protection, and a scepter, symbolizing her authority as queen of the gods.

Associations with the Month of June: The month of June is thought to be named after Juno. It was considered an auspicious month for weddings, aligning with Juno's role as a goddess of marriage.

Role in Roman Mythology: Juno appears in various Roman myths, often in her capacity as the wife of Jupiter and as a central figure in stories involving the protection of the Roman state and the divine lineage of Rome.

Mythological Children: Juno is the mother of several important deities, including Mars (god of war) and Vulcan (god of fire and craftsmanship). In some traditions, she is also considered the mother of Juventas, the goddess of youth.

Epithets: Juno had various epithets reflecting her different aspects, such as Juno Lucina (goddess of childbirth), Juno Moneta (goddess of advice), and Juno Sospita (goddess of protection).

Juno's significance in Roman mythology is underscored by her multifaceted role as a matron goddess, queen of the gods, and protector of various aspects of Roman life, including marriage and childbirth.

Selene (Greek)

Goddess of the Moon: Selene is a Greek goddess associated with the moon. She is often depicted driving a chariot drawn by two horses across the night sky, illuminating the Earth with her moonlight.

Parentage: In various traditions, Selene is described as the daughter of the Titans Hyperion (Titan of the sun) and Theia (Titaness of sight), making her a sister to Helios (the sun) and Eos (the dawn).

Lover of Endymion: One of the most famous myths involving Selene is her love affair with the mortal shepherd Endymion. According to the myth, Selene fell in love with Endymion and requested from Zeus that he be granted eternal youth and eternal sleep so that she could visit him every night.

Offspring: Selene is said to be the mother of several children, including Pandeia, who was born from her union with Zeus.

Titans and Titansomachy: As a Titaness, Selene was part of the generation of Titans that preceded the Olympian gods. She did not play a prominent role in the Titanomachy, the war between the Titans and Olympians, which led to the establishment of the Olympian order.

Worship: Selene had temples and cults dedicated to her in various parts of ancient Greece, but her worship was not as widespread as that of some other major deities.

Epithets: Selene was known by various epithets, reflecting her role and characteristics. One such epithet is "Phoebe," meaning bright or shining, associated with her moonlight.

Moon as a Symbol: Selene's association with the moon has made her a symbolic figure representing the changing phases of the lunar cycle. The moon is often personified as Selene in various Greek myths and poetry.

Cultural Influence: Selene's imagery and symbolism have impacted art, literature, and culture. She is often referenced in poetry and is depicted in various works of art across different historical periods.

Roman Equivalent: In Roman mythology, Selene is equated with Luna, the Roman goddess of the moon. While Luna shares similarities with Selene, there are also differences in their cultural and mythological contexts.

Selu (Cherokee)

Selu, also known as Selu Selu or Corn Mother, is a figure in Cherokee mythology.

Goddess of Corn: Selu is considered the Corn Mother and is revered as the goddess of corn and agriculture in Cherokee mythology.

Creation of Humans: In some versions of the myth, Selu plays a role in the creation of humans. According to the story, the first humans were created from the dust on Selu's body.

Gift of Corn: Selu is associated with the gift of corn, a staple crop for the Cherokee people. In the myth, she provides the people with the knowledge of planting, cultivating, and harvesting corn, ensuring their sustenance.

Fertility and Nourishment: Selu is a symbol of fertility and nourishment. Her role in providing corn signifies her importance in sustaining the Cherokee people and ensuring their well-being.

Duality with Kanati: In some versions of the myth, Selu is the wife of Kanati, the Lucky Hunter or Spirit of the Hunt. Together, they represent the dual aspects of agricultural and hunting societies, reflecting the balance in Cherokee life.

Cultural Importance: The story of Selu is not just a myth but also a cultural teaching. It imparts important lessons about agriculture, sustainability, and the relationship between humans and the natural world.

Harvest Ceremonies: The Cherokee people traditionally held ceremonies to honor Selu and express gratitude for the corn harvest. These ceremonies often involved rituals, dances, and expressions of thanks for the abundance provided by Selu.

Seasonal Connection: Selu's mythology intertwines seasonal planting cycles, growth, and harvest. The Cherokee people recognize the importance of living in harmony with the Earth and respecting the natural cycles.

Adaptation: The myth of Selu has been passed down through generations and adapted to different regional variations among the Cherokee people. Other communities may have nuanced versions of the story.

Cultural Continuity: Despite the challenges faced by the Cherokee people throughout history, the mythology of Selu remains an essential part of their cultural identity. The story is often shared to preserve traditional knowledge and values.

Selu's significance lies in her role as a provider, nurturing the Cherokee people through the gift of corn. Her mythology reflects the deep connection between the Cherokee culture and the natural world, emphasizing sustainable practices and respect for the Earth.

Vesta (Roman)

Goddess of the Hearth: Vesta is the Roman goddess of the hearth, home, and family. She is considered the guardian of the sacred fire and the well-being of the household.

Virgin Goddess: Vesta is one of the few Roman goddesses honored as a virgin. Her priestesses, known as the Vestal Virgins, were dedicated to maintaining the sacred fire and observing their vow of chastity.

Parentage: In Roman mythology, Vesta is often identified as one of the daughters of Saturn (Cronus in Greek mythology) and Ops (Rhea in Greek mythology). She is a sister to Jupiter (Zeus), Juno (Hera), Ceres (Demeter), and Neptune (Poseidon).

Cult of Vesta: Vesta's cult was one of Rome's most ancient and revered. The focus of her worship was the hearth fire, which symbolized the heart of the family and the Roman state.

Vestal Virgins: The Vestal Virgins were priestesses dedicated to Vesta's service. Chosen at a young age, they were required to maintain the eternal flame in the Temple of Vesta and uphold their vow of celibacy for 30 years.

Penalties for Neglect: Neglect of the sacred fire by the Vestal Virgins was considered a serious offense. If the flame were to extinguish, it was believed to bring ill fortune to Rome. Vestal Virgins who broke their vow of chastity could face severe penalties, including burial alive.

Public and Private Worship: Vesta's worship extended beyond private homes to the civic realm. The Temple of Vesta, located in the Roman Forum, housed the sacred flame tended by the Vestal Virgins. Public ceremonies and rites were conducted at this temple.

Festivals: Vesta was honored in various Roman festivals, including the Vestalia, which took place in June. During this festival, the Vestal Virgins would open the doors of the Temple of Vesta to allow the public to make offerings and participate in rituals.

Symbolism: Vesta's symbolism extended beyond the hearth to include the idea of communal harmony, domestic order, and the stability of the Roman state.

Roman Equivalent: Vesta is often associated with the Greek goddess Hestia, who presided over the hearth and was honored as a virgin goddess.

Vesta's importance in Roman religious and civic life was reflected in the meticulous care given to her sacred flame and the significant role of the Vestal Virgins in Roman society.

Bragi(Norse)

Norse God of Poetry and Music: Bragi is a god in Norse mythology associated with poetry, music, and eloquence. He is known as the son of Odin, the chief god, and the giantess Gunnlod.

Attributes: Bragi is often depicted as a wise and eloquent figure, embodying the qualities of inspiration and creativity. He is renowned for his ability to compose beautiful and persuasive poetry.

Husband of Idunn: Bragi is married to Idunn, the goddess of youth and keeper of the golden apples that grant the gods their immortality.

Progeny: Bragi and Idunn have two sons, Forseti and Eiríkr, who are associated with justice and healing, respectively.

Hall of Bragi: In Asgard, the realm of the gods, there is a hall named "Bragi's Hall" where the righteous and heroic dead are said to gather.

Mead of Poetry: A notable myth involves Bragi and the Mead of Poetry. The mead is a magical drink that grants the gift of poetic inspiration. Bragi is often linked to this mead and is considered one of the few who can partake of it.

Kennings and Epithets: In Old Norse poetry, kennings (figurative expressions) and epithets often refer to Bragi to invoke the inspiration and eloquence associated with him.

Skaldic Tradition: Bragi is particularly revered in the skaldic tradition of Norse poetry. Skalds, the poets of Viking Age Scandinavia, often invoke Bragi for inspiration and guidance in their craft.

Surviving Texts: While references to Bragi are found in various Old Norse texts, such as the Prose Edda and the Poetic Edda, detailed information about him is relatively sparse compared to some other Norse gods.

End Times Prophecy: In some Norse mythology prophecies, including the Poetic Edda's Voluspa, Bragi is mentioned as one of the few surviving gods after the events of Ragnarok, the end of the world.

Bragi's role as the god of poetry and music underscores the importance of these arts in Norse culture, and his association with eloquence and inspiration makes him a revered figure in the pantheon.

Cupid/Amor (Roman)

God of Love: Cupid, known as Amor in Latin, is the Roman god of love and desire. He is often depicted as a mischievous, winged child carrying a bow and arrows.

Parentage: In Roman mythology, Cupid is the son of Venus (Aphrodite in Greek mythology), the goddess of love and beauty. His father's identity varies in different myths, with Mars (Ares in Greek mythology) being a common choice.

Attributes: Cupid is typically portrayed with a bow and arrows, which he uses to shoot people with love-inducing arrows. The arrows can make individuals fall deeply in love with the first person they see.

Mischievous Nature: Cupid is often depicted as mischievous and playful. His actions can be unpredictable, causing both gods and mortals to fall in love unexpectedly.

Psyche and Cupid: One of the most famous stories involving Cupid is the myth of Cupid and Psyche. In this tale, Cupid falls in love with the mortal Psyche. The story involves trials and tribulations, ultimately culminating in their union.

Roman Adaptation: Cupid's mythology shares similarities with the Greek god Eros, but the Roman version often emphasizes his playful and mischievous nature rather than just his role in promoting romantic love.

Associations with the Arts: Cupid is sometimes depicted as an attendant to the Muses, associating him with the arts and inspiration. This aligns with the idea that love and passion can be sources of artistic creativity.

Symbol of Love: Cupid became an enduring symbol of love and desire in Western art and literature. His image often represents Valentine's Day and other romantic themes.

Cultural Influence: Cupid's imagery and symbolism have permeated various aspects of Western culture, including art, literature, and popular culture. He is familiar in classical art, Renaissance paintings, and contemporary media.

Roman Equivalent: While Cupid is the Roman god of love, his Greek equivalent is Eros. The two deities share many characteristics, but their cultural contexts and stories may differ.

Cupid's playful and enchanting nature and his association with romantic love have made him an enduring and recognizable figure in Roman mythology and beyond.

Dian Cecht (Irish)

God of Healing: Dian Cecht is a deity in Irish mythology associated with healing and medicine. He is often regarded as the physician or healer among the Tuatha Dé Danann, a mythical race in Irish mythology.

Parentage: Dian Cecht is the son of the god Cermait and the grandson of the Dagda, a major figure in the Tuatha Dé Danann.

Healing Well: Dian Cecht is credited with creating a magical well called Sláine, which possessed the power to heal wounds and cure ailments. This well played a crucial role in healing the wounded warriors of the Tuatha Dé Danann.

Sons: Dian Cecht had three sons, each skilled in various aspects of healing. Miach, his most talented son, was particularly gifted in restoring life and limb.

Jealousy and Conflict: Dian Cecht grew jealous of his son Miach's superior healing abilities. In a fit of envy, he killed Miach. However, Miach's sister, Airmid, collected and arranged his body parts, and he was miraculously restored to life.

Dian Cecht's Contributions: Despite the conflicts within his family, Dian Cecht remained an important figure in Irish mythology due to his association with healing. His contributions, including the creation of the healing well and his expertise in medicine, benefited the Tuatha Dé Danann during times of conflict and war.

Lugh's Wrath: Dian Cecht's role in the death of his son Miach led to the wrath of Miach's brother, Lugh. Lugh confronted Dian Cecht and his supporters, seeking justice for Miach's death.

Dian Cecht's Hand: Dian Cecht lost his hand during the battle with Lugh. Following the confrontation, Dian Cecht abdicated his position as the healer of the Tuatha Dé Danann, passing the role to his son Miach, who had been resurrected.

Death: The details of Dian Cecht's death are not explicitly mentioned in surviving texts. However, his role as the healer of the Tuatha Dé Danann came to an end, and he faded into obscurity.
Dian Cecht's significance lies in his association with healing and medicine in Irish mythology, and his story highlights themes of family conflict and jealousy within the divine realm of the Tuatha Dé Danann.

Dumuzi (Sumerian)

God of Vegetation and Fertility: Dumuzi, also known as Tammuz, is a Sumerian god associated with vegetation, fertility, and the annual cycle of growth and decay.

Divine Shepherd: Dumuzi is often depicted as a divine shepherd, emphasizing his connection to Sumerian life's pastoral and agricultural aspects.

Sacred Marriage Rite: Dumuzi is a central figure in the sacred marriage rite, an important ritual in Sumerian religious practices. The ritual involved the symbolic union of the goddess Inanna (Ishtar) with Dumuzi, representing the union of the divine and earthly realms.

Marriage to Inanna: Dumuzi becomes the consort of Inanna, the goddess of love, fertility, and war. Their sacred marriage is celebrated in myths and rituals, and it is believed to ensure the fertility of the land.

Descent to the Underworld: Dumuzi plays a crucial role in the myth of Inanna's Descent to the Underworld. After Inanna descends to the Underworld, Dumuzi is left in charge of the throne. However, he eventually meets a tragic fate and is taken to the Underworld as a substitute for Inanna.

Grief and Mourning: Inanna's descent results in Dumuzi's death, leading to mourning and grief in the myth. The mourning rituals for Dumuzi and Inanna are associated with the changing seasons, reflecting the cycle of life, death, and rebirth.

Resurrection: Dumuzi's death and descent to the Underworld are not final. In some versions of the myth, Dumuzi can return to the earthly realm for part of the year, representing the cyclical nature of vegetation and fertility.

Parallel with Other Deities: Dumuzi's death and resurrection parallels ancient Near Eastern mythologies, such as the Babylonian myth of Tammuz and the Phoenician myth of Adonis. These myths share similar themes of divine sacrifice and rebirth.

Symbol of Nature's Renewal: Dumuzi's myth is often interpreted as a symbolic representation of the seasonal cycle, where his death and resurrection mirror the death and rebirth of vegetation in the agricultural calendar.

Cultural Influence: The worship of Dumuzi and Inanna, along with the associated rituals and myths, significantly influenced Sumerian religious practices. Later cultures in the ancient Near East adopted and adapted elements of these myths.

Dumuzi's mythology is an allegory for the natural cycles of life, death, and renewal, reflecting the importance of agriculture and fertility in the ancient Sumerian worldview.

Eros (Greek)

God of Love and Desire: Eros is the Greek god of love, desire, and attraction. He is often portrayed as a young winged god with a bow and arrows, which he uses to incite love in the hearts of gods and mortals.

Parentage: In various myths, Eros is depicted as the son of Aphrodite (Venus in Roman mythology) and Ares (Mars in Roman mythology), or in some versions, he is considered one of the primordial deities born from Chaos.

Mythological Roles: Eros plays a role in several myths, often acting as a mischievous and capricious figure. Notably, he is involved in the love stories of gods and mortals, using his arrows to manipulate their emotions.

Psyche and Eros: One of the most famous stories involving Eros is the myth of Eros and Psyche. Eros falls in love with the mortal Psyche, and their story involves trials, separation, and eventual reunification.

Worship and Cult: Eros was not extensively worshipped in formal cults in ancient Greece. However, his presence in art, literature, and everyday life emphasized the pervasive influence of love and desire in Greek culture.

Februus (Roman)

God of Purification: Februus is a god in Roman mythology associated with purification and the expiation of sins. His name is linked to the Latin word "februare," meaning "to purify" or "to expiate."

Parentage: Februus is sometimes identified as the son of Mars, the god of war, and Venus, the goddess of love and beauty.

Festival of Februa: Februus is particularly associated with the festival of Februa, which is celebrated annually on February 15th. This festival was a time of purification and cleansing.

Februa Implements: The implements used in the rituals of Februa included strips of goat skin called "februa," which were used to whip or touch people and livestock for purification.

Februatio: The entire month of February is believed to have derived its name from Februus, emphasizing the association with purification rituals performed during this time.

End of the Roman Year: The festival of Februa marked the end of the Roman year in the ancient lunar calendar. It was a time to cleanse and purify oneself in preparation for the new year.

Linked to Lupercalia: The festival of Februa has some connections to the more well-known festival of Lupercalia, which was also celebrated in mid-February. Both festivals involved purification rites and were seen as a way to ward off evil.

Cultural Influence: The concept of purification associated with Februus aligns with Roman beliefs in the importance of ritual cleanliness and the expiation of sins. While Februus himself may not have had a comprehensive mythology, the rituals and festivals associated with him held cultural significance in ancient Rome.

Februus, as a god associated with purification and the end of the Roman year, played a role in ancient Rome's religious and cultural practices. The rituals and festivals connected to Februus reflected the Roman emphasis on spiritual renewal and cleanliness.

CHAPTER 11

Quicky
Duties

African Deities

Ala-Ibo, Nigeria: Mother goddess, ruler of the underworld, goddess of fertility
Amma-Dogon, Mali: Supreme god
Cagn-Bushmen, Southwestern Africa: Creator god
Eshu- Yoruba, Nigeria: Trickster and messenger god
Katonda-Buganda, East Africa: Creator god, father of the gods, king and judge of the universe
Kibuka-Buganda, East Africa: War god
Leza- Bantu, Central and South Africa: Creator and sky god
Mujaji-Lovedu, South Africa: Rain goddess
Nyame-Ashanti and Akan, Ghana: Creator god associated with the Sun and moon
Ogun-Yoruba, West Africa: God of war and iron
Olorun-Yoruba, West Africa: Sky god and supreme deity

Aztec Deities

Coatlicue: Lady of the Serpent, Earth goddess
Huitzilopochtli: Hummingbird of the South sun and war god
Ometecuhtli: Dual Lord creator god
Quetzalcoatl: Feathered Serpent god of twins and learning
Tezcatlipoca: Lord of the Smoking Mirror, god of the night sky
Tlaloc: Growth-maker god of rain and fertility
Xipe Totec: Flayed Lord god of vegetation, torture, and sacrifice

Celtic Deities

Goddesses

Brigantia: Goddess of rivers and waters, poetry and crafts
Brigit: Goddess of fire, fertility, healing, cattle, and poetry
Ceridwen: Goddess and sorceress, poetic wisdom, prophecy, magic, and rebirth
Epona: Horse goddess, fertility and cornucopias, horses, and mules
Medb: Goddess of sovereignty and motherhood
Morrigan: Goddess of war and death, fate and battle
Nehalennia: Goddess of seafarers, fertility, and abundance
Nemausicae: Mother goddess, fertility, and healing
Nerthus: Goddess of fertility, peace, and prosperity
Saitada: Goddess of grief

Gods

Alator: God of war and protection, the name means "he who nourishes the people."
Albiorix: God of protection and war, means "king of the world."
Belenus: God of healing, the name means "bright one."
Borvo: God of healing waters and minerals
Bres: God of fertility, the tyrant ruler
Cernunnos: Horned god of nature, fertility, the underworld, wealth, and fruit
Esus: God of strength and human sacrifice
Lenus: God of healing, associated with the Roman god Mars
Lugh: God of the sun and craftsmanship, justice, and rulership
Maponus: God of music, poetry, and youth
Nuada: God of healing, the sea, and warfare

Egyptian Deities

Goddesses

Bastet: Goddess of protection, takes the form of a cat or lioness

Bat: Cow goddess of the sky

Hathor: Goddess of the sky, sun, sexuality, motherhood, music and dance, the afterlife

Imentet: Goddess of the afterlife, friend of the dead

Isis: Goddess of motherhood, protection, and magic

Kauket: Goddess of chaos and darkness

Maat: Goddess of truth, justice, and order

Menhit: Goddess of war, foreign war, took the form of a lioness

Neith: Goddess of creation and hunting, patron of the city Sais

Nekhbet: Vulture goddess, goddess of protection

Nepit: Goddess of grain, counterpart to Neper

Nut: Sky goddess, arched over the heavens

Pakhet: Lioness goddess, goddess of war

Sekhmet: Goddess of destruction and violence, warder of disease, protector of pharaohs, consort of Ptah

Wajdet: Cobra goddess, protective of the earth and pharaohs

Gods

Aker: God of the Earth and horizon, protection

Anhur: God of war and hunting

Anubis: God of the dead, conductor of souls, has the head of a jackal

Bennu: God of the sun, rebirth, and creation. Geb: God of the Earth, physically supports the world

Horus: God of the sky, sun, protection, kingship and healing

Khepri, God of the morning/rising sun, has a scarab beetle as a face

Montu: God of war and the sun

Nefertum: God of the lotus flower and youth Nemty: Falcon god, Ferryman for the gods Osiris: God of death, resurrection, rebirth, ruler of the Underworld

Ptah: God of craftsmen and creation

Ra: Ruler of all Gods, god of the sun, god of creation and afterlife

Set: God of deserts, storms, violence, disorder, and foreigners

Shu: God of the air, wind, and supporter of the sky

Thoth: God of the moon, writing and scribes, master of physical and moral law

Wadj-Wer: God of the sea and fertility

Greek Deities

Goddesses
Aphrodite: Goddess of love, beauty, passion, sex
Artemis: Goddess of the hunt, wild nature, chastity
Athena: Goddess of wisdom and war, peace and crafts, spinning and weaving
Demeter: Goddess of agriculture, fertility, harvest, and sacred law
Gaia: Goddess of the Earth, Mother Earth, the great mother
Hecate: Goddess of magic, witchcraft, the other, spirit
Hera: Goddess of goddesses, women, marriage, Queen of the Gods
Hestia: Goddess of the home and hearth, architecture, family, domestic affairs
Iris: Goddess of the rainbow, messenger of the gods
Nike: Goddess of victory, known as the Winged Goddess of Victory
Nyx: Goddess of the night and darkness
Persephone: Goddess of Spring and vegetation, Queen of the Underworld
Selene: Goddess of the moon and sleep
Themis: Goddess of natural and divine order, law and custom

Gods
Apollo: God of music, art, poetry, medicine, knowledge
Ares: God of war, aggression, violence, untamed physical action
Charon, Ferryman of Hades, took newly dead people to the Underworld
Dionysus: God of the grape harvest, wine, ritual madness, ecstasy and theatre
Hades: God of the dead and the Underworld, riches, rebirth
Hermes: God of trade, travelers, guide to the Underworld, messenger of the gods
Kratos: God of strength, power and war
Pan: God of nature, shepherds, sexuality, and goats
Poseidon: Greek god of the sea, earthquakes, horses, storms
Prometheus: God of forethought and craft, molded humans from clay
Thanatos: God of gentle, peaceful death
Triton: Messenger of the sea, son of Poseidon
Zeus: God of the sky, thunder, order, justice, King of all Gods and men

Norse Deities

Goddesses
Eir: Goddess of healing and medical skill
Eostre: Goddess of spring and dawn
Freyja: Goddess of love, fertility, battle and witchcraft
Frigg: Goddess of marriage and motherhood, Queen of the gods
Gefjun: Goddess of fertility and plow, abundance and prosperity
Hlin: Goddess of consolation and protection
Jord: Goddess of the Earth, Mother Earth
Nanna: Goddess of joy, peace, and the moon
Nott: Goddess of the night and darkness
Sif: Goddess of the harvest, grain, and earth
Sigyn: Goddess of fidelity, mercy, and mourning
Skadi: Goddess of winter, mountains and skiing
Sol: Goddess of the sun and healing
Vor: Goddess of wisdom, knowledge, and awareness

Gods
Baldur: God of beauty, peace, innocence, rebirth
Bragi: God of poetry, music, the harp
Frey: God of fertility, peace, the sun and rain
Hodr: God of winter, blind god, god of darkness
Hoenir: God of silence, passion, spirituality, poetry
Kvasir: God of inspiration, god of wisdom
Loki: God of trickery and mischief
Magni: God of strength and bravery
Mani, God of the moon, pulled the moon across the sky
Njord: God of the sea, wind. fish and wealth
Odin: The Allfather, God of war, poetry, magic and wisdom
Thor: God of thunder and battle, protection of mankind
Tyr: God of war and justice, god of the skies
Ullr: God of skis and bows, god of winter
Vali: God of revenge and vengeance

Roman Deities

Goddesses
Aurora: Goddess of the dawn
Bellona: Goddess of war and battle
Ceres: Goddess of the harvest and agriculture
Concordia: Goddess of agreement, understanding, and harmony in marriage
Diana: Goddess of the hunt, the moon, childbirth and virginity
Fortuna: Goddess of fortune, chance and luck
Juno: Queen of the gods, goddess of matrimony and marriage
Luna: Goddess of the moon, also known as the goddess Selene
Minerva: Goddess of wisdom, war, the arts, trade, and craft
Nemesis: Goddess of revenge and divine retribution
Nox: Goddess of the night and darkness
Pax: Goddess of peace and harmony
Venus: Goddess of love, sexuality, beauty and gardens
Vesta: Goddess of the hearth and sacred fire, family and home

Gods
Apollo: God of the sun, poetry, healing, truth, music and archery
Bacchus: God of wine, sexuality, and truth
Cupid: God of love, a messenger of love
Hercules: God of strength, adventure, and heroism
Lucifer: God of the morning star and dawn
Mars: God of war and military, protector of agriculture
Mercury: Messenger of the gods, bearer of souls to the Underworld. Neptune: God of the sea, horses, and earthquakes
Orcus: God of the Underworld, punisher of broken oaths
Pluto: Ruler of the Underworld and the dead
Saturn: God of harvest and agriculture, sowing and seed
Vulcan: God of fire and blacksmiths, volcanoes and destruction

Love Deities of World Mythology

A love deity in mythology is associated with sexual love, lust, fertility, or sexuality. Love deities are common in mythology and may be found in many polytheistic religion. These are but a few of the many that exist.

Kamadeva
Hindu God of Human Love and Desire

Laka
Hawaiian Goddess of Fertility

Erzulie Freda
Haitian African Loa of Love and Beauty

Turan
Etruscan Goddess of Love, Fertility and Vitality

Oshun
Yoruban Orisha of Love, Sexuality, Beauty, and Pleasure

Aphrodite/Venus
Greek/Roman Goddess of Love and Beauty

Nanaya
Sumerian Goddess of Sexuality

Astghik
Armenian Deity of Fertility and Love

Rati
Hindu Goddess of Love, Carnal Desire, Lust, Passion and Sexual Pleasure

Ziva
Slavic Goddess of Life and Fertility

Qetesh
Canaanite Goddess of Sacred Ecstasy and Sexual Pleasure

Prende
Albanian Goddess of Love

Inari Okami
Japanse Kami of Fertility

Atabey
Taino Goddess of Fertility

Aengus
Iris, God of Love, Youth, and Poetic Inspiration

Inanna/Ishtar
Sumerian Goddess of Love, Beauty, Sex and War

Freyja
Norse Goddess of Love, Beauty and Attraction

Xochipilli
Aztec God of Flowers

Yue-Lao
Chinese God of Love and Marriage

Hathor
Egyptian Goddess of Joy, Feminine Love and Motherhood

The Erotes
Greek Gods of Love

Shauska
Hittite Goddess of Fertility, War and Healing

CHAPTER 12

Magical Creatures and Beings

Ammit-Egyptian

Ammit, or Ammut or Ahemait, is a significant figure in ancient Egyptian mythology. Ammit is a mythical creature called the "Devourer of the Dead" or "Eater of Hearts." It plays a role in the judgment of souls in the afterlife.

Key features of Ammit

Appearance: Ammit is depicted as a composite creature with the head of a crocodile, a lion's forelimbs, and a hippopotamus's hind legs. This combination of fierce animal features symbolizes its role as a fearsome and devouring force.

Role in the Afterlife: In ancient Egyptian belief, when a person died, their heart was weighed against the feather of Ma'at (the goddess of truth and justice) during the judgment process in the Hall of Ma'at. The soul could proceed to the afterlife if the heart were deemed pure and lighter than the feather. However, if the heart were heavy with wrongdoing, Ammit would devour it, condemning the soul to eternal restlessness.

Symbolism: Ammit served as a symbol of the consequences of a sinful life. The idea of being consumed by Ammit was a powerful deterrent against wrongdoing in the eyes of the ancient Egyptians.

Judgment Scene: Depictions of the judgment scene in Egyptian funerary texts often show Ammit standing beside the scales used to weigh the heart. The god Anubis, associated with mummification and the afterlife, is typically depicted overseeing the judgment process.

Purification Rituals: Ancient Egyptians believed in various rituals and spells to ensure the purity of the heart and safeguard against the threat of Ammit. These rituals aimed to secure a favorable outcome in the afterlife.

Ammit's role in the judgment of souls reflects the ancient Egyptian emphasis on moral conduct and the concept of justice in the afterlife. The image of Ammit as the "Eater of Hearts" added a profound and vivid element to the mythology surrounding death and the journey to the next realm.

Bake-Kujira - Japan

"Bake Kujira," which translates to "ghost whale" in Japanese, is a yokai—a supernatural creature or ghost—in Japanese folklore. This mythical creature is often depicted as the ghostly apparition of a whale that brings misfortune and disaster.

Key features of Bake Kujira

Apparition of a Whale: Bake Kujira is said to appear as the spectral form of a whale, often accompanied by strange lights. Its ghostly presence is associated with eerie occurrences and is considered an omen of impending disaster.

Ghostly Flames: Witnesses of Bake Kujira sightings often describe the presence of mysterious flames or lights accompanying the ghost whale. These ghostly flames are part of the supernatural phenomena associated with the creature.

Crying Sounds: In some accounts, Bake Kujira is said to emit mournful and eerie cries, adding to the unsettling nature of its appearances. The sounds are believed to foretell calamities or misfortunes.

Curse and Misfortune: The belief is that encountering Bake Kujira brings curses and misfortune to the nearby people or communities. Its ghostly presence is considered a harbinger of tragedy.

Origins: The legend of Bake Kujira has variations in different regions of Japan, and its origins are rooted in traditional folklore. The stories surrounding Bake Kujira often serve as cautionary tales about respecting nature and the consequences of human actions.

Connection to Whaling: Some interpretations of Bake Kujira stories link the creature to the historical practice of whaling. The vengeful spirit of a whale might manifest as Bake Kujira in response to the exploitation of whales.

Symbolic Meaning: Beyond its supernatural aspects, Bake Kujira is sometimes seen as a symbolic representation of environmental concerns and the consequences of disrupting the balance of nature.

Bake Kujira, like many yokai in Japanese folklore, reflects cultural attitudes, environmental awareness, and the storytelling traditions of different regions in Japan. The tales of ghostly whales serve as a reminder of the interconnectedness of humans and nature and the potential consequences of ecological imbalances.

Baku-Chinese

In Japanese folklore, a Baku is a mythical creature known for its ability to devour dreams and nightmares. The Baku is often considered a protective spirit that can ward off evil dreams and bring good fortune to those it visits.

Key features of Baku

Appearance: The Baku is commonly depicted as a chimera-like creature with the body of a bear, the face of an elephant, the tail of an ox, and tiger-like paws. This unique combination of features gives the Baku a distinctive and fantastical appearance.

Dream Eater: The primary role of the Baku is to eat dreams. In Japanese folklore, people would invoke Baku's assistance by praying to it when plagued by nightmares. The belief is that by consuming bad dreams, Baku could provide protection and ensure peaceful sleep.

Nightmare Repellent: The Baku is often considered a guardian against malevolent spirits and nightmares. Hanging an image or charm depicting Baku in the bedroom is believed to prevent bad dreams and bring a sense of security.

Origins: The concept of the Baku has roots in Chinese mythology, where a similar creature, known as the "Mo," also possesses the ability to devour dreams. Over time, the idea of Baku made its way into Japanese folklore.

Cultural Influence: Baku has had a lasting impact on Japanese culture and art. It is featured in various forms, including paintings, sculptures, and talismans, often as a protective charm for children.

Baku in Popular Culture: Baku has appeared in modern Japanese literature, anime, and popular culture. It continues to be a symbol of protection against nightmares and malevolent forces.

Wordplay: In Japanese, the word "Baku" is also used to refer to tapirs, a type of mammal. This linguistic connection adds an interesting layer to the cultural understanding of Baku.

The Baku's role as a dream-eating creature and protector against nightmares reflects its positive and benevolent nature in Japanese folklore. It remains a fascinating and culturally significant figure, often associated with dreams and the pursuit of restful sleep.

Camazotz-Mayan

Camazotz is a figure found in Mesoamerican mythology, particularly in the traditions of the Maya civilization. The name "Camazotz" is derived from the K'iche' language of the Maya people and can be translated as "death bat" or "snatch bat." Camazotz is often associated with death, the underworld, and certain aspects of warfare.

Key features of Camazotz

Bat Deity: Camazotz is commonly depicted as a bat god. The association with bats is significant, as bats were considered mysterious creatures and were often linked to the underworld in various Mesoamerican cultures.

Underworld Connection: In some Mayan beliefs, Camazotz is associated with the underworld or Xibalba, a realm of death and afterlife in Maya cosmology. It is sometimes portrayed as a servant or inhabitant of the underworld.

Violent Attributes: Camazotz is often depicted as a violent and fearsome deity. In certain mythologies, it is associated with acts of bloodletting, sacrifice, and war.

Hero Twins Mythology: In the Popol Vuh, a sacred text of the K'iche' Maya, Camazotz plays a role in the story of the Hero Twins, Hunahpu, and Xbalanque. The Hero Twins engage in a ballgame with the Lords of Xibalba, and one of the challenges involves facing Camazotz, who is said to decapitate victims with a single bite.

Cultural Significance: Camazotz, like other deities in Mesoamerican mythology, played a role in the religious and cosmological beliefs of the Maya people. Rituals, ceremonies, and myths involving Camazotz were likely part of the cultural and spiritual practices of the ancient Maya civilization.

It's important to note that interpretations of Camazotz and other figures in Mesoamerican mythology can vary, and the details of these myths may have regional differences. Understanding these deities is often based on archaeological findings, inscriptions, and the study of ancient texts like the Popol Vuh.

Cerberus-Greek

Cerberus is a mythical creature in Greek mythology, and it is often depicted as a multi-headed dog guarding the entrance to the Underworld. As a monstrous and formidable beast, Cerberus plays a significant role in Greek mythology and the tales of heroes venturing into the realm of the dead.

Key features of Cerberus

Guardian of the Underworld: Cerberus is the three-headed dog that guards the entrance to the Underworld, preventing the living from entering and the dead from escaping.

Parentage: In most accounts, Cerberus is the offspring of Typhon and Echidna, two monstrous figures in Greek mythology. Typhon is often considered one of the deadliest creatures, and Echidna is a serpent-like monster.

Appearance: Cerberus is typically depicted with three heads, although some variations mention fifty or even a hundred heads. The number of heads may vary, but the three-headed portrayal is the most common.

Hades and Capture: As part of the Twelve Labors of Heracles (Hercules), the hero is tasked with capturing Cerberus. Heracles ventures into the Underworld and successfully brings Cerberus to the surface, showcasing his strength and prowess.

Hercules' Capture: In the myth of Heracles and Cerberus, Heracles can take Cerberus from the Underworld because he subdues the creature without using weapons. Heracles accomplishes this by using his strength to wrestle Cerberus into submission.

Symbolic Role: Cerberus serves as a symbolic guardian, representing the boundary between the world of the living and the realm of the dead. Its presence underscores the seriousness of crossing into the afterlife.

Heraldic Symbol: Cerberus has been used as a heraldic symbol and is often associated with guardianship and protection. Its representation in various art forms and coats of arms emphasizes its role as a mythical guardian.

Influence in Popular Culture: Cerberus remains popular in literature, art, and popular culture. Its portrayal as a fierce, multi-headed dog guarding the entrance to the Underworld has made it an iconic symbol.

Cerberus remains one of the most recognizable and enduring creatures in Greek mythology, symbolizing the transition between life and death and the challenges heroes face in their quests.

Cipactli-Aztec

Cipactli is a mythical creature from Aztec mythology, and it plays a significant role in the creation story according to Aztec cosmology.

Key features of Cipactli

Appearance: Cipactli is often described as a monstrous crocodile -like creature. It has aquatic and terrestrial features, symbolizing merging elements from the land and water.

Creation Myth: According to Aztec mythology, in the beginning, the gods Tezcatlipoca and Quetzalcoatl sought to create the world. They descended into the primeval waters and encountered Cipactli. In a cosmic struggle, Tezcatlipoca and Quetzalcoatl managed to defeat Cipactli.

Transformation: After defeating Cipactli, Tezcatlipoca and Quetzalcoatl transformed its body to create the different aspects of the world. Cipactli's body was used to form the Earth's land, mountains, valleys, and other features.

Symbolism: Cipactli is symbolic of chaos and the primordial state before the ordered creation of the world. Its defeat and transformation represent establishing order from the initial chaotic conditions.

Cycles of Creation and Destruction: In Aztec cosmology, the world undergoes cycles of creation and destruction. The creation story involving Cipactli is a foundational myth that explains how the world came into existence after a period of chaos.

Cipactli's role in the creation narrative highlights the Aztec understanding of the cyclical nature of the cosmos, with the world going through phases of creation, destruction, and rebirth. This mythic creature represents the transformative power leading to the ordered world's formation.

Cwn Annwn-Welsh

Cŵn Annwn, often called the "Hounds of Annwn," is a mythical and supernatural entity in Welsh folklore. Annwn is considered the Otherworld in Welsh mythology, and Cŵn Annwn are spectral dogs associated with this realm.

Key features of Cŵn Annwn

Guardians of the Otherworld: Cŵn Annwn are believed to be otherworldly hounds that serve as guardians or hunting companions of Annwn, the Welsh Otherworld. Annwn is often seen as a mysterious realm separate from the world of the living.

Appearance: Descriptions of Cŵn Annwn vary, but they are commonly depicted as large, ghostly white dogs with red ears. These spectral hounds are sometimes associated with the appearance of the Wild Hunt, a supernatural procession often led by a spectral figure.

The Wild Hunt: Cŵn Annwn are sometimes linked to the Wild Hunt, a motif in various European folklore. In the Wild Hunt, a group of spectral beings, often led by a supernatural figure, rides across the sky or through the land, sometimes accompanied by a pack of spectral hounds.

Connection to Death: In some Welsh traditions, Cŵn Annwn are seen as psychopomps, guiding souls to the Otherworld or serving as heralds of death. Their appearance could signal the imminent passing of a person or a significant event.

Hunting Souls: It is believed that Cŵn Annwn roam the countryside, especially during specific times like Samhain (Halloween) or other liminal periods, hunting for souls or guiding them to the Otherworld.

Literary References: Cŵn Annwn has appeared in various Welsh myths and medieval literature. In "The Spoils of Annwn," a poem found in the Welsh collection known as the "Book of Taliesin," King Arthur and his warriors encounter the otherworldly hounds during a journey to Annwn.

Cultural Symbolism: Cŵn Annwn, associated with the Otherworld and death, is symbolic in Welsh folklore. They embody the mysterious and supernatural elements present in the cultural imagination.

Cŵn Annwn continues to capture the imagination, and their presence in Welsh folklore adds an eerie and mythical dimension to the Otherworldly realms, emphasizing the liminality between life and death.

Garuda-Hindu

Garuda is a legendary bird or bird-like creature in Hindu, Buddhist, and Jain mythology. It is often depicted as a large eagle or hawk and is considered the mount (vahana) of the Hindu god Vishnu. Garuda is a prominent and revered figure in various cultural and religious traditions.

Key features of Garuda

Physical Appearance: Garuda is typically portrayed as a large bird with golden feathers, a white face, a sharp beak, and a wingspan that can block the sun. Its appearance is majestic and symbolizes power.

Vahana of Vishnu: In Hindu mythology, Garuda serves as the mount and the devoted vehicle of Lord Vishnu, one of the principal deities in the Hindu pantheon. Garuda is often depicted carrying Vishnu on its back.

Symbolism: Garuda symbolizes power, strength, speed, and freedom. It is also associated with dharma (righteousness) and protects against evil forces.

Hymns and Texts: The "Garuda Purana" is one of the texts in Hinduism named after Garuda. While this text primarily focuses on funerary rites, it also includes sections about cosmology, mythology, and the nature of the soul.

Role in Epics: Garuda plays a significant role in Hindu epics, particularly in the "Mahabharata." The epic recounts the story of Garuda obtaining the nectar of immortality (amrita) from the gods to free his mother from the enslavement of the serpentine Nagas.

Buddhist and Jain Traditions: Garuda is also present in Buddhist and Jain traditions. In Buddhism, Garuda is often associated with the concept of enlightenment. In Jainism, Garuda is considered a symbol of the cycle of birth and death (samsara).

National Symbol: Garuda is Indonesia's national emblem, known as "Garuda Pancasila." The mythical bird is prominently featured on the country's coat of arms and symbolizes Indonesia's national ideology.

Garuda's symbolism and significance extend beyond mythology, influencing various cultures' art, literature, and national symbolism. As the vahana of Vishnu, Garuda represents the divine force that carries the god across the celestial realms.

Griffin-Multiple Cultures

The Griffin, also spelled Gryphon or Gryphon, is a mythical creature with the body of a lion and the head of an eagle. It is a legendary creature that has been part of various mythologies and is often depicted as a symbol of strength, majesty, and protection.

Key features of the Griffin

Lion and Eagle Combination: The Griffin is typically portrayed with the body of a lion, representing courage and strength, and the head of an eagle, symbolizing keen vision and nobility. This unique combination of features makes it a powerful and majestic creature.

Guardian and Protector: In many mythological traditions, the Griffin is considered a guardian and protector of treasures. It is often depicted as standing watch over valuable possessions or sacred places.

Symbol of Divinity: The Griffin is sometimes associated with divine qualities and symbolizes divine power and protection. Its dual nature, combining the king of beasts (lion) with the king of birds (eagle), reinforces its symbolic significance.

Mythological Origins: The Griffin has roots in ancient mythology and is found in the traditions of various cultures, including Greek, Persian, and medieval European folklore. It has been mentioned in works such as Aesop's Fables and appears in the art and literature of different civilizations.

Protector of the Divine: In ancient Greek mythology, Griffins were associated with the god Apollo, and they were believed to guard his treasures. They were also associated with the sun, and their feathers were considered protective.

Heraldic Symbol: The Griffin has been widely used in heraldry, often symbolizing courage, strength, and guardianship. It is frequently depicted on coats of arms, shields, and crests of noble families.

Literary and Popular Culture: The Griffin has continued to capture the imagination and appears in various works of literature and popular culture. It is featured in fantasy novels, films, and games, often embodying characteristics of nobility and mythical prowess.

Variations: Different cultures and periods have depicted Griffins with variations in their characteristics. Some versions may include wings, while others portray the creature with additional elements like serpent tails.

The Griffin's enduring presence in mythology and its symbolic representation in various cultures reflect its universal appeal as a mythical creature embodying strength, courage, and protection.

Jormungandr-Norse

Jormungandr, also known as the Midgard Serpent or World Serpent, is a prominent figure in Norse mythology. A gigantic serpent encircles the Earth, grasping its own tail. Jormungandr is one of the three children of Loki, the trickster god, and plays a significant role in Norse cosmology.

Key features of Jormungandr

Origins: Jormungandr is one of the offspring of the trickster god Loki and the giantess Angrboða. The other two children are the wolf Fenrir and the half-dead, half-living Hel.

Size and Appearance: Jormungandr is often described as a colossal serpent that can encircle the entire Earth. Its sheer size and fearsome appearance make it a formidable and awe-inspiring creature.

Encircling the Earth: According to Norse mythology, Odin, the All-Father, cast Jormungandr into the sea surrounding Midgard (Earth). The serpent grew so large that it eventually encircled the entire world, grasping its tail. This act symbolizes an eternal cycle or continuity.

Prophesied Role in Ragnarok: Jormungandr plays a crucial role in the events leading up to Ragnarok, the Norse apocalypse. It is foretold that Jormungandr will rise from the ocean's depths during Ragnarok and engage in a fateful battle with the god Thor. Thor is prophesied to slay Jormungandr in this battle, but the serpent's venomous breath will also fatally poison Thor.

Symbolic Meaning: The symbolism of Jormungandr encompasses themes of cyclical nature, the interconnectedness of all things, and the inevitability of fate. Its encircling of the Earth represents the continuity of life and death.

Influence on Popular Culture: Jormungandr has significantly impacted popular culture and has appeared in various forms of literature, art, and media. Its depiction in Norse mythology and its association with Ragnarok have made it a memorable and iconic figure.

Jormungandr's presence in Norse mythology contributes to the rich tapestry of cosmic events and prophesied destinies. The World Serpent remains a powerful and enigmatic symbol within the Norse mythological tradition.

Kraken-Icelandic

The Kraken is a legendary sea monster often mentioned in Norse mythology and later popularized in various works of literature and popular culture. It is typically depicted as a gigantic, tentacled creature dwelling off the coasts of Norway and Greenland.

Key features of the Kraken

Appearance: The Kraken is commonly described as a massive, cephalopod-like creature with enormous tentacles. In many depictions, it is likened to a giant octopus or squid, capable of dragging entire ships and crews underwater.

Mythological Origins: The Kraken's roots can be traced back to Norse mythology, where it is mentioned in sagas and folklore. It is often associated with the sea and is considered a dangerous force that can create whirlpools and drown sailors.

Legends and Lore: Throughout history, sailors have shared tales of encounters with sea monsters, and these stories have contributed to the legend of the Kraken. In some accounts, the Kraken is said to surface near ships, causing havoc and destruction.

Literary References: The Kraken gained significant popularity through literature, including works like Alfred Lord Tennyson's poem "The Kraken" and Jules Verne's "Twenty Thousand Leagues Under the Sea." The Kraken is portrayed as a mysterious and fearsome creature in these works.

Pop Culture Influence:
The Kraken has become an iconic figure in popular culture, appearing in various films, books, and art. It is often featured as a formidable sea monster that challenges sailors and adventurers.

Release the Kraken: The catchphrase "Release the Kraken" became popular in modern times, especially after its use in the 1981 film "Clash of the Titans" and later in the 2010 remake. The phrase is often used to suggest unleashing a powerful or unstoppable force.

Cryptid or Fictional Creature: While the Kraken is firmly rooted in mythology and folklore, there is no scientific evidence to support the existence of such a creature. The legend of the Kraken is considered a fictional or mythological creation.

The Kraken's mystique and representation in literature and media continue to captivate imaginations, making it one of popular culture's most enduring and recognizable sea monsters.

Pegasus-Greek

Pegasus is a mythical winged horse in Greek mythology. It is one of the most famous and iconic creatures from ancient Greek lore and has become a symbol of poetic inspiration and flight.

Key features of Pegasus

Origin: Pegasus is said to have sprung from the blood of the Gorgon Medusa when she was slain by the hero Perseus. In some versions of the myth, Pegasus is born from the sea foam created by Medusa's blood mingling with the ocean.

Winged Horse: Pegasus is often depicted as a magnificent white horse with wings that allow it to fly. The wings are a distinguishing feature and a source of association with the ability to soar through the skies.

Captured by Bellerophon: In one of the most well-known myths involving Pegasus, the hero Bellerophon captures and tames the winged horse with the help of a golden bridle given to him by the goddess Athena. Together, Bellerophon and Pegasus embark on various heroic adventures.

Defeating the Chimera: Bellerophon, riding Pegasus, confronts and defeats the Chimera, a monstrous creature with the body of a lion, the head of a goat, and a serpent's tail. Pegasus aids Bellerophon by allowing him to fly and attack the Chimera from above.

Hippocrene Spring: According to mythology, Pegasus's hoof struck the ground on Mount Helicon, giving rise to the Hippocrene, a spring sacred to the Muses. This association with the Muses reinforces the symbolic connection between Pegasus and artistic inspiration.

Fountain of the Muses: Pegasus is often considered a symbol of poetic inspiration and the arts. The image of Pegasus is frequently found in classical art, literature, and later cultural references to represent creativity and pursue higher ideals.

Constellation: In astronomy, the Pegasus constellation is named after the mythical winged horse. It is a prominent constellation in the northern hemisphere sky.

The legend of Pegasus has endured through the ages, and the creature remains an enduring symbol of imagination, inspiration, and the boundless spirit of flight. Pegasus has left an indelible mark on Western mythology and is a popular and recognizable figure in art and literature.

Qilin-Chinese

The Qilin, also spelled "Kirin" in Japanese, is a mythical creature in East Asian folklore, and it holds significance in both Chinese and other East Asian cultures. The Qilin is often described as a hybrid creature with attributes of various animals, and it is associated with good fortune, prosperity, and auspicious events.

Key features of the Qilin

Appearance: The Qilin is typically depicted as a creature with the body of a deer, hooves like a horse, tail resembling an ox or lion, and a single horn on its head. It may also have scales and a mane.

Symbolism: The Qilin is regarded as a symbol of good luck, prosperity, and serenity. It is believed to appear during times of peace or when a virtuous ruler is in power.

Association with Confucianism: In Confucian philosophy, the Qilin is associated with the virtue of righteousness. According to some legends, it is said that a Qilin appeared to announce the birth of Confucius.

Harbinger of Good Events: The sighting of a Qilin was traditionally considered an auspicious omen associated with the birth or death of a great leader, the beginning of a new era, or the arrival of a virtuous ruler.

Gentle Nature: Despite its fearsome appearance, the Qilin is often depicted as a gentle and benevolent creature. It is said to avoid harming living things, even plants, and is sometimes associated with vegetarianism.

Guardian of Dharma: In Buddhism, the Qilin is considered a guardian of the Dharma (teachings) and is said to protect those who follow the Buddhist path.

Cultural Significance: Images of the Qilin are often seen in traditional East Asian art, sculptures, and even on currency. It has become a cultural symbol representing positive attributes and values.

Similarities to Other Mythical Creatures: The Qilin shares similarities with other mythical creatures in different cultures, such as the unicorn in Western mythology. However, the Qilin is distinct in its combination of features from various animals.

The Qilin's enduring presence in East Asian culture reflects its role as a symbol of positive virtues and a bringer of good fortune. It has become an iconic and beloved mythical creature with deep cultural and symbolic significance.

Roc-Arabic

The Roc, also known as Rukh or Ruhk, is a mythical giant bird of prey in Arabic and Persian mythology. The Roc is often described as an enormous eagle or falcon, sometimes with features reminiscent of a mythical bird known as the Simurgh. It has been a popular element in Middle Eastern folklore and has made its way into various stories and literature.

Key features of the Roc

Enormous Size: The Roc is typically depicted as an immense bird, often said to be large enough to carry off elephants or even whales. Its size varies in different accounts but is consistently portrayed as gigantic.

Origins in Arabic Literature: The Roc appears prominently in Arabic literature, particularly in "One Thousand and One Nights" (Arabian Nights). In these tales, the Roc is featured in various stories and adventures.

Nesting on Mount Qaf: According to some versions of the mythology, the Roc is said to nest on Mount Qaf, a mythical mountain often associated with the divine and the cosmic.

Carrying Off Elephants: One famous story about the Roc involves the bird carrying off elephants. This theme underscores the Roc's incredible strength and size.

Simurgh Connection: The Roc is sometimes associated with the Simurgh, a mythical bird in Persian folklore. While the Simurgh is often depicted as benevolent and wise, the Roc is sometimes portrayed as more fearsome.

Influence in Other Cultures: The concept of a gigantic bird resembling the Roc has found its way into various cultures and has been referenced in European literature and fantasy works.

Cultural Symbolism: The Roc represents nature's majestic and powerful aspects in Arabic and Persian mythology. Its mythical size and abilities make it a symbol of both awe and danger.

The Roc's depiction in Arabic and Persian folklore has had a lasting impact, and its legendary size and strength have made it an enduring figure in the rich tapestry of mythological traditions.

Selkie-Irish

A Selkie is a mythical creature found in the folklore of the Orkney and Shetland Islands of Scotland and in Irish and Faroese traditions. The Selkie is often depicted as a seal that can transform into a human by shedding its seal skin. This transformation allows the Selkie to dwell on land temporarily.

Key features of the Selkie myth

Seal Transformation: The core aspect of the Selkie myth is the creature's ability to transform between a seal and a human form. The Selkie is often described as a beautiful and enchanting being in its human form.

Human Encounters: Stories about Selkies frequently involve interactions between humans and Selkies. In some tales, a human discovers the Selkie's discarded seal skin, which the Selkie needs to resume its aquatic form. Without the skin, the Selkie is bound to remain in human form.

Love Stories: Many Selkie legends involve romantic relationships between humans and Selkies. A common narrative is that a human falls in love with a Selkie, often after finding and hiding the seal's skin. Eventually, the Selkie discovers its hidden skin and returns to the sea, leaving the human lover behind.

Tragic Themes: Selkie stories often carry elements of tragedy, as the separation between the Selkie and its human lover is typically inevitable. The themes of love, loss, and the yearning for freedom are prevalent in these narratives.

Clothing Symbolism: The seal skin is crucial in Selkie's stories. It represents the connection between the Selkie and its natural habitat. In human form, the Selkie is vulnerable without skin, and hiding or stealing the skin becomes a central plot point in many tales.

Cultural Variations: While the core concept of the Selkie is shared across different cultures, specific details and variations exist in Scottish, Irish, and Faroese folklore. The stories are often passed down through oral traditions and may differ in their regional nuances.

Selkie myths continue to captivate people's imaginations, inspiring literature, art, and adaptations in various forms of media. The tales of Selkies often explore themes of love, identity, and the connection between the human and natural worlds.

Simurgh-Persian

In Persian mythology and literature, the Simurgh (سیمرغ) is a mythical bird, often associated with wisdom, benevolence, and protection. The Simurgh is a significant and revered creature in Persian culture and has appeared in various works of Persian literature, including epic poems.

Key features of the Simurgh

Appearance: The Simurgh is often described as a large and majestic bird, sometimes with the features of other animals. It is said to have a dog's head, a lion's claws, a bird's wings, and a peacock's tail.

Wisdom and Knowledge: The Simurgh is considered a symbol of wisdom and knowledge in Persian mythology. It is often portrayed as a wise and benevolent figure possessing profound understanding and insight.

Guardian and Protector: The Simurgh is sometimes depicted as a guardian or protector, especially in assisting heroes on their quests or protecting individuals in need.

Immortality: In some myths, the Simurgh is said to be a creature of great age and wisdom, possibly representing immortality or the cycle of life.

Connection to Epic Literature: The Simurgh plays a notable role in Persian epics, such as the "Shahnameh" (Book of Kings) by Ferdowsi. In the "Shahnameh," the Simurgh is portrayed as a wise and compassionate being, offering guidance and support to the heroes.

Symbolism: The Simurgh carries rich symbolism, representing the union of opposites, the quest for knowledge, and the pursuit of spiritual growth. It is sometimes associated with the idea of self-discovery and transformation.

Simurgh in Art and Culture: The Simurgh has been depicted in Persian art, literature, and culture for centuries. Its image has graced manuscripts, carpets, and other artistic creations, contributing to its enduring presence in Persian heritage.

The Simurgh remains a fascinating and enduring symbol in Persian mythology, representing values that include wisdom, protection, and the pursuit of higher knowledge. Its mythical characteristics have made it a subject of intrigue and inspiration in Persian literature and culture.

Taniwha-Māori

In Māori mythology, a Taniwha is a supernatural creature or being that is often associated with bodies of water, such as rivers, lakes, and coastal areas. Taniwha can be depicted as both benevolent guardians and malevolent entities, and they are believed to possess shape-shifting abilities.

Key features of Taniwha

Guardianship: In some traditions, Taniwha are seen as protective guardians of specific geographic locations, especially bodies of water. They may be regarded as spiritual entities responsible for safeguarding people and places.

Shape-Shifting: Taniwha is believed to have the ability to shape-shift, assuming various forms, including that of a sea creature, reptile, or even a log or stone. This shape-shifting ability allows them to move between the supernatural and physical realms.

Variety of Forms: Taniwha can take on different forms, and their appearance varies in Māori mythology. Some are described as resembling large sea serpents, while others may appear more reptilian or monstrous.

Cultural Significance: Taniwha plays a significant role in Māori culture and mythology, and their stories are often intertwined with the history of specific tribes and regions. The belief in Taniwha is part of the broader spiritual and cultural landscape of the Māori people.

Connection to Water: Many Taniwha are associated with water bodies, reflecting the importance of water in Māori culture. Rivers and coastal areas are often regarded as the domains of Taniwha.

Relationship with Humans: The relationship between Taniwha and humans can vary. While some Taniwha are considered protective and benevolent, others are viewed as dangerous or malicious, capable of causing harm to those who encounter them.

Modern Perspectives: The belief in Taniwha continues to influence cultural practices and perspectives in modern New Zealand. Respect for Taniwha and acknowledgment of their presence are considerations in various development projects and activities near water bodies.

Taniwha remains an important element of Māori mythology and cultural identity, contributing to the rich tapestry of stories that connect the Māori people to their ancestral lands and the spiritual forces that inhabit them.

Wendigo-Algonquin

The Wendigo is a mythical creature or monster from Algonquian folklore, particularly among the Algonquin-speaking peoples of North America, including the Ojibwe, Cree, and Algonquin tribes. The Wendigo is often depicted as a malevolent, cannibalistic spirit or creature associated with winter, famine, and the harsh northern wilderness.

Key features of the Wendigo

Cannibalistic Nature: The Wendigo is strongly associated with the act of cannibalism. Some legends believe that consuming human flesh, particularly during times of famine, can transform a person into a Wendigo.

Giant and Emaciated Appearance: The Wendigo is often described as a tall, emaciated, and skeletal creature. It is sometimes portrayed as having a heart of ice and antlers on its head. Its gaunt appearance is indicative of its insatiable hunger.

Never Satisfied: One of the defining characteristics of the Wendigo is its unending hunger. No matter how much it consumes, it remains hungry and seeks more victims.

Association with the Cold: The Wendigo is often linked to winter, cold, and desolation. Its presence is thought to coincide with harsh winter conditions, and its howls are said to carry on the icy winds.

Transformation: Some Wendigo legends involve transforming humans into Wendigos due to resorting to cannibalism. The act is considered taboo, and those who partake in it risk becoming possessed by the Wendigo spirit.

Supernatural Abilities: Wendigos are sometimes attributed to supernatural abilities, including the ability to control the weather, mimic human voices, and lure people into the wilderness.

Cultural Significance: The legend of the Wendigo serves as a cautionary tale against cannibalism and the consequences of violating traditional taboos. It also reflects the harsh realities of survival in the challenging northern environments.

Pop Culture Influence: The Wendigo has appeared in various forms of popular culture, including literature, films, and video games. Its haunting and mysterious nature has contributed to its enduring presence in horror and folklore.

The Wendigo remains a powerful and evocative figure in Native American folklore, representing a supernatural threat and embodying cultural values and warnings against taboo actions. Different tribes may have variations in the Wendigo legend, but its common theme revolves around the consequences of succumbing to the darkest aspects of human nature.

CHAPTER 13

The Moon

The Phases of the Moon

New

Sometimes called the Crescent Moon, when you can see the very first sliver of light in the sky. This phase promotes new beginnings, new endeavors, and new relationships. It is the time to make positive changes and plant seeds of ideas that will be harvested later.

Waxing

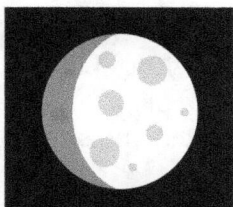

In this phase, the Moon appears to be growing in size, shifting from new to full as though it's gaining strength. It makes sense, then, that this is an excellent time to focus on increasing your knowledge, bank accounts, and relationships. This phase promotes healing.

Full

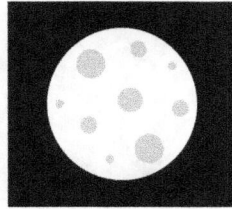

The Moon's most potent phase is when we see her entire illuminated face. This is a time of fulfillment, activity, and increased psychic ability for perfecting ideas, in other words, "getting your act together," celebrations, or renewing commitments to people or projects—the best time for spells of any kind.

Waning

The Moon is decreasing in size as it journeys from full to dark. The waning Moon is a time of decrease, release, letting go, and completion. It is an excellent time to begin dieting, breaking bad habits, breaking off relationships, or dealing with legal matters.

February Moon

Despite winter's lingering presence, there is a noticeable change in nature, with sunlight growing stronger and days longer. Even the birds seem to sing a little louder. We sense a quickening deep within the Earth as it begins its journey toward spring.

As the Moon waxes, we draw in the renewed energy of the Earth and allow it to invigorate and motivate us. Conversely, during the waning of the Moon, we let go of any negative emotions, such as fatigue and fear, which may hold us back from making plans or setting goals.

March Moon

During March, the Earth finds itself in a state of equilibrium, a perfect balance between light and darkness. The worms emerge from the ground as the planet begins to warm, and the sap flows through the trees. Life itself seems to awaken and stretch towards the sun, eager to fulfill its potential.

As the Moon begins to wax, we, too, seek to draw strength from within ourselves, opening up to inspiration and our own inner reserves of power. As the Moon wanes, we take the opportunity to release any fatigue or reluctance that may be holding us back, freeing ourselves from feelings of inadequacy and embracing the limitless possibilities that lie ahead.

Moons of the Year

A rare second Full Moon in a single month is called a "Blue Moon." A rare second New Moon in a month is called a "Black Moon."

Different cultures gave the Moon different titles to express what the Moon means to them in a given month. As a result, some of the moon names make sense, while others may not make any sense.

Full Moon – January
Native American Tribes: Old Moon, Wolf Moon, Ice Moon, Moon after Yule, and Winter Moon
Siouan (Assiniboines) Tribe: Hard Time Moon
Inuit People of Northern Canada: Dwarf Seal Moon
Celtic: Wolf Moon, Stay Home Moon, Moon after Yule
Chinese: Holiday Moon
Fairy: Icicle Moon

Full Moon – February
Native American Tribes: Hunger or Starvation Moon, Storm Moon, Trapper's Moon, Moon of Ice, and Tree Moon
Siouan (Assiniboines) Tribe: Long Day Moon
Inuit People of Northern Canada: Seal Pup Moon
Celtic: Storm Moon, Ice Moon, and Snow moon
Chinese: Budding Moon
Fairy: Snowdrop Moon

Full Moon – March
Native American Tribes: Worm Moon, Crow Moon, Moon of Winds, Sap Moon, Fish Moon, Chaste Moon, and Death Moon
Siouan (Assiniboines) Tribe: Sore Eye Moon
Inuit People of Northern Canada: Snow Bird Moon
Celtic: Plough Moon, Wind Moon, Lenten (lengthening) Moon
Chinese: Sleeping Moon
Fairy: Waking Wood Moon

Moons of the Year

Full Moon – April
Native American Tribes: Pink Moon, Seed Moon, Frog Moon, Egg Moon, and Awakening Moon
Siouan (Assiniboines) Tribe: Frog's Moon
Inuit People of Northern Canada: Snow Melt Moon
Celtic: Budding Moon, New Shoots Moon, and Seed Moon
Chinese: Peony Moon
Fairy: Birthing Moon

Full Moon – May
Native American Tribes: Flower Moon, Hare Moon, Milk Moon, and Grass Moon
Siouan (Assiniboines) Tribe: Idle Moon
Inuit People of Northern Canada: Goose Moon
Celtic: Mother's Moon and Bright Moon
Chinese: Dragon Moon
Fairy: Moon of White Petals

Full Moon – June
Native American Tribes: Strawberry Moon, Planting Moon, and Green Corn Moon
Siouan (Assiniboines) Tribe: Full Leaf Moon
Inuit People of Northern Canada: Hunting Moon
Celtic: Mead Moon, Horse Moon, Dyan Moon, and Rose Moon
Chinese: Lotus Moon
Fairy: Wild Cherry Moon

Full Moon – July
Native American Tribes: Hay Moon, Summer Moon, Thunder Moon, and Buck Moon
Siouan (Assiniboines) Tribe: Red Berries Moon
Inuit People of Northern Canada: Dry Moon
Celtic: Claiming Moon, Wyrt or Herb Moon, and Mead Moon
Chinese: Hungry Ghost Moon
Fairy: Dancing Delight Moon

Full Moon – August
Native American Tribes: Sturgeon Moon, Corn Moon, Green Corn Moon, Dog Days Moon, and Lightening Moon
Siouan (Assiniboines) Tribe: Black Cherries Moon
Inuit People of Northern Canada: Swan Flight Moon
Celtic: Dispute Moon, Lynx Moon, and Grain Moon
Chinese: Harvest Moon
Fairy: Blackberry Harvest Moon

Moons of the Year

Full Moon – September
Native American Tribes: Singing Moon and Barley Moon
Siouan (Assiniboines) Tribe: Yellow Leaf Moon
Inuit People of Northern Canada: Harpoon Moon
Celtic: Wine Moon, Song Moon, Harvest Moon, and Barley Moon
Chinese: Chrysanthemum Moon
Fairy: Chestnut Moon

Full Moon – October
Native American Tribes: Traveller's Moon and Blackberry Moon
Siouan (Assiniboines) Tribe: Gophur Looks Back Moon
Inuit People of Northern Canada: Ice Moon
Celtic: Hunter's Moon, Blood Moon, and Seed Fall Moon
Chinese: Kindly Moon
Fairy: Moon of the Wild Hunt

Full Moon - November
Native American Tribes: Frosty Moon, Beaver Moon, Dark Moon, Tree Moon, Snow Moon, Freezing Moon, Ice Moon, and Migrating Moon
Siouan (Assiniboines) Tribe: Frost Moon
Inuit People of Northern Canada: Freezing Mist Moon
Celtic: Mourning Moon and Darkest Depths Moon
Chinese: White Moon
Fairy: Moon of the Wild Hunt

Full Moon – December
Native American Tribes: Cold Moon, Long Night Moon,
Siouan (Assiniboines) Tribe: Younger Hard Time Moon
Inuit People of Northern Canada: Dark Night Moon
Celtic: Oak Moon, Full Cold Moon
Chinese: Bitter Moon
Fairy: Mistletoe Moon

CHAPTER 14

Days of the
Week
for Spells

Days of the Week for Spells and Rituals

Monday
Best for psychic endeavors, invoking power, creative ideas, divine/inspirational messages, and healing.

Tuesday
Best for protection and building the strength of mind, body, and confidence.

Wednesday
Best for career/job issues, intellectual pursuits, travel planning and research.

Thursday
Best for finances, legal matters, spirituality, and development.

Friday
Best for romantic attraction, all relationships, reconciliation, physical makeovers, and beautifying your environment.

Saturday
Best for home-related issues, brainstorming future projects, committing to personal goals, weight loss, releasing bad habits, ending relationships, etc.

Sunday
Best for healing (body, mind, soul), management/decision-making, insights into problem-solving, divine intervention/miracles, and unique friendships.

Do what makes you comfortable waiting for the "right" day to perform rituals or divination is unnecessary. So you do you, Boo!

THIS WEEK

Monday

Zodiac: Cancer
Solar System: Moon
Rune: Lagu
Numbers: 2, 9
Colors: Blue (pale), Gray, Silver, White
Tarot: High Priestess, Moon
Trees: Birch, Elder, Myrtle, Willow
Misc. Plants: Moonwort, Wormwood
Herb and Garden: Bluebell, Chamomile, Gardenia, Jasmine, Poppy, Rose (white), Violet
Gemstones and Minerals: Emerald, Moonstone, Quartz (clear, white), Sapphire
Metal: Silver
From the Sea: Pearl
Goddesses: Hecate, Selene
Gods: Aegir, Thoth
Angel or Magical Beings: Gabriel
Issues, Intentions, and Powers: astral realm, clairvoyance, creativity, dream work, emotions, family, fertility, healing, the home, illumination, inspiration, intuition, love, magic (general, moon), prophecy, protection, psychic ability, travel, truth

Tuesday

Zodiac: Aries, Scorpio
Solar System: Mars
Rune: Tyr
Number: 5
Colors: Black, Orange, Red, Scarlet
Tarot: Strength, Wands (5, 6)
Trees: Cedar, Elm, Holly, Palm (dragon's blood)
Misc. Plants: Allspice, Ginger, Patchouli, Thistle
Herb and Garden: Basil, Garlic, Snapdragon
Gemstones and Minerals: Bloodstone, Emerald, Garnet, Ruby, Sapphire (star), Topaz
Metal: Iron
From the Sea:
Goddess:
God: Mars
Angel or Magical Beings: Elves
Issues, Intentions, and Powers: action, aggression, assertiveness, battle/war, challenges, courage, discipline, energy, healing, honor, integrity, justice, passion, purification, strength, truth

Wednesday

Zodiac: Gemini
Solar System: Mercury
Rune: Odal
Number: 3
Colors: Orange, Purple, Silver, Violet, Yellow
Tarot: The Magician, Wheel of Fortune, Pentacles (8)
Trees: Aspen, Hazel, Rowan
Misc. Plant: Fern
Herb and Garden: Dill, Jasmine, Lavender, Lily of the Valley
Gemstones and Minerals: Agate, Amethyst, Aventurine, Lodestone, Opal, Ruby (star), Turquoise
Metal: Mercury
From the Sea:
Goddess: Athena
Gods: Hermes, Mercury, Odin
Angel or Magical Beings: Raphael
Issues, Intentions, and Powers: business, cleverness, communication, creativity, crossroads, divination, fear, improvement (self), insight, intelligence, introspection, knowledge, loss, money, problems, skills, travel, wisdom

Thursday

Zodiac: Capricorn, Pisces
Solar System: Jupiter
Rune: Thorn
Numbers: 4, 8
Colors: Blue (royal), Green, Indigo, Purple
Tarot: Pentacles (ace, 9, 10)
Trees: Laurel, Maple, Oak, Pine
Misc. Plants: Cinnamon, Cinquefoil, Grain (wheat), Nutmeg
Herb and Garden: Honeysuckle, Sage
Gems and Minerals: Amethyst, Carnelian, Cat's Eye, Chrysoberyl, Sapphire, Turquoise
Metal: Tin
From the Sea:
Goddess: Juno
Gods: Jupiter, Thor, Zeus
Angel or Magical Beings:
Issues, Intentions, and Powers: abundance, business, desire, endurance, fidelity, honor, justice (legal matters), leadership, loyalty, luck, money, prosperity, relationships, success, well-being

Friday

Zodiac: Taurus
Solar System: Venus
Rune: Peorth
Numbers: 6, 9
Colors: Aqua, Blue, Green, Indigo, Pink
Tarot: Empress, Lovers, Cups (2)
Trees: Apple, Birch, Myrtle
Misc. Plants: Saffron, Sandalwood
Herb and Garden: Feverfew, Raspberry, Rose, Strawberry, Thyme, Violet
Gemstones and Minerals: Alexandrite, Amber, Cat's Eye, Chrysoberyl, Emerald, Rose Quartz, Ruby
Metal: Copper
From the Sea:
Goddesses: Aphrodite, Freya, Frigg, Lakshmi, Venus
God: Eros
Angel or Magical Beings: Auriel
Issues, Intentions, and Powers: beauty, emotions, fertility, friend/ ship, happiness, love, magic, passion, pleasure, romance, sex/uality, wisdom

Saturday

Zodiac: Aquarius
Solar System: Saturn
Rune: Dag
Number: 7
Colors: Black, Gray (dark), Indigo, Purple (dark)
Tarot: Temperance, Swords (knight, 2)
Trees: Alder, Cypress, Hawthorn, Pomegranate
Misc. Plants: Mullein, Myrrh
Herb and Garden: Morning Glory, Thyme
Gems and Minerals: Amethyst, Apache Tears, Diamond, Hematite, Jet, Labradorite, Turquoise
From the Sea:
Goddess: Hecate
God: Saturn
Angel or Magical Beings: Fairies
Issues, Intentions, and Powers: banish, bind, business, death, discipline (self), freedom, justice, karma, life, limitations/ boundaries, money, motivation, negativity, obstacles, peace, problems, protection, willpower, wisdom

Sunday

Zodiac: Leo
Solar System: Sun
Rune: Sigel
Number: 1
Colors: Gold, Gray, Orange, Pink, White, Yellow
Tarot: Chariot, Sun, Wands (ace)
Trees: Ash, Birch, Laurel
Misc. Plants: Cinnamon, Frankincense
Herb and Garden: Carnation, Marigold, St. John's Wort, Sunflower
Gemstones and Minerals: Amber, Carnelian, Diamond, Quartz (clear), Sunstone, Tiger's Eye, Topaz
Metal: Gold
From the Sea: Pearl
Goddess: Brigid
God: Helios
Angel or Magical Beings: Elves
Issues, Intentions, and Powers: accomplishment, action, ambition, attraction, authority, beauty, confidence, creativity, energy (solar), fame, freedom, friend/ship, goals, growth (personal), healing, hope, illumination, justice, leadership, light, money power (personal), pride, prosperity, protection, spirituality, strength, success, visions, warmth, well-being

Time of the Day for Spells and Rituals

Dawn

At dawn, the sun's fragile rays spread like a blanket of hope over an awakening world. At this time, choices are made, and paths unfold before us, full of life-giving potentiality.

Midday/Noon

Midday is when sunlight shines the strongest - a reminder of our strength and courage to tackle whatever lies ahead. It provides the motivation we need to persevere, no matter what obstacle stands in our way.

Dusk/Twilight

As dusk approaches, the sun bids a wistful farewell to the sky. Its goodbye is made of change and final goodbyes, an invitation to new beginnings if we're brave enough to open our hearts.

Midnight

At midnight, we come to the precipice of a journey into uncertainty; here is where paths diverge, and endings have no choice but to be accepted. It's an inevitable transition from one day to another, filled with promise yet also cloaked in sadness.

Do what makes you feel comfortable. There's no need to wait for the "right" time to perform rituals or divination. You do you, Boo!

Dawn

Zodiac:
Solar System: Venus
Runes: Beorc, Hagal, Thorn
Number:
Color:
Tarot: Swords
Trees:
Misc. Plants:
Herb and Garden:
Gemstones and Minerals:
Metal:
From the Sea:
Goddess: Brigid
Gods: Byelobog, Janus, Njord, Surya
Angel or Magical Beings: Raphael
Issues, Intentions, and Powers: activate/awaken, beginnings, crossroads, fertility, hope, life (vitality), light, nurture, purpose, romance, youth

Midday/Noon

Zodiac: Leo
Solar System: Sun
Runes: Dag, Rad, Sigel
Number:
Color:
Tarot: Wands
Trees:
Misc. Plants:
Herb and Garden:
Gemstones and Minerals:
Metal:
From the Sea:
Goddess:
God: Byelobog
Angel or Magical Beings: Michael
Issues, Intentions, and Powers: determination, obstacles, strength, willpower

Dusk/Twilight

Zodiac: Cancer
Solar System: Venus
Runes: Feoh, Jer, Peorth
Numbers:
Colors:
Tarot: Cups
Trees:
Misc. Plants:
Herb and Garden:
Gemstones and Minerals:
Metal:
From the Sea:
Goddess:
God: Gabriel
Issues, Intentions, and Powers: banish, change/s, endings, the otherworld/underworld, sorrow

Midnight

Zodiac: Taurus
Solar System: Earth, Venus
Runes: Is, Tyr, Ur
Number:
Color:
Tarot: Pentacles
Trees:
Misc. Plants:
Herb and Garden:
Gemstones and Minerals:
Metal:
From the Sea:
Goddess:
God:
Angel or Magical Beings: Auriel
Issues, Intentions, and Powers: crossroads, endings, release

CHAPTER 15

Astrology

February Energy Quicky

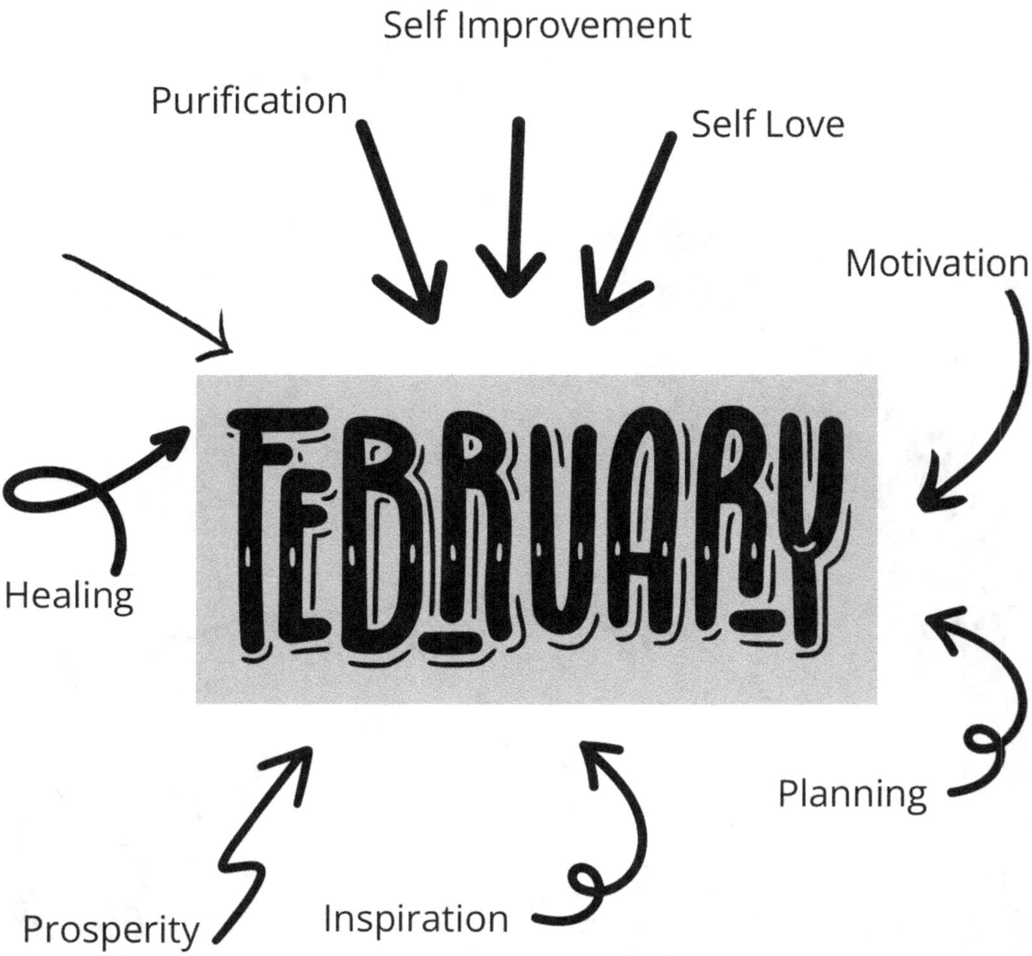

Self Improvement

Purification

Self Love

Motivation

FEBRUARY

Healing

Planning

Prosperity

Inspiration

February Focus

February's Focus: Self-Love and Renewal

This month, love is in the air and starts with loving yourself. It's time to revisit the goals you set for yourself last month, assess your progress, and rid yourself of any negativity that may be hindering your progress. Take this opportunity to recommit to your passions, spiritual journey, deities, and more. Prioritize your mental, physical, emotional, and spiritual well-being to move forward into the year with a refreshed and revitalized outlook. Wishing you love, light, and abundance in all your endeavors this year.

March Energy Quicky

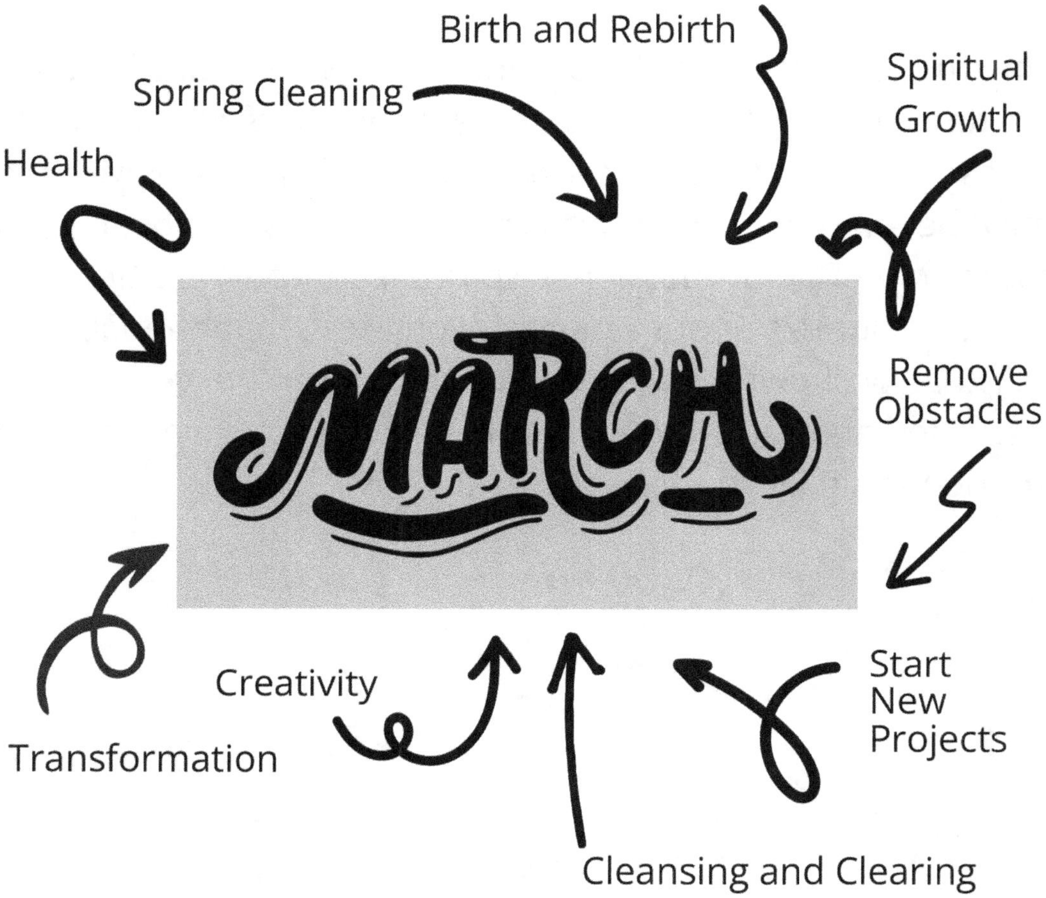

Birth and Rebirth

Spring Cleaning

Spiritual Growth

Health

MARCH

Remove Obstacles

Transformation

Creativity

Start New Projects

Cleansing and Clearing

March Focus

Harnessing the Energy of March for Growth, Prosperity, and Abundance

March presents the ideal environment for growth, prosperity, and fruitfulness. Start planting the seeds both in the physical and metaphysical sense for what you desire to harvest later in the year. Additionally, engage in spring cleaning to eliminate negativity and blockages that could hinder the manifestation of your dreams. Remember to stay connected with the Earth and to focus on grounding yourself to attract prosperity and love. Be kind to yourself, expand your knowledge, and grow spiritually this March.

Birth Chart Meanings

Your **Sun** is about yourself.

Your **Moon** is your heart.

Your **Rising** is how you look.

Your **Mercury** is the way you think.

Your **Venus** is how you love.

Your **Mars** is how you deal with life.

Your **Jupiter** is your luck.

Your **Saturn** is how you discipline yourself and your responsibilities.

Your **Uranus** is how unique you are.

Your **Neptune** is your imagination.

Your **Pluto** is your transformation.

Your **Chiron** is how you heal.

Your **Ceres** is how you take care of yourself.

Your **Pallas** is your relationship.

Your **Juno** is beauty and influence.

Your **Vesta** is your potential and your organization.

Your **North Node** is how you develop in your current life.

Your **South Node** is how you developed in your past life.

Your **Midheaven** is your career; how others view you.

Your **Lilith** is your hidden emotions.

For help with your birth chart try:
https://astro.cafeastrology.com/natal.php

Astrological Signs

Aries
March 21 - April 19
for those born under the sign of
The Ram

Taurus
April 20 - May 20
for those born under the sign of
The Bull

Gemini
May 21 - June 20
for those born under the sign of
The Twins

Cancer
June 21 - July 22
for those born under the sign of
The Crab

Leo
July 23 - August 22
for those born under the sign of
The Lion

Virgo
August 23 - September 22
for those born under the sign of
The Virgin

Libra
September 23 - October 22
for those born under the sign of
The Scales

Scorpio
October 23 - November 21
for those born under the sign of
The Scorpion

Sagittarius
November 22 - December 21
for those born under the sign of
The Archer

Capricorn
December 22 - January 19
for those born under the sign of
The Goat

Aquarius
January 20 - February 18
for those born under the sign of
The Water Bearer

Pisces
February 19 - March 20
for those born under the sign of
The Fishes

Aboriginal Astrology

Aboriginal astronomy is a term used to describe the astronomical knowledge and practices of Indigenous Australian cultures. It is essential to note that the concept of "Aboriginal astrology" might be a misnomer, as Indigenous Australians didn't traditionally have a system comparable to Western or Eastern astrology. However, their understanding of the night sky is deeply connected to their cultural and spiritual beliefs. Here are key aspects:

Dreamtime Stories: Aboriginal astronomy is intertwined with Dreamtime stories, which are central to Indigenous Australian cultures. The Dreamtime is a spiritual dimension where ancestral beings created the world and its features. Many celestial features, such as stars and the Milky Way, are believed to be reflections of Dreamtime events.

Seasonal Markers: Indigenous Australians used celestial bodies to mark seasons and guide activities like hunting and gathering.

The rising and setting of specific stars and constellations signaled changes in weather and the availability of resources.

Oral Traditions: Knowledge of the night sky was passed down through oral traditions. Elders and knowledgeable community members were crucial in preserving and transmitting this astronomical knowledge.

Star Clusters and Constellations:
Different Aboriginal groups recognized various star clusters and constellations. For example, the Pleiades, known as the Seven Sisters, is a significant celestial feature in many Indigenous Australian cultures.

Practical Navigation: Indigenous
Australians used the stars for practical purposes, such as navigation. Certain stars and celestial features served as guides during journeys across the land.

Ceremonial Significance: Celestial events often held ceremonial significance. The timing of rituals and ceremonies was linked to astronomical occurrences, reinforcing the connection between the spiritual and natural worlds.

While Aboriginal astronomy is not astrology in the conventional sense, it reflects a profound and holistic understanding of the cosmos. It emphasizes the interconnectedness of the land, sky, and spiritual dimensions within Indigenous Australian cultures. The study of Aboriginal astronomy is an ongoing effort to preserve and respect the astronomical knowledge embedded in these rich traditions.

Arabic Astrology

Arabic Astrology refers to astrological practices that originated in the Arab world, particularly during the Islamic Golden Age (8th to 14th centuries). It encompasses a diverse range of astrological traditions, blending elements of Hellenistic astrology with Arabic and Islamic influences. Here are key aspects of Arabic Astrology:

Translation Movement: During the Islamic Golden Age, scholars in the Arab world played a crucial role in preserving and translating ancient Greek and Roman texts, Including astrological works by Ptolemy and others. This led to the assimilation and adaptation of Hellenistic astrology into Arabic culture.

Astrological Houses and Planets: Arabic astrologers continued to use the concept of houses and planets, as seen in Hellenistic astrology. The seven classical planets-Moon, Mercury, Venus, Sun, Mars, Jupiter, and Saturn-retained their significance.

Arabic Parts: The concept of Arabic Parts, also known as "Lots" or "Arabic Points," gained prominence in Arabic Astrology.

These are sensitive points in the horoscope, calculated based on mathematical relationships between planets, and are associated with specific life themes. Influence on Western Astrology: Arabic astrological texts profoundly impacted the development of Western astrology during the medieval period. Many Arabic astrological works were translated into Latin, contributing to the synthesis of astrological knowledge in Europe.

Fixed Stars: Arabic astrologers made significant contributions to studying fixed stars. They identified and named numerous stars, incorporating their influence into astrological interpretations.

Solar and Lunar Mansions: Arabic Astrology uses a system of 28 lunar mansions or "manazil," each associated with specific qualities and influences. The "solar mansions" or "houses of the sun" are also considered in Arabic astrological practices.

Istikhara and Electional Astrology: Arabic Astrology influenced practical applications, such as electional astrology, to determine auspicious times for various activities. "Istikhara" is a form of divination to seek guidance in decision-making, often incorporating astrological considerations.

Integration with Islamic Traditions: Arabic Astrology was often integrated with Islamic mysticism and spirituality.

While Arabic Astrology has historical significance and has influenced the development of astrology in various cultures, including the West, it's important to note that many contemporary Islamic scholars consider astrology with caution or skepticism, as it might conflict with certain Islamic beliefs.

Aztec Astrology

Aztec Astrology, also known as Tonalamati, is an ancient Mesoamerican astrological system developed by the Aztecs, a civilization that flourished in central Mexico from the 14th to the early 16th century. Unlike Western astrology, Aztec Astrology does not focus on celestial bodies like planets and stars. Instead, it revolves around a complex calendrical system based on two interlocking cycles: the Tonalpohualli and the Xiuhpohualli.

Tonalpohualli: The Tonalpohualli is a sacred 260-day calendar known as the "Divine Count" or "Count of Days." It consists of 20 periods, each associated with a unique day sign and a number from 1 to 13. The combination of 20-day signs and 13 numbers results in a cycle of 260 days. A distinct symbol represents each day's sign, often depicted as an animal, deity, or other significant cultural symbol.

Day Signs: The 20-day signs in the Tonalpohualli include names like Cipactli (Crocodile), Ehecat/ (Wind), Calli (House),(Crocodile), Ehecat/ (Wind), Calli (House), Cuetzpallin (Lizard), and Xochit! (Flower), among others. Each sign is believed to possess distinct characteristics and influences.

Numbers 1-13: The numbers 1 through 13 are associated with each day sign in the Tonalpohualli, creating unique combinations that repeat every 260 days. The combination of a day sign and a number is thought to influence an individual's desire and personality.

Xiuhpohualli: The Xiuhpohualli, often called the "Solar Count," is a 365-day agricultural calendar that aligns with the solar year. It consists of 18 periods, each lasting 20 days, plus a short final period of five "empty" or "unlucky" days. The Xiuhpohualli runs parallel to the Tonalpohualli but at a different pace.

Ceremonial Calendar: Aztec Astrology played a significant role in guiding religious and ceremonial practices. Certain days were considered more auspicious for specific rituals, celebrations, and events.

Life Path and Personality: Aztec Astrology is believed to influence an individual's life path and personality traits based on the combination of day signs and numbers in the Tonalpohualli. People born under specific combinations were thought to possess certain strengths, weaknesses, and destinies.

Aztec Astrology

Divination and Guidance: Aztec priests and spiritual leaders used the Tonalpohualli for divination and guidance. The calendar was consulted to make decisions, predict outcomes, and understand the spiritual aspects of daily life.

Aztec Astrology reflects the interconnectedness of time, nature, and spirituality in Aztec culture. It played a crucial role in shaping the religious and social practices of the Aztec civilization, offering a unique perspective on the relationship between individuals and the cosmic forces at play in their lives.

African Astrology

African astrology encompasses various systems used across the continent, each tied to cultural and regional beliefs. One notable example is the Akan system from Ghana, which includes 12 animal totems, such as the crocodile and leopard, each corresponding to a specific birth period. These totems are associated with personality traits and characteristics.

Another system is the Yoruba astrology, rooted in Nigeria. It features 16 primary signs called "Odu" linked to the Yoruba divination system. Each Odu represents a combination of 2 binary code systems, resulting in unique divination verses that guide spiritual practices and offer insights into individual destinies.

African astrology often intertwines with spiritual practices, emphasizing the interconnectedness of individuals with nature and the cosmos. Interpretations may involve rituals, divination, and storytelling, highlighting the diverse African continent's rich cultural and spiritual tapestry.

Balinese Astrology

Balinese Astrology is deeply rooted in the cultural and religious traditions of Bali, Indonesia. Its unique system combines Hindu-Buddhist cosmology, animism, and local beliefs. Here are key elements of Balinese Astrology:

Pawukon Calendar: The Balinese use the Pawukon calendar, which consists of ten concurrent weeks, each containing one to ten days. This calendar is used for various purposes, including determining auspicious times for ceremonies, rituals, and important life events. Each week, called a "wuku," has its unique characteristics.

Wayang Kulit and Topeng Performances:
Traditional Balinese arts, such as Wayang Kulit (shadow puppetry) and Topeng (mask) performances, often incorporate astrological themes. Characters in these performances may represent astrological archetypes, and the stories may align with celestial events.

Balinese Zodiac: Unlike the 12-animal zodiac system found in Chinese astrology, Balinese Astrology has a 35-week cycle with animals ass' ted with each week. These animals include a mix of real and mythical creatures, such as a tiger, dragon, elephant, monkey, and more.

Temple Festivals and Galungan: Balinese temple festivals, especially the major celebration of Galungan, are influenced by astrological considerations. The timing of these festivals is often determined based on the Pawukon calendar and other astrological factors.

Galungan and Kuningan: The Balinese celebrate Galungan, a festival marking the victory of dharma (good) over adharma (evil). Kuningan, which follows Galungan, is when ancestral spirits are believed to return to the heavens. The Pawukon calendar influences the timing of these festivals.

Ceremonial Practices: Balinese ceremonies, including weddings and rites of passage, are often scheduled based on astrological considerations. The alignment with auspicious times is believed to bring blessings and positive energies.

Astrological Guidance: Balinese individuals may consult astrological practitioners for guidance on important life decisions, such as marriage, naming ceremonies, or starting a business.

Astrologers analyze the Pawukon calendar and other astrological factors to offer insights. Balinese Astrology is integral to the island's daily life and cultural practices. It reflects the Balinese people's deep connection with the spiritual and natural world, incorporating celestial observations into their religious ceremonies, arts, and everyday activities.

Burmese Astrology

Burmese Astrology, also known as Burmese Zodiac or Mahabote Astrology, is a traditional astrological system practiced in Myanmar (Burma). It is deeply rooted in Burmese culture and Buddhism and shares some similarities with other Southeast Asian astrological systems. Here are key features of Burmese Astrology:

Mahabote: The core of Burmese Astrology is the Mahabote, a system that assigns one of eight animal symbols to each day of the week. These symbols are Rat, Elephant, Tiger, Rabbit, Dragon, Snake, Horse, and Garuda (mythical bird). Each day is also associated with a guardian planet.

Daily Birth Animal: In Burmese Astrology, individuals are assigned a "zodiac animal" based on the day of the week they were born. This daily birth animal is significant in understanding one's personality traits, characteristics, and destiny.

Eight-Planetary System: Burmese Astrology integrates an eight-planetary system, associating each planet with a specific day and animal. For example, Sunday is related to the Sun and the mythical bird Garuda, while Monday is linked to the Moon and the Rat.

Guardian Spirit: Besides the daily birth animal, Burmese Astrology considers a guardian spirit associated with the time of birth. This guardian spirit is known as the "Yahu," and its influence is believed to shape an individual's nature.

Directional Astrology: Burmese Astrology includes directional astrology, linking each zodiac animal with a cardinal direction. This connection is significant in various aspects of life, including choosing a favorable direction for important activities.

Astrological Amulets: Burmese people often wear astrological amulets or talismans based on their Mahabote to attract positive energies and protection. These amulets may feature symbols associated with the daily birth animal.

Spiritual Significance: Burmese Astrology is intertwined with Buddhist beliefs and practices. Astrology is used for personal insights and to determine auspicious times for religious ceremonies, festivals, and other important events.

Ceremonial Occasions: Burmese Astrology is crucial in determining auspicious times for various ceremonial occasions, such as weddings, naming ceremonies, and other significant life events.

It's important to note that Burmese Astrology is deeply ingrained in Myanmar's cultural and religious fabric. While it shares some similarities with other Asian astrological systems, its unique features, such as the Mahabote and the eight-planetary system, distinguish it as a distinct and culturally significant practice in the region.

Celtic Astrology

Celtic astrology, also known as Druid astrology, is rooted in the Celtic traditions of ancient Europe. Unlike the more widely known Western astrology with its zodiac signs, Celtic astrology is based on trees and their associated qualities. There are thirteen tree signs in Celtic astrology, each corresponding to a lunar month.

Birch (Beth): December 24 - January 20
Rowan (Luis): January 21 - February 17
Ash (Nion): February 18 - March 17
Alder (Fearn): March 18 - April 14
Willow (Saille) + ril 15 - May 12
Hawthorn (Uati: Mav 13 - June 9
Hawthorn (Uath): May 13 - June 9
Oak (Duir): June 10 - July 7
Holly (Tinne): July 8 - August 4
Hazel (Coll): August 5 - September 1
Vine (Muin): September 2 - September 29
Ivy (Gort): September 30 - October 27
Reed (Ngetal): October 28 - November 24
Elder (Ruis): November 25 - December 23

Each tree sign is associated with specific personality traits, characteristics, and symbolic meanings. For instance, Willow individuals may be intuitive and empathetic, while Oak individuals are often seen as strong and resilient. Celtic astrology incorporates the natural world and lunar cycles, reflecting the Celtic people's deep connection to nature and their reverence for life cycles.

Chinese Astrology

Chinese Astrology is a traditional system that assigns animal signs and elements each year in a repeating 12-year cycle. This system is based on the lunar calendar and is deeply rooted in Chinese philosophy, particularly Taoism and Confucianism. Here are the key components:

Animal Signs: The Chinese Zodiac consists of 12 animal signs, each representing a different personality type.

The animals are Rat, Ox, Tiger, Rabbit, Dragon, Snake, Horse, Goat (or Sheep), Monkey, Rooster, Dog, and Pig. People are associated with the sign of the year they were born.

The Five Elements: Each animal sign is associated with one of the five elements: Wood, Fire, Earth, Metal, and Water. The combination of the animal and element creates a 60-year cycle (12 animal signs x 5 elements).

12-Year Cycle: The Chinese Zodiac operates on a 12-year cycle, with each year associated with a specific animal sign. The cycle repeats, and each person experiences their Chinese Zodiac sign every 12 years.

Yin and Yang: Within the 12 animal signs, there is a further division into Yin and Yang attributes. The Rat, Tiger, Dragon, Horse, Monkey, and Dog are considered Yang, representing assertive and active qualities.
The Ox, Rabbit, Snake, Goat, Rooster, and Pig are Yin, symbolizing receptive and passive characteristics.

Compatibility and Characteristics:
Chinese Astrology offers insights into compatibility between individuals based on their animal signs. It also provides general characteristics of each sign, offering a broad understanding of personality traits.

Four Pillars of Destiny (Ba Zi): In addition to the yearly animal sign, Chinese Astrology often involves analyzing a person's complete birth chart, known as the Four Pillars of Destiny. This chart includes the year, month, day, and time of birth, providing a more detailed and personalized profile.

Chinese Astrology is widely used for various purposes, including personal guidance, compatibility assessment, and forecasting. It is an integral part of Chinese culture, influencing decisions related to marriage, career, and life events. While it's not considered a predictive science, many value its insights and symbolism.

Egyptian Astrology

Egyptian Astrology is a system of astrology that emerged in ancient Egypt, and while it shares some similarities with Western and other astrological systems, it has distinct features. Here's an overview:

12 Egyptian Zodiac Signs: Egyptian Astrology is based on a system of 12 zodiac signs, each associated with specific time periods. These signs are related to the 12 months of the Egyptian calendar.

Connection to Egyptian Deities: Each Egyptian zodiac sign is linked to a particular deity or god. For example, Aries is associated with Amon-Ra, Taurus with Hathor, and so on. The influence of these deities is believed to shape the characteristics and destiny of individuals born under each sign.

Three Decans: In addition to the 12 zodiac signs, Egyptian Astrology includes the concept of decans. Each zodiac sign is divided into three decans, making a total of 36 decans in the entire zodiac. Each decan is associated with its own set of characteristics.

Influence of the Nile River: The Nile River plays a significant role in Egyptian Astrology. The rising and falling of the Nile were linked to the zodiac signs, and this connection influenced the agricultural and societal activities of the time.

Birth Charts and Destiny: Similar to other astrological systems, Egyptian Astrology involves creating birth charts based on the positions of celestial bodies at the time of an individual's birth. These charts were consulted for guidance on various aspects of life, including career, relationships, and destiny.

Hieroglyphs and Symbols: Symbols and hieroglyphs associated with each zodiac sign were used in Egyptian Astrology.

These symbols often represented animals, gods, or objects related to the associated deity.

It's important to note that while Egyptian Astrology has historical and cultural significance, its practices and interpretations may vary, and the surviving knowledge about it is somewhat limited compared to other ancient astrological systems. Additionally, modern interpretations of Egyptian Astrology often involve a blending of historical elements with more contemporary astrological concepts. As with many ancient astrological systems, the accuracy and scientific basis of Egyptian Astrology are subjects of debate and skepticism.

Greek Astrology

Greek Astrology, also known as Hellenistic Astrology, refers to the astrological practices that emerged and developed in ancient Greece during the Hellenistic period (approximately the 4th century BCE to the 5th century CE). It played a foundational role in the development of Western astrology. Here's an overview:

Zodiac Signs: Greek Astrology, like its modern Western counterpart, is based on the zodiac, a belt in the sky divided into 12 equal parts, each associated with a specific constellation. The zodiac signs are Aries, Taurus, Gemini, Cancer, Leo, Virgo, Libra, Scorpio, Sagittarius, Capricorn, Aquarius, and Pisces.

Planetary Influences: The ancient Greeks recognized seven classical planets, including the Sun and Moon, as significant influences in astrology. Each planet was associated with certain qualities and attributes. This planetary system laid the foundation for much of Western astrological tradition.

Houses and Aspects: Greek astrologers introduced the concept of dividing the astrological chart into houses, each representing different areas of life.

Aspects, or geometric angles between planets, were also considered in interpreting the chart.

Ascendant and Descendant: The Ascendant (rising sign) and Descendant (setting sign) became integral components of Greek Astrology, influencing an individual's overall personality and characteristics.

Concept of Lots or Parts: Greeks introduced the concept of "Lots" or "Arabic Parts" in astrology. These are sensitive points in the chart calculated based on mathematical relationships between planets, providing insights into specific areas of life.

Philosophical Influences: Greek philosophy, particularly the teachings of philosophers like Plato and Aristotle, profoundly impacted the development of Greek Astrology. Astrology was often intertwined with philosophical and metaphysical discussions about fate, free will, and the interconnectedness of the cosmos.

Timing Techniques: Greek astrologers developed various timing techniques, such as annual profections and solar returns, to provide insights into different periods of an individual's life.

Greek Astrology laid the groundwork for the evolution of astrology in the Western world. While the specifics of techniques and interpretations have evolved over time, the fundamental concepts introduced by ancient Greek astrologers continue to shape the astrological practice today.

Indonesian Astrology

Indonesian Astrology is a broad term encompassing a variety of traditional astrological practices found across the diverse cultures of Indonesia. Due to the archipelago's rich tapestry of ethnicities and belief systems, astrological traditions can differ significantly from one region to another. Here are some general aspects:

Javanese Astrology: Javanese Astrology holds significance in Java, the most populous island of Indonesia. It is influenced by Javanese mysticism, which integrates elements of Hindu-Buddhist traditions, Islamic mysticism, and indigenous beliefs. The Javanese calendar incorporates lunar cycles and is used for astrological and divinatory purposes.

Wayang Kulit and Topeng Performances: Wayang Kulit (shadow puppetry) and Topeng (mask) performances often incorporate astrological themes.

Characters in these traditional arts may represent astrological archetypes or have characteristics associated with specific zodiac signs.

Balinese Pawukon Calendar: In Bali, the Pawukon calendar is used for various purposes, including determining auspicious times for ceremonies and activities. It consists of ten concurrent weeks, each with ten days, reflecting a unique astrological perspective.

Day Names: Some Indonesian cultures associate each day of the week with particular deities or celestial bodies, influencing activities and decisions. For example, certain days may be considered more auspicious for specific events in Javanese culture.

Traditional Healers and Dukun: Traditional healers, known as "dukun," may use astrological insights in their practices. They may assess an individual's birth chart or consult celestial events to guide health, relationships, and other aspects of life.

Austronesian Cultural Influences: Across the Indonesian archipelago, various ethnic groups with Austronesian roots may incorporate celestial observations into their cultural practices. This can include navigation by the stars, lunar calendars, and folklore connecting celestial events with local myths.

Traditional Healers and Dukun: Traditional healers, known as "dukun," may use astrological insights in their practices. They may assess an individual's birth chart or consult celestial events to guide health, relationships, and other aspects of life.

Indonesian Astrology

Cultural Diversity: Indonesia's diverse cultures contribute to various astrological beliefs and practices. Local variations can be observed in Kalimantan, Sumatra, Sulawesi, and other regions, each with its unique interpretations and applications of astrology.

It's important to approach Indonesian Astrology with an awareness of its cultural diversity and the specific practices within each community. While there may be shared in each community. While there may be shared elements, the astrological traditions in Indonesia are deeply intertwined with local customs, beliefs, and historical influences.

Mayan Astrology

Haab's Calendar: Mayan Astrology also incorporates the Haab' calendar, a solar calendar of 365 days divided into 18 months of 20 days each, plus a final month of 5 "empty" or unlucky days. Combining the Tzolk'in and Haab' calendars creates the Calendar Round, a 52-year cycle with no repeating combinations.

Long Count Calendar: The Mayans also used the Long Count calendar to track longer periods. This calendar system was crucial for recording historical events and predicting future occurrences.

Personal Energy: In Mayan Astrology, individuals are associated with a specific day sign and number based on their birthdate in the Tzolk'in. This combination is believed to influence a person's energy, characteristics, and destiny.

Mayan Astrology is deeply intertwined with the Mayan religious and cultural beliefs. It was used for various purposes, including divination, agricultural planning, and determining auspicious ceremony times.

Mayan Astrology is deeply intertwined with the Mayan religious and cultural beliefs. It was used for various purposes, including divination, agricultural planning, and determining auspicious ceremony times.

While not widely practiced today, some people still explore Mayan Astrology for spiritual and historical insights. It's important to note that Mayan Astrology is distinct from the popularized notion of the "Mayan calendar" predicting apocalyptic events, which is a misinterpretation of the Long Count calendar.

Iranian Astrology

Iranian Astrology, also known as Persian Astrology or Iranian Astrology System (IAS), is a unique astrological system developed in contemporary Iran by Mahmoud Ghasemi. Ghasemi introduced this system in the late 20th century as an alternative to traditional Western astrology. Here are key aspects of Iranian Astrology:

Planetary Periods: A fundamental concept in Iranian Astrology uses planetary periods or "Dasha" periods, similar to the Vedic astrological system. These periods, ranging from one to ten years, are associated with specific planets. The sequence of planetary periods in Iranian Astrology is Sun, Moon, Mercury, Venus, Mars, Jupiter, Saturn, Uranus, Neptune, and Pluto.

Dwads: Iranian Astrology uses a zodiacal subdivision known as "dwads." The dwad is a 2.5-degree segment of a zodiac sign, and each planet is assigned a specific dwad position in a sign. Dwads are used to gain additional insights into the qualities and characteristics of planets within a sign.

Midpoints: Midpoints, the middle point between two planets or points in a chart, are emphasized in Iranian Astrology. These midpoints are believed to represent sensitive areas in a person's life and can be interpreted to reveal specific themes or events.

Uranian Astrology Techniques: Iranian Astrology incorporates techniques associated with the Uranian system, developed by the Hamburg School. This includes using hypothetical planets like Cupido, Hades, Zeus, and Kronos and sensitive points known as "Arabians."

Solar and Lunar Returns: Like Western astrology, Iranian Astrology utilizes Solar Returns (annual charts cast for the moment the Sun returns to its natal position) and Lunar Returns (monthly charts based on the Moon's return to its natal position) for predictive purposes.

Astrological Counseling: Iranian Astrology often emphasizes counseling and psychological interpretation of the birth chart. Practitioners may use the chart for self-awareness, personal development, and understanding life patterns.

Modern and Global Perspective: Iranian Astrology aims to provide a contemporary and global perspective, integrating both traditional and modern astrological traditional and modern astrological concepts. It is designed to be adaptable to the evolving needs and consciousness of individuals in the contemporary world.

Iranian Astrology, as introduced by Mahmoud Ghasemi, represents a departure from traditional Western astrology while incorporating elements from various astrological traditions. It emphasizes predictive techniques, psychological insights, and a holistic approach to understanding.

Japanese Astrology

Unlike Western or Chinese astrology, Japanese Astrology does not have a well-established system comparable to the zodiacs commonly known in the West or the Chinese animal signs. However, Japan's traditional astrological and divinatory practices are rooted in Shinto and Buddhist beliefs. Here are some aspects to consider:

Shichijuuni-shi (tt=*): This term, translated as "seventy-two signs," is a Japanese astrological concept derived from the Chinese sexagenary cycle, which combines ten heavenly stems and twelve earthly branches. While not as prominently used as the Chinese zodiac, it has been historically referenced in Japanese divination.

Traditional Calendar and Festivals:
Japanese festivals and celebrations often align with lunar and solar events. The lunar calendar has been historically influential in determining the timing of events and festivals, connecting celestial cycles to earthly activities.

Shinto and Celestial Worship: Shinto, the indigenous spirituality of Japan, emphasizes the reverence for natural elements and celestial bodies. Some Shinto rituals and festivals are linked to celestial events, reflecting a connection between the divine, nature, and the cosmos.

Astrology in Japanese Culture: While not as prominent as in some other cultures, astrology has left its mark on Japanese literature, art, and folklore. Elements of divination and fortune-telling, such as interpreting celestial phenomena, can be found in historical Japanese texts.

Influence of Chinese Astrology: with its zodiac signs and elements, Chinese astrology has impacted Japanese divination practices. The Chinese zodiac, in particular, is well-known in Japan and celebrated during the New Year.

Modern Astrology Practices: Western and traditional astrology have gained popularity in contemporary Japan. Some people consult horoscopes, birth charts, and astrological readings for guidance in various aspects of life.

It's important to note that while there are traces of astrological and divinatory practices in Japan, the country's approach to these matters is diverse and has evolved. Modern Japan, with its blend of traditional and global influences, incorporates various astrological systems, reflecting the adaptability and openness of Japanese culture.

Native American Astrology

Native American Astrology, unlike the Western zodiac system, is diverse and varies among different tribes and nations. It often involves a close connection with nature, animals, and the elements. Here's a general overview:

Animal Totems: Many Native American tribes associate specific animals with birthdates, creating a system of animal totems or spirit animals. These totems are believed to reflect an individual's personality traits and life path.

Medicine Wheel: Some Native American cultures use a Medicine Wheel, a sacred hoop divided into four quadrants, each representing a cardinal direction and associated with specific qualities, colors, and animals. The wheel is a symbolic and spiritual tool, offering guidance and insight.

Seasonal Influences: Native American Astrology often considers the natural cycles of the seasons. Different tribes may associate specific qualities or animals with each season, influencing the characteristics of individuals born during those times.

Connection to Elements: The elements— earth, air, fire, and water-play a significant role in Native American Astrology. Each element is associated with certain qualities and is believed to influence an individual's nature based on birthdate.

Lunar Influences: Some tribes incorporate lunar cycles into their astrological beliefs. Full moons, in particular, may be associated with specific energies or events.

Cultural Variations: It's crucial to recognize that Native American cultures are diverse, with each tribe having unique beliefs and practices. There isn't a single, unified Native American Astrology system, and interpretations can differ widely among tribes.

Ceremonial Practices: Astrological insights may be integrated into ceremonial practices and rituals. Birth and naming ceremonies, for example, may involve spiritual leaders providing guidance based on astrological considerations.

It's important to approach Native American Astrology with cultural sensitivity and respect, as these traditions hold deep spiritual significance for indigenous communities.

Additionally, many aspects of Native American Astrology are sacred and not meant for casual or commercial use. As with any cultural or spiritual practice, understanding and appreciating the context and diversity of beliefs is essential.

Orisha Astrology

Orisha astrology is rooted in the Yoruba religion, which originated in West Africa and has spread to various parts of the world, particularly the Americas, through the African diaspora. Orisha refers to the deities or divine forces worshiped in the Yoruba tradition. The Yoruba people have a rich cosmology that includes a system of divination known as Ifa, which is central to Orisha astrology.

In Orisha astrology, individuals are associated with specific Orishas based on their birth date, similar to how Western astrology assigns zodiac signs.

Ifa divination uses a set of 256 Odus (divination signs) combined with the casting of sacred palm nuts or cowrie shells to provide guidance and insight into one's destiny, challenges, and spiritual path.

Key Orishas include:
Orunmila: The Orisha of wisdom, knowledge, and divination.
Eshu (Elegua): The trickster and messenger Orisha, often invoked at the beginning of rituals.
Ogun: The Orisha of iron, war, and labor, associated with strength and determination.
Yemoja: The motherly Orisha of the Ogun River, symbolizing motherhood, fertility, and the sea.
Shango: The Orisha of thunder, lightning, and fire, embodying power and masculinity.

Orisha astrology intertwines with daily life, ceremonies, and rituals. Individuals may receive guidance on offerings, ceremonies, and lifestyle choices based on their Orisha alignment. The system reflects the Yoruba people's deep spiritual connection, emphasizing the importance of harmony with the divine forces for a balanced and fulfilling life.

Roman Astrology

Roman Astrology, also known as Roman Zodiac, is a term often used to describe the astrology practiced in ancient Rome.

However, it's important to note that Roman astrology largely adopted and adapted the Greek astrological traditions. The Romans were heavily influenced by Greek culture, including their astrology. Here's a brief overview:

Adoption of Greek Astrology: The Romans borrowed heavily from Greek Astrology, adopting the Greek zodiac signs, planets, and astrological techniques. For example, the planetary names in Latin closely resemble their Greek counterparts.

Zodiac Signs: The Roman zodiac signs are the same as the Greek ones and include Aries, Taurus, Gemini, Cancer, Leo, Virgo, Libra, Scorpio, Sagittarius, Capricorn, Aquarius, and Pisces.

Planetary Influences: The Roman astrological system recognized seven classical planets, including the Sun and Moon, each associated with specific qualities and characteristics. The influences of these planets were thought to affect different aspects of an individual's life.

Hellenistic Techniques: Many Hellenistic astrological techniques, such as houses, aspects, and the concept of Lots, were incorporated into Roman Astrology.

The Greeks had a profound influence on Roman philosophical and astrological thought.

Roman Interpretations: While the Romans largely adopted Greek astrological principles, they sometimes interpreted the symbolism and meanings of signs and planets in ways that aligned with their own cultural context and mythology.

Integration with Roman Religion:
Astrology was integrated into various aspects of Roman life, including religious practices. The Romans had a tradition of consulting the heavens for omens, and astrology became a part of this divinatory system.

Astrological Influence on Roman Society:
Astrology played a role in Roman politics, with emperors and leaders often consulting astrologers for guidance. However, there were times when the practice faced restrictions, as some rulers were skeptical of its influence.

It's important to recognize that Roman Astrology is more of an extension or adaptation of Greek Astrology rather than an independent system. Blending these traditions shaped the astrological practices that later influenced medieval and Renaissance astrology in Europe.

Tibetan Astrology

Tibetan Astrology, also known as Tibetan Elemental Astrology or "Nagtsi," is a traditional system rooted in Tibetan Buddhism and the Bon religion. It incorporates astrological principles to guide various aspects of life, including personal conduct, agriculture, and religious practices. Here are key elements of Tibetan Astrology:

Five Elements: Tibetan Astrology is centered around the five elements—earth, water, fire, air, and space.
These elements are believed to influence both individuals and the world at large. The interactions and relationships between these elements form the basis of astrological calculations.

Twelve Animal Signs: Similar to Chinese Astrology, Tibetan Astrology uses a twelve-animal cycle associated with each year.

However, the specific animals in the Tibetan system differ, including the Garuda, Monkey, Deer, Owl, Garuda, Mouse, Hare, Dragon, Snake, Horse, Sheep, and Monkey.
Astrological Calendar: The Tibetan astrological calendar, based on lunar months, determines auspicious and inauspicious times for various activities. This calendar considers the movement of the moon and specific celestial events.

Calculating Personal Elements: Tibetan Astrology involves calculating personal astrological elements based on the time, day, month, and year of an individual's birth. These elements include the "Mewa" (personal number) and "Lung-Ta" (wind horse), providing insights into one's nature and tendencies.

Divination Practices: Astrological divination is a common practice in Tibetan culture. Lamas and practitioners use various methods, such as casting dice or analyzing the positions of celestial bodies, to offer guidance on decisions and events.

Muhurta: Similar to the concept in Vedic Astrology, Tibetan Astrology emphasizes selecting auspicious times for various activities. "Muhurta" refers to choosing a favorable moment for events like weddings, travel, or starting a new endeavor.

Religious Significance: Tibetan Astrology is closely tied to religious practices and rituals. It is often used in planning ceremonies, festivals, and religious events.
Monasteries and practitioners may consult astrological guidance before important religious activities.

It's important to approach Tibetan Astrology with an understanding of its cultural and religious context. While it may share some similarities with other astrological systems, its unique elements and incorporation of Buddhist and Bon religious principles distinguish it as a distinct and culturally embedded practice in Tibetan society.

Vedic Astrology

Vedic Astrology, also known as Jyotish, is an ancient system of astrology that originated in India and is deeply rooted in Hindu traditions.

It shares some similarities with Western Astrology but has distinct principles and methods. Here's an overview:

Zodiac Signs and Planets: Vedic Astrology also uses a 12-sign zodiac, but the signs have different names and are based on fixed star constellations. The planets considered are similar to Western Astrology, including the Sun, Moon, Mars, Venus, Mercury, Jupiter, Saturn, Rahu (North Node), and Ketu (South Node).

Nakshatras: Besides the zodiac signs, Vedic Astrology divides the ecliptic into 27 lunar mansions or Nakshatras. Each Nakshatra has its characteristics and is associated with a ruling deity.

Houses: Similar to Western Astrology, Vedic Astrology uses a system of 12 houses, each representing different aspects of life. The houses are crucial in interpreting the chart.

Dasha System: Vedic Astrology employs a unique time-measuring system called dashas, which divides a person's life into major and minor periods ruled by specific planets. This system is used for timing events and predicting life trends.

Yogas and Doshas: Vedic Astrology includes combinations of planets called yogas, which can indicate auspicious or challenging conditions in a person's chart.

Doshas, on the other hand, represent imbalances that might affect health or other aspects of life.

Ascendant (Lagna): The Ascendant or Lagna in Vedic Astrology is as significant as in Western Astrology. It represents the rising sign on the eastern horizon at birth and sets the tone for the entire chart.

Vedic Astrology is deeply connected to Hindu philosophy, and spirituality is often used to guide various life decisions, including marriage, career, and spirituality. Like Western Astrology, its efficacy is subjective, and its practices are rooted in cultural and historical traditions.

Western Astrology

Western Astrology is a system that interprets the positions and movements of celestial bodies, such as planets and stars, to understand and predict human affairs and natural phenomena. It is based on the zodiac concept, a belt in the sky divided into 12 equal parts, each associated with a specific constellation.
Here's a brief overview of the key components:

Zodiac Signs: There are 12 signs, each representing a specific segment of the ecliptic. The signs are Aries, Taurus, Gemini, Cancer, Leo, Virgo, Libra, Scorpio, Sagittarius, Capricorn, Aquarius, and Pisces.

Planets: Astrology considers the positions of planets at the time of a person's birth. The Sun and Moon are crucial, along with Mercury, Venus, Mars, Jupiter, Saturn, Uranus, Neptune, and Pluto.

Houses: The birth chart is divided into 12 sections, known as houses, each representing different aspects of life, such as career, relationships, and home.

Aspects: These are angles between planets, indicating their relationships. Common aspects include conjunctions, sextiles, squares, trines, and oppositions.

Ascendant and Descendant: The Ascendant, or rising sign, is the zodiac sign rising on the eastern horizon at birth. The Descendant is its opposite point.

Moon Phases: The phase of the Moon at birth is considered to influence emotional traits.

Astrologers interpret these elements to create a natal or birth chart, providing insights into an individual's personality, strengths, challenges, and potential life path.

CHAPTER 16

Solar System

The boundless expanse of the universe holds a captivating realm known as the solar system, a complex web of celestial bodies that has fascinated humanity for generations. At the heart of this cosmic spectacle is the radiant and mighty Sun, a colossal star that provides the life-giving energy that fuels our world. Orbiting Earth, our loyal companion, the Moon, enchants us with its shimmering phases and mysterious allure. Together, these elements paint a mesmerizing portrait of the grandeur and diversity present in our cosmic neighborhood. In this journey of exploration, we'll delve into the wondrous dynamics that define the solar system, bask in the brilliance of the Sun, and unravel the enigma of the Moon's influence on our planet.

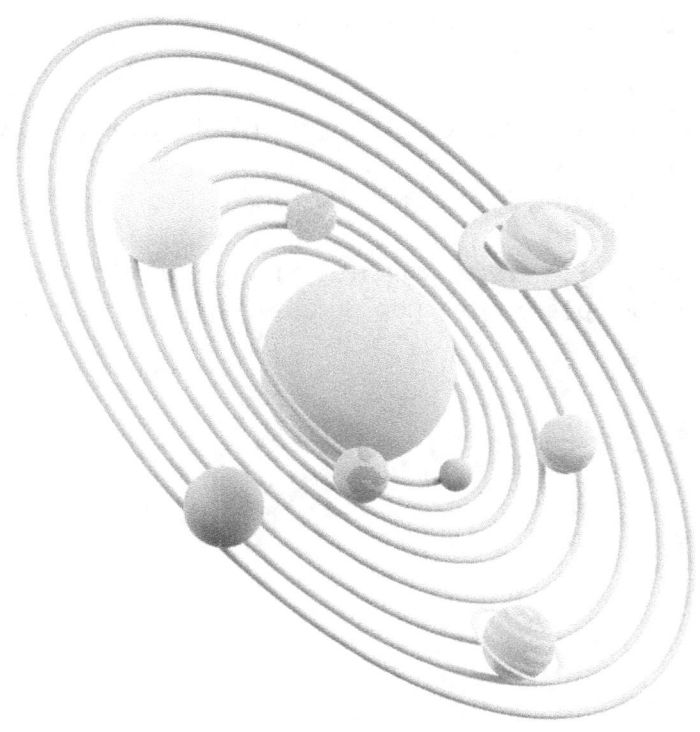

Earth

Solar System: Earth
Zodiac: Capricorn, Taurus, and Virgo
Chakra: Root
Celebrations: Earth Day and Walpurgis
Season: Winter
Day:
Time of Day: Midnight
Rune:
Number: 4
Colors: Black, Brown, Green, and White
Tarot:
Trees: Acacia and Oak
Misc. Plant: Grain
Herb and Garden:
Gemstones and Minerals: Agate (brown), Ametrine, Andalusite, Bloodstone, Carnelian, Chrysoprase, Citrine, Diopside, and Moss Agate
Metal:
From the Sea:
Goddesses: Anat, Ceres, Coatlicue, Cybele, Demeter, Gaia, Inanna, Isis, Maia, and Nanna
Gods: Adonis, Attis, Dionysus, Dumuzi, Ea, Enki, Faunus, Geb, and Vertimnus
Angel: Auriel
Issues, Intentions, and Powers: agriculture, creativity, grounding, healing, the home, magic (animal), nurture, peace, protection, purpose, revenge, and spirits

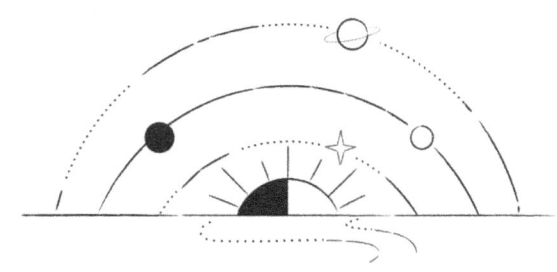

Jupiter

Solar System: Jupiter
Zodiac: Pisces and Sagittarius
Chakras: 3rd Eye, Heart, and Solar Plexus
Celebrations:
Season:
Day: Thursday
Time of Day:
Rune: Man
Numbers: 3, 4, and 5
Colors: Blue, Green (light, sea), Indigo, Purple, Turquoise, and Violet
Tarot: Wheel of Fortune
Trees: Birch, Cedar, Chestnut, Fir, Horse Chestnut, Linden, Magnolia, Maple, Oak, Olive, Palm (coconut), Pine, Sycamore, Walnut, and Yew
Misc. Plant: Aloe, Anise, Betony, Cinquefoil, Meadowsweet, Myrrh, Nutmeg, and Star Anise
Herb and Garden: Agrimony, Borage, Clove, Dandelion, Honeysuckle, Lemon Balm, and Sage
Gemstones and Minerals: Amethyst, Ametrine, Diopside, Emerald, Lepidolite, Sapphire,
Sugilite, Turquoise, and Zircon (red)
Metal: Tin
From the Sea:
Goddesses: Devi, Hera, Justitia, and Nut
Gods: Baal, Indra, Jupiter, Marduk, and Zeus
Mythical Being: Unicorn
Issues, Intentions, and Powers: abundance, astral realm, authority, business, control, dignity, discipline, favors, generosity, honor, influence, intuition, justice, kindness, leadership, luck, the mind, money, opportunities, optimism, power, pride, problems, prosperity, responsibility, spirituality, success, wealth, well-being, and wisdom

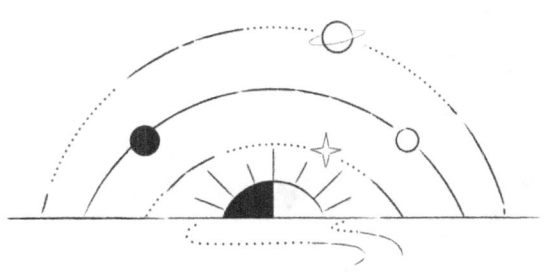

Mars

Solar System: Mars
Zodiac: Aries and Scorpio
Chakras: Root, Sacral, Solar Plexus, and Throat
Celebrations:
Season:
Day: Tuesday
Time of Day:
Rune: Man
Numbers: 2, 3, 5, and 9
Colors: Crimson, Maroon, Orange, Pink, and Red
Tarot: Devil, Emperor, and Tower
Trees: Alder, Blackthorn, Fir, Hawthorn, Holly, Juniper, Palm (dragon's blood), Pine, and Yew
Misc. Plant: Allspice, Anise, Asafoetida, Black Cohosh, Blessed Thistle, Bloodroot, Coriander, Cumin, Deer's Tongue, Galangal, Ginger, High John, Mustard, Nettle, Pepper, Reed, Thistle, and Wormwood
Herb and Garden: Anemone, Basil, Broom, Garlic, Gorse, Honeysuckle, Pennyroyal, Rue, Snapdragon, and Sweet Woodruff
Gemstones and Minerals: Beryl, Bloodstone, Citrine, Diamond, Garnet, Hematite, Jasper (red), Onyx, Pyrite, Rhodochrosite, Rhodonite, Ruby, Sard, Sardonyx, Tourmaline (red, watermelon), Tsavorite, and Zircon (red)
Metals: Iron and Steel
From the Sea: Coral (red)
Goddesses: Anat, Astarte, Badb, Durga, Macha, Maeve, Minerva, and Nanna
Gods: Ares, Indra, Mars, Nergal, Odin, Set, and Thor
Mythical Being: Unicorn
Issues, Intentions, and Powers: action, aggression, anger, assertiveness, battle/war, beginnings, courage, death, defense, desire, determination, emotions, endurance, energy (sexual), enmity, growth, justice, life, lust, magic (general, defensive, dragon, sex), passion, power, sexuality (male), skills, strength, and willpower

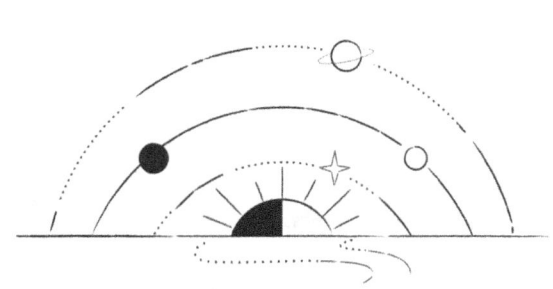

Mercury

Solar System: Mercury
Zodiac: Gemini and Virgo
Chakras: 3rd Eye, Root, Sacral, Solar Plexus, and Throat
Celebrations:
Season:
Day: Wednesday
Time of Day:
Rune:
Numbers: 1, 4, 5, and 8
Colors: Blue (navy), Gray, Green, Orange, Purple, Silver, Violet, and Yellow
Tarot: Hermit, Lovers, and Magician
Trees: Ash, Aspen, Cedar, Cherry, Elder, Hazel, Juniper, Linden, Olive, Pomegranate, and Acacia
Misc. Plants: Anise, Betony, Bittersweet, Cinquefoil, Flax, Horehound, Mandrake, Mistletoe, and Sandalwood
Herb and Garden: Agrimony, Bergamot, Clover, Dandelion, Dill, Fennel, Fern, Honeysuckle, Jasmine, Lavender, Lilac, Lily of the Valley, Marjoram, Peppermint, Periwinkle, Rosemary, Sage, and Valerian
Gemstones and Minerals: Agate (fire, green, red, snakeskin, tree), Amber, Aventurine, Blue Lace Agate, Carnelian, Cat's Eye, Citrine, Fluorite, Hematite, Jasper, Moss Agate, Onyx, Opal, Peridot, Rhodochrosite, Sardonyx, Sodalite, Sphene, and Topaz
Metals: Aluminum and Mercury
From the Sea: Coral (red)
Goddesses: Athena, Maat, Maia, Minerva, and Seshat
Gods: Anubis, Arawn, Coyote, Hermes, Loki, Lugh, Mercury, Odin, Ogma, Thor, and Thoth
Angels: Michael and Raphael
Issues, Intentions, and Powers: adaptability, balance, business, change(s), cleverness, communication, creativity, crossroads, deceit, divination, fear, improvement, inspiration, intelligence, justice, learning, love, magic, memory/memories, messages/ omens, the mind, money, moods, power, rebirth, renewal, skills, travel, wealth, and wisdom

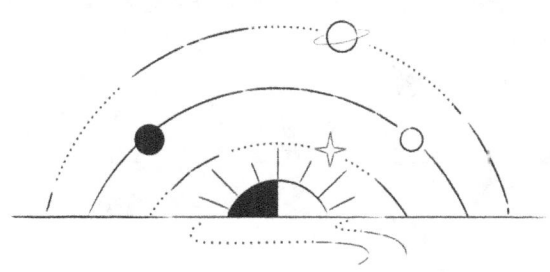

Moon

Solar System: Moon
Zodiac: Cancer
Chakra: Sacral
Celebrations: Beltane, Imbolc, Lughnasadh, and Samhain
Season:
Day: Monday
Time of Day:
Runes: Is and Lagu
Numbers: 2, 3, 0, and 13
Colors: Blue, Gray Green (sea), Orange, Silver, and White
Tarot: Chariot, High Priestess, and Moon
Trees: Birch, Mesquite, Olive, Palm, Rowan, and Willow
Misc. Plants: Aloe, Lotus, Moonwort, Myrrh, Nutmeg, Saffron, and Sandalwood
Herb and Garden: Bergamot, Blackberry/Bramble, Gardenia, Grape, Iris, Jasmine, Lemon Balm Lily, Poppy, and Rosemary
Gemstones and Minerals: Agate, Angelite, Aquamarine, Beryl, Calcite (clear), Herkimer Diamond, Moonstone, Morganite, Opal, Quartz, Sapphire, Selenite, and Turquoise
Metal: Silver
From the Sea: Coral (white), Moon Snail, Mother-of-Pearl, Mussel, and Pearl
Goddesses: Aine, Aphrodite, Ariadne, Arianrhod, Artemis, Cerridwen, Diana, Freya, Hecate, Ishtar, Isis, Juno, Luna, Nanna, Persephone, Rhiannon, Sedna, Selene, and Spiderwoman
Gods: Aegir, Hermes, Horus, Janus, Jupiter, Khensu, Shiva, and Thoth
Angel: Gabriel
Magical Beings: Fairies, Mermaids and Dragons
Issues, Intentions, and Powers: action, agriculture, animals, balance (inner), beginnings, change(s), consciousness (and subconscious), creativity, cycles, darkness, death, divination, dream work, emotions, enchantment, endings, energy (general, receptive), family, fertility, growth, guidance, healing, hexes, the home, illumination, imagination, inspiration, intuition, jealousy, life (rhythms), light, loneliness, love, magic (general, crone, moon, night), manifestation, moods, negativity, night-mares, obstacles, peace, power, pregnancy/childbirth, protection, psychic ability, rebirth/renewal, secrets, self-work, sensitivity, sorrow, spirits, transformation, wisdom, and witches/ witchcraft

Neptune

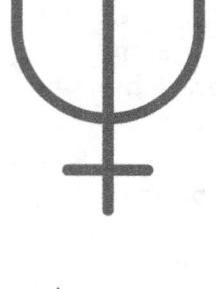

Solar System: Neptune
Zodiac: Aquarius and Pisces
Chakras: 3rd Eye and Crown
Celebrations:
Season:
Day:
Time of Day:
Rune:
Number: 7
Colors: Blue, Green (light, sea), Indigo, Lavender, Purple, and Turquoise
Tarot: Hanged Man
Trees: Ash
Misc. Plants:
Herb and Garden:
Gemstones and Minerals: Amethyst, Angelite, Aquamarine, Beryl, Celestite, Fluorite, Jade, Labradorite, Lapis Lazuli, Lepidolite, Sapphire, and Turquoise
Metal:
From the Sea: Coral and Mother-of-Pearl
Goddesses: Amphitrite, Brigid, Ran, Sedna and Tiamat
Gods: Aegir, Manannan, Neptune, and Poseidon
Angel:
Magical Beings: Fairies and Mermaids
Issues, Intentions, and Powers: awareness (expand), clairvoyance, community, consciousness (subconscious), creativity, dream work, enchantment, energy (psychic), guardian, guidance, inspiration, intuition, life, the otherworld/ underworld, power, protection, psychic ability, sensitivity, visions

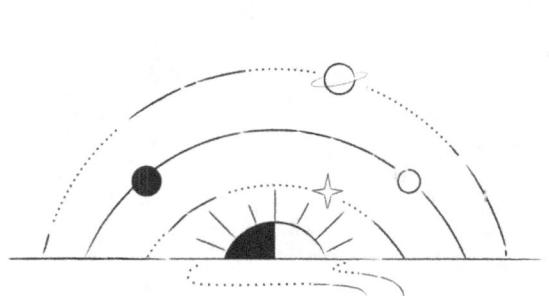

Pluto

Solar System: Pluto
Zodiac: Cancer and Scorpio
Chakra: Sacral
Celebrations:
Season:
Day:
Time of Day:
Rune:
Number:
Colors: Blue, Green (light, sea), Indigo, Lavender, Purple, and Turquoise
Tarot: Hanged Man
Tree: Cypress
Misc. Plants: Belladonna, Bittersweet, Nettle, and Reed
Herb and Garden: Basil and Fern (bear paw)
Gemstones and Minerals: Amethyst, Garnet, Jet, Kunzite, Labradorite, Obsidian, Quartz (tourmalated), Spinel, Tourmaline, and Tsavorite
Metal:
From the Sea:
Goddesses: Ereshkigal, Hathor, Hecate, Hel, Hera, Kali, the Morrigan, and Persephone
Gods: Pluto and Osiris
Angel:
Magical Beings:
Issues, Intentions, and Powers: the afterlife, changes, danger, darkness (inner), death, dream work, justice, karma, memory/memories, the otherworld/underworld, rebirth/renewal, secrets, sexuality, spirituality, transformation, and wealth

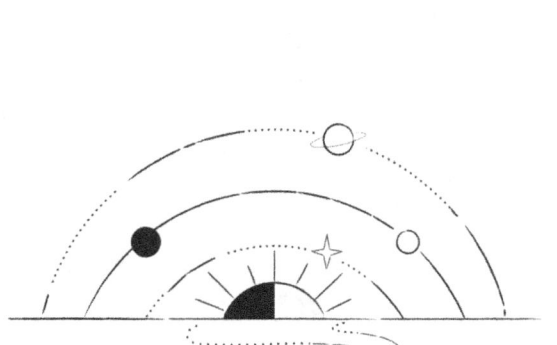

Saturn

Solar System: Saturn
Zodiac: Aquarius, Capricorn, and Libra
Chakra: Crown, Heart, Root, and Throat
Celebrations:
Season:
Day: Saturday
Time of Day:
Rune: Peorth
Numbers: 3, 7, and 8
Colors: Black, Blue (navy), Brown, Gray (dark), Green (dark), Indigo, and Yellow (light)
Tarot: Death, Hanged Man, and World
Tree: Aspen, Beech, Blackthorn, Cypress, Elm, Fir, Holly, Magnolia, Mesquite, Mimosa, Pine, Poplar, Rowan, Witch Hazel, and Yew
Misc. Plants: Cinnamon, Clove, Bamboo, Eyebright, Frankincense, Galangal, Ginseng, Grain
Herb and Garden: Amaranth, Carnation, Comfrey, Ivy, Monkshood, Morning Glory, Rue, and Solomon's Seal
Gemstones and Minerals: Apache Tears, Azurite, Carnelian, Hematite, Jasper (brown), Jet, Obsidian, Onyx, Sapphire, Sardonyx, Serpentine, and Tourmaline (black)
Metal: Lead
From the Sea: Coral (black)
Goddesses: Ariadne, Ceres, Demeter, Dôn, Durga, Hecate, Hera, Juno, Kali, and Rhea
Gods: Amun, Khensu Saturn
Angel:
Magical Beings:
Issues, Intentions, and Powers: agriculture, ambition, astral realm, authority, banish, bind, business, concentration/ focus, darkness, death, discipline, endings, endurance, freedom, goals, grounding, justice, karma, knowledge, limitations/ boundaries, longevity, loyalty, lust, the mind, obstacles, peace, purification, relationships, stability, strength.

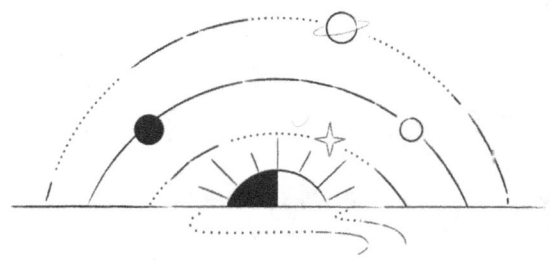

Sun

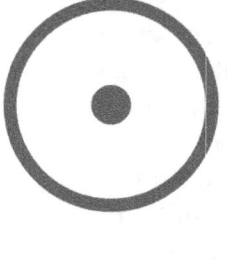

Solar System: Sun
Zodiac: Aries, Cancer, and Leo
Chakra: Solar Plexus
Celebrations: Litha, Mabon, Ostara, Walpurgis, and Yule
Season:
Day: Sunday
Time of Day: Noon
Rune: Jera and Sigel
Numbers: 1 and 6
Colors: Gold, Orange, and Yellow
Tarot: Death, Hanged Man, and World
Tree: Acacia, Ash, Birch, Cedar, Chestnut, Hazel, Horse Chestnut, Juniper, Laurel, Linden, Oak, Olive, Palm, Rowan, Walnut, and Witch Hazel
Misc. Plants: Belladonna, Bittersweet, Henbane, Lady's Slipper, Mandrake, Mullein, Patchouli, Skullcap, and Thornapple
Herb and Garden: Angelica, Broom, Carnation, Chamomile, Chrysanthemum, Daffodil, Daisy, Goldenseal, Gorse, Heliotrope, Lovage, Marigold, Peony, Rosemary, St. John's Wort, and Sunflower (com), Lotus, Mistletoe, and Saffron
Gemstones and Minerals: Amber, Ametrine, Beryl (golden), Calcite (orange, red), Carnelian, Chrysoberyl, Citrine, Diamond, Herkimer Diamond, Peridot, Quartz, Ruby, Sunstone, Tiger's Eye, Topaz, Tourmaline (black), and Zircon
From the Sea: Coral (black)
Goddesses: Aine, Amaterasu, Bast, Brigid, Hathor, Phoebe, Sekhmet, and Spider Woman
Gods: Adonis, Agni, Amun, Apollo, Baal, Belenus, Helios, Horus, Jupiter, Lugh, Marduk, Mithras, Ogma, Osiris, Pushan, Ra, Shiva, Surya, and Vishnu
Angel: Raphael
Magical Beings: Dragon, Griffin, Phoenix, Sphinx, Unicorn, Dragon, Griffin, Phoenix, Sphinx, and Unicorn
Issues, Intentions, and Powers:

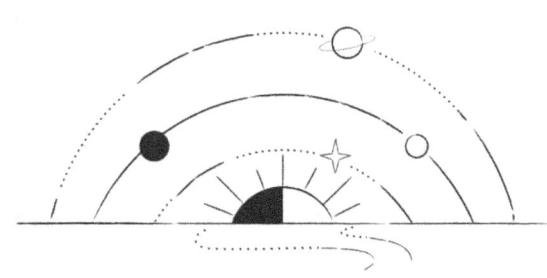

Uranus

Solar System: Uranus
Zodiac: Aquarius and Gemini
Chakras: Brow, Crown, and Throat
Celebrations:
Season:
Day: Sunday
Time of Day:
Rune:
Number: 4
Colors: Indigo and Yellow (light)
Tarot: Fool, Star, and Tower
Tree: Ash and Rowan
Misc. Plants: Belladonna, Bittersweet, Henbane, Lady's Slipper, Mandrake, Mullein, Patchouli, Skullcap, and Thornapple
Herb and Garden: Angelica, Broom, Carnation, Chamomile, Chrysanthemum, Daffodil, Daisy, Goldenseal, Gorse, Heliotrope, Lovage, Marigold, Peony, Rosemary, St. John's Wort, and Sunflower (com), Lotus, Mistletoe, and Saffron
Gemstones and Minerals: Amazonite, Aventurine, Herkimer Diamond, Labradorite, and Quartz
From the Sea: Coral (black)
Goddesses: Anat, Aphrodite, Danu, Inanna, Ishtar, and Isis
Gods:
Angel:
Magical Beings:
Issues, Intentions, and Powers: ambition, anger, change(s), community, cooperation, freedom, goals, hope, illumination, improvement, intuition, motivation, power, and relationships

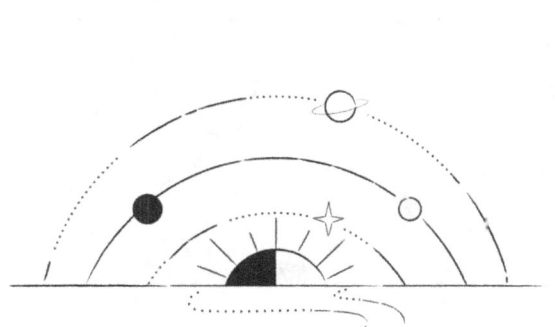

Venus

Solar System: Venus, Also known as the Morning and Evening Star
Zodiac: 3rd Eye, Heart, Sacral, and Throat
Chakras: Brow, Crown, and Throat
Celebrations:
Season:
Day: Friday
Time of Day: Dawn, Dusk, and Midnight
Rune: As and Ken
Numbers: 5, 6, and 7
Colors: Aqua, Blue (light), Green, Indigo, Lavender, Mauve, Pink, Rose, White, and Yellow (light)
Tarot: Empress, Justice, and Star
Tree: Alder, Apple, Aspen, Birch, Cherry, Elder, Magnolia, Myrtle, Sycamore, and Willow
Misc. Plants: loe, Burdock, Cardamom, Coltsfoot, Cowslip, Dittany, Orris Root, and Sandalwood
Gemstones and Minerals: Alexandrite, Aventurine, Azurite, Calcite, Carnelian, Cat's Eye, Celeste Chrysoberyl, Chrysocolla, Chrysoprase, Desert Rose, Diamond, Dioptase, Emerald, Jade, Jasper (green), Kunzite, Lapis Lazuli, Lodestone, Malachite, Peridot, Rhodochrosite, Rose Quart, Sapphire, Sodalite, Tourmaline (blue, green, pink, watermelon), Tsavorite, Turquoise
Metal: Copper
From the Sea:
Goddesses: Astarte, Ishtar, and Venus
Gods: Quetzalcoatl
Angel:
Magical Beings:
Issues, Intentions, and Powers: affection, agriculture, astral realm, attraction, beauty, beginnings, connections, creativity, desire, emotions, energy (receptive, sexual), fertility, friendship, gentleness, happiness, harmony: kindness, love, lust, magic (sex), needs, passion, pleasure rebirth/renewal, relationships, reversal, romance, sensuality, sexuality, stress, and unity

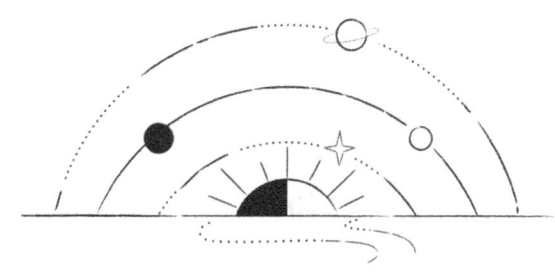

Retrogrades

What is retrograde?

A planet could be retrograde—meaning that it appears to be spinning backward from the vantage point of Earth. What's happening? The Earth is completing its orbit around the Sun faster than other planets outside its orbit. Periodically, it will outpace them— that's when retrograde mayhem breaks loose!

Much like a speeding car or train passing a slower one, the planet being passed will appear to stop and move backward—the apparent retrograde period.
Then, once the Earth completely passes this planet in its orbit, the motion appears normal again, and the planet is said to be "direct" or "prograde" (to use the short scientific term). Chances are, you've been in a vehicle before that felt like it was moving in reverse when it was passed; this is just like that!

What about the "shadow" period?

It isn't over 'til it's over! Each retrograde cycle has a "shadow period" — the awkward adjustment of the retrograde planet from apparent backward to forward motion...and vice-versa. For that reason, you may feel the stirrings of a retrograde cycle for several days, even weeks, before it officially begins.

Pluto
Saturn
Neptune
Chiron
Jupiter
Uranus
Mars
Venus

Planetary Retrogrades

Planetary retrograde is an astrological occurrence that happens when a planet seems to move backward in its orbit from the perspective of Earth. This happens due to differences in the orbital speed of the planets relative to Earth's position. It's important to note that planets don't actually change their direction, but the apparent retrograde motion occurs due to how the Earth orbits around the Sun.

Astrologers believe that planetary retrogrades can influence the energy and vibration of the planet in question, which can affect us. During a retrograde, the planetary energy is said to turn inward, and its impact can be felt more strongly in our lives. Different planets are believed to affect us differently, and their retrogrades may also have other effects.

Mercury Retrograde occurs three to four times a year for around three weeks. It is known for causing communication issues, technology malfunction, and travel delays. It's essential to take extra care when making important decisions or signing contracts during this time.

Venus Retrograde: This happens every eighteen months for about 40-43 days. It's a time for re-evaluating relationships, romantic connections, and money matters. It's a good time for reflection and introspection on handling these areas.

Mars Retrograde: This happens every two years for two months
It brings up feelings of frustration, anger, and aggression. It is important to be patient and avoid impulsive actions during this time.

Jupiter Retrograde: This happens every thirteen months for around four months. It can be a time for introspection and personal growth, but it can also cause setbacks in areas of expansion and growth.

Saturn Retrograde: This occurs every year for around four months. It is time to take stock of responsibilities and make necessary changes. obstacles and lead to personal growth and development.ItCanBringChallengesAnd

Uranus Retrograde: This happens every year for around five months. It can bring unexpected changes and upheavals, but it can also bring innovation and new ideas.

Neptune Retrograde: This occurs every year for around five months; it's time for spiritual growth and reflection but can also cause confusion and delusion.

Pluto Retrograde: This happens every year for around six months. It's a time for transformation and personal growth but can also bring power struggles and intense emotional experiences.

Retrogrades

Mercury Retrograde:
Mercury takes 88 days to make one complete revolution around the Sun. Mercury moves into retrograde three times per year for anywhere between 19 to 24 days. When Mercury retrogrades, mistakes, misunderstandings, and problems in communication and transportation are likely. Do not sign contracts, buy new items, or begin new projects. It is an excellent time to plan, research, and prepare for something that will happen later. Try to evaluate how you communicate and actively remain present.

Venus Retrograde:
Venus takes 225 days to make a complete revolution around the Sun and is stationary for between a few hours or 3 or 4 days. Venus moves into retrograde every 18 months and then stays that way for about 6 weeks. When Venus goes retrograde, money and love areas are reviewed, and old relations could return to resume or be completed. New love relationships may produce a change of heart when Venus goes direct. Investments done during the retrograde phase of Venus could lose value. Old relationship issues you thought were settled rear their ugly heads. Heal those issues.

Mars Retrograde:
Mars takes approximately 2 years or 687 days to complete a revolution around the Sun. Mars moves into retrograde every 2 years and 2 months and then stays that way for about 55 to 80 days. When Mars goes retrograde, any direct action becomes difficult. Traveling within, finishing incomplete tasks, redoing, renovating, and repairing will work better than pushing forward with any new direct ventures. Look your issues in the eye and tackle them once and for all. Self-care is your best friend during these times.

Jupiter Retrograde:
Jupiter takes around 12 years to make a complete revolution around the Sun. After that, Jupiter goes retrograde every year for about 120 days. When Jupiter goes retrograde, reviewing our visions, ideals, and belief systems in life is good. This reminds us that we need to work to achieve our dreams and re-align with our authentic selves.

Saturn Retrograde:
Saturn takes around 29.5 years to make a complete revolution around the Sun. Saturn goes retrograde every year for about 140 days. When Saturn goes retrograde, it is an excellent time to revisit our relationship and work on long-term goals, responsibilities, and duties. It is a time to restructure how we manifest our reality and find a new attitude towards obstacles—a chance to revisit karmic lessons, which are gentler and more familiar than new ones. Focus on self-discipline.

Retrogrades

Uranus Retrograde:
Uranus takes about 84 years to make a complete revolution around the Sun, thus spending almost 7 years in each sign of the Zodiac. Uranus moves into retrograde approximately every year for around 148 days. When Uranus goes retrograde, our inner freedom is the focus. It is an excellent time for us to look for new paths toward accomplishing older intentions, using its energy to help us think creatively.

Neptune Retrograde:
Neptune takes about 164 years to make a complete revolution around the Sun, thus spending almost 14 years in each sign of the Zodiac. Neptune moves into retrograde approximately every year for around 150 days. When Neptune retrogrades, our spirituality, inner tranquility, and vision become the focus. Smashes illusion, giving us the sometimes-surprising opportunity to see ourselves more clearly, unlike the other retrogrades. It forces you out of your comfort zone.

Chiron Retrograde:
It is a comet between Saturn and Uranus; Chiron takes about four years to move from sign to sign, although it spends 7 to 8 years in Aries and Pisces and only one to two years in Virgo and Libra. It entered Aries on April 17, 2018, retrograded back into Pisces on September 25, 2018, and finally moved back into the cardinal fire sign on February 18, 2019, which will remain until June 19, 2026. Chiron retrograde can be valuable for paying attention to your dreams, journaling, or addressing past trauma alongside a therapist.

Pluto Retrograde:
Pluto takes 248 years to make a complete revolution around the Sun, thus spending, on average, about 21 years in each sign of the Zodiac. Pluto moves into retrograde approximately every year for around 5 or 6 months. When Pluto goes retrograde, reflecting on how we are doing with change and transformation is good. It urges us to evaluate our relationship with power. Embrace your inner strength and use it to empower others.

CHAPTER 17

Elemental
Magic

Elemental Magic

The elements are another essential aspect of Witchcraft; we often call on them during spells and rituals. There are four primary elements, each of which has particular associations. Each element represents a different type of energy that you can harness.

Earth Magic - The element of Earth is the foundation of all life. The color green and the northern quarter align with the element of Earth. It is potent in spells that require wisdom and spells for fertility, prosperity, strength, and wealth.

Air Magic - The element of air is light fuel for all living things. It is represented by the color yellow and the eastern quarter when casting a circle. Spells for renewal, change, intuition, and knowledge call upon the air.

Fire Magic - The element of fire is a source of creation and destruction of life. It is represented by the color red and the southern quarter when casting a circle. Spells for passion, inspiration, intuition, creativity, and protection use fire.

Water Magic - Water represents the flow of life. It is represented by the color blue and the western quarter when casting a circle. It is powerful in spells for healing, peace, and compassion.

Air

Symbol: △
Number: 5
Solar System: Jupiter, Mercury, and Uranus
Zodiac: Aquarius, Gemini, and Libra
Celebration: Ostara
Season: Spring
Time of Day: Dawn
Runes: Beorc, Hagal, and Thorn
Ogham: Onn
Tarot: Fool, Swords, and Wands
Direction: East
Sense: Smell
Energy: Yang
Chakras: Crown, Heart, and Throat
Colors: Blue (light), Gray, Lavender, Pink, Red, Silver, White, and Yellow (bright, light)
Trees: Acacia, Alder, Apple, Ash, Aspen, Cedar, Chestnut, Elder, Elm Fir, Hawthorn, Hazel, Holly, Horse Chestnut, Laurel, Linden, Maple, Mesquite, Oak, Olive, Palm, Pine, Sycamore, Walnut, and Yew
Herbs and Flowers: Agrimony, Anemone, Bergamot, Borage, Broom, Clover, Comfrey, Dandelion, Fern, Ivy, Lavender, Lily of the Valley, Marjoram, Marigold, Mugwort, Peppermint, Primrose, Sage, Spearmint, Thyme, Vervain, Violet, and Yarrow
Misc. Plants: Anise, Bamboo, Bittersweet, Eyebright, Frankincense, Goldenrod, Horehound, Meadowsweet, Mistletoe, Myrrh, Nutmeg, Reed, Sandalwood, Star Anise, and Wormwood
Gemstones and Minerals: Agate (tree), Ametrine, Angelite, Aragonite, Aventurine, Blue Lace Agate, Celestite, Chrysoberyl, Desert Rose, Moldavite, Opal, Quartz (clear), Sodalite, Sphene, Staurolite, Topaz (blue), and Tourmaline (blue)
Metals: Aluminum, Mercury, and Tin
From the Sea: Angel Wing and Jingle

Air

Angels: Michael and Raphael
Goddesses: Amaterasu, Athena, Arianrhod, Hera, Nut, and Phoebe
Gods: Hermes, Khnum, Mimir, Mercury, Quetzalcoatl, Thoth, and Zeus
Magical Beings: Elves, Fairies, Pixies
Animal: Gazelle
Birds: Albatross, Condor, Eagle, Falcon, Hawk, and Seagull
Reptile:
Insect/Misc.: Firefly
Mythical: Dragon, Sphinx, and Thunderbird
Ritual Tools: Athame, Incense, and Sword
Principle: To Know
Issues, Intentions, and Powers: acceptance, action, Astral Realm, beginnings, business, clairvoyance, clarity, communication, concentration/ focus, consecrate/bless, creativity, divination, enchantment, energy, enlightenment, fairness, freedom, harmony, healing, imagination, inspiration, intelligence, intuition, justice, knowledge, learning, life, light, loss, magic (animal, dragon), memory/memories, the mind, money, motivation, order/ organize, power, protection, psychic ability, purification, relationships, release, the senses (hearing, smell, touch), shamanic work, spirits, spirituality, travel, visions, weather (general, lightning, storms), willpower, and wisdom

Earth

Symbol: ▽
Numbers: 4, 6, 8
Solar System: Earth, Saturn, and Venus
Zodiac: Capricorn, Taurus, and Virgo
Celebrations: Earth Day, Hunting of the Wren, and Yule
Season: Winter
Time of Day: Midnight
Runes: Is, Tyr, and Ur
Ogham: Ioho
Tarot: Pentacles
Direction: North
Sense: Touch
Energy: Yin
Chakra: Root
Colors: Black, Brown, Green, and White
Trees: Ash, Blackthorn, Cedar, Cypress, Elder, Elm, Holly, Juniper, Locust, Magnolia, Maple, Oak, Olive, Pine, Pomegranate, Rowan, Spruce, and Witch Hazel
Herbs and Flowers: Comfrey, Fern, Honeysuckle, Ivy, Jasmine, Mugwort, Primrose, Sage, and Vervain
Misc. Plants: Cinquefoil, Clove, Grains, Henbane, High John, Horehound, Mandrake, Patchouli, and Reed
Gemstones and Minerals: Agate, Alexandrite, Amazonite, Amber, Andalusite, Apophyllite, Calcite (green), Cat's Eye, Cerussite, Chrysocol a, Chrysoprase, Diopside, Emerald, Fluorite, Hematite, Jade, Jasper, Jet, Kunzite, Malachite, Moss Agate, Peridot, Petrified Wood, Quartz (rutilated), Salt, Smoky Quartz, Staurolite, Sugilite, Tourmaline (black, brown, green, watermelon), Turquoise, and Unakite
Metals: Lead and Mercury
From the Sea: Coral (black)

Earth

Angels: Gabriel and Auriel

Goddesses: Anat, Ariadne, Artemis, Asherah, Bertha, Ceres, Demeter, Gaia, Kore, Nephthys, Persephone, Rhea, and Rhiannon

Gods: Adonis, Arawn, Cernunnos, Dionysus, Geb, the Green Man, Khnum, Marduk, Mimir, Pan, Prometheus and Vishnu

Magical Beings: Brownies, Dryads, Elves, Fairies, Gnomes, Pixies

Animals: Antelope, Armadillo, Badger, Bear, Boar, Buffalo / Bison, Cattle, Deer (stag), Dog, Elephant, Goat, Groundhog, Hippopotamus, Jaguar, Mole, Otter, Pig, Prairie Dog, and Wolverine.

Birds: Blue Jay, Chicken, Crow, Goose, Sparrow, Swan, Turkey, and Woodpecker

Reptiles: Crocodile, Snake, Toad, Tortoise, and Turtle

Insect/Misc: Dragonfly

Mythical: Dragon and Selkies

Ritual Tool: Pentacle

Principle: To Be Silent

Issues, Intentions, and Powers: abundance, acceptance, agriculture, anxiety, balance, beginnings, business, comfort, communication, consecrate/bless, consciousness, creativity, cycles, death, endurance, energy (general, receptive), family, fertility, gentleness, grounding, growth, healing, hexes, the home, justice, life, magic (dragon), manifestation, money, nurture, the otherworld/underworld, patience, peace, pregnancy/childbirth, prosperity, protection, purpose, rebirth/renewal, relationships, the senses (smell, touch), sensuality, sexuality, spirits (nature spirits), stability, strength, success, support, travel, warmth, wealth, weather, well-being, willpower, and wisdom

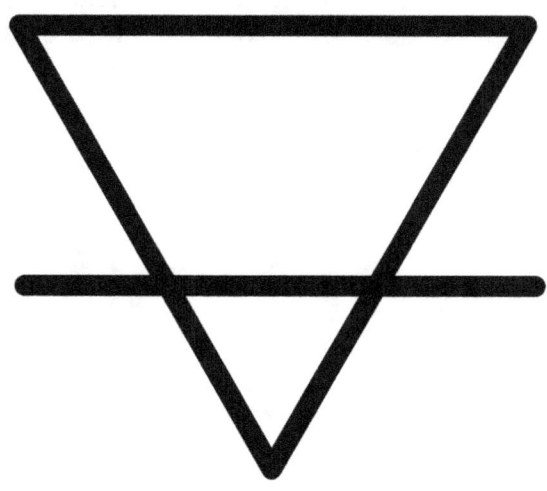

Fire

Symbol:
Numbers: 1, 3, 9
Solar System: Jupiter, Mars, and Sun
Zodiac: Aries, Leo, and Sagittarius
Celebrations: Beltane, Imbolc, and Litha
Season: Summer
Time of Day: Midday
Runes: Dag, Ken, Rad, and Sigel
Ogham: Ur
Tarot: Judgement, Swords, and Wands
Direction: South
Sense: Sight
Energy: Yang
Chakra: Solar Plexus
Colors: Crimson, Gold, Orange, Pink, Red, White, and Yellow
Trees: Alder, Ash, Beech, Blackthorn, Cedar, Cherry, Chestnut, Elder, Hawthorn, Holly, Horse Chestnut, Juniper, Laurel, Mesquite, Oak, Olive, Palm (dragon's blood), Pine, Pomegranate, Rowan, Walnut, Willow, Witch Hazel, and Yew
Herbs & Flowers: Amaranth, Anemone, Angelica, Basil, Carnation, Chrysanthemum, Dill, Fennel, Garlic, Goldenseal, Gorse, Heliotrope, Hibiscus, Holy Basil, Lovage, Marigold, Pennyroyal, Peony, Peppermint, Poppy, Primrose. Rosemary, Rue, St. John's Wort, Snapdragon, Sunflower, Sweet Woodruff, and Vervain
Misc. Plants: Allspice, Asafetida, Betony, Black Cohosh, Blessed Thistle, Bloodroot, Cinnamon, Cinquefoil, Clove, Coriander, Cumin, Deer's Tongue, Flax, Frankincense, Galangal, Ginger, Ginseng, High John, Mandrake, Mullein, Mustard, Nettle, Nutmeg, Pepper, Thistle, and Wormwood
Gemstones & Minerals: Agate (banded, black, brown, fire, red, red-banded, snakeskin), Amber, Amet-rine, Apache Tears, Beryl (golden), Bloodstone, Calcite (orange, red), Carnelian, Citrine, Diamond, Garnet, Hematite, Herkimer Diamond, Jasper (red), Obsidian, Onyx, Opal (fire), Peridot, Pyrite, Quartz, Rhodochrosite, Rhodonite, Ruby, Sard, Sardonyx, Serpentine, Smoky Quartz, Spinel, Staurolite, Sunstone, Tiger's Eye, Topaz, Tourmaline (red), Tsavorite, and Zircon (red)
Metals: Antimony, Brass, Gold, Iron, and Steel
From the Sea: Coral (red)

Fire

Angel: Michael

Goddesses: Aine, Amaterasu, Bertha, Brigid, Danu, Durga, Freya, Hestia, Kupala, Pele, Phoebe, Sekhmet, Spider-Woman, and Vesta

Gods: Agni, Belenus, Brahma, Dionysus, Hephaestus, Horus, Inari, Indra, Khnum, Mimir, Nergal, Nord, Perun, Prometheus, and Vulcan

Magical Beings: Mermaids and Salamanders

Animals: Goat, Hedgehog, Horse, Lion, Porcupine, Sheep (ram), and Tiger

Birds: Crane, Eagle, Falcon, Heron, Macaw, Peacock, Quail, Robin, Swallow, Woodpecker, and Wren

Reptiles: Lizard, Salamander, and Snake

Insects/Misc.: Bee, Cicada, Firefly, Ladybug, Praying Mantis, and Scorpion

Mythical: Dragon and Phoenix

Ritual Tools: Censer and Wand

Principle: To Will

Issues, Intentions, and Powers: action, activate/awaken, ambition, anger, authority, battle/war, cheerfulness, communication, concentration/ focus, confidence, consecrate/bless, courage, creativity, defense, desire, destruction, divination, energy, faith, freedom, healing, honor, illumination, influence, inspiration, intelligence, intuition, justice, leadership, life, light, love, lust, magic (general, defensive, dragon, sex), the mind, motivation, passion, power, protection, psychic ability, purification, purity, purpose, release, revenge, sexuality, stimulation, transformation, truth, warmth, weather (general, lightning), and willpower

Water

Symbol:
Numbers: 2, 7
Solar System: Mercury, Moon, Neptune, Pluto, and Saturn
Zodiac: Cancer, Pisces, and Scorpio
Celebrations: Mabon and Neptunalia
Season: Autumn
Time of Day: Dusk
Runes: Feoh, Jera, Lagu, and Peorth
Ogham: Eadha, and Eamhancholl
Tarot: Cups, Hanged Man, and Moon
Direction: West
Sense: Taste
Energy: Yin
Chakra: Sacral
Colors: Aqua, Black, Blue, Gray, Green (blue, sea), Indigo, Lilac, Purple, Silver, Turquoise, Violet, and White
Trees: Alder, Apple, Ash, Aspen, Beech, Birch, Cedar, Cherry, Chestnut, Cypress, Elder, Elm, Hazel, Horse Chestnut, Locust, Magnolia, Mesquite, Mimosa, Myrtle, Olive, Poplar, Spindle-tree, Spruce, Sycamore, Willow, Witch Hazel, and Yew
Herbs & Flowers: Aster, Blackberry / Bramble, Catnip, Chamomile, Columbine, Comfrey, Daffodil, Daisy, Feverfew, Foxglove, Gardenia, Geranium, Grape, Heather, Hibiscus, Hyacinth, Iris, Ivy, Jasmine, Lady's Mantle, Lemon Balm, Lilac, Lily, Monkshood, Morning Glory, Passionflower, Periwinkle, Poppy, Raspberry, Rose, Solomon's Seal, Spearmint, Strawberry, Thyme, Valerian, Violet, and Yarrow
Misc. Plants: Aloe, Belladonna, Burdock, Cardamom, Coltsfoot, Cowslip, Dittany, Henbane, Lady's Slipper, Lotus, Meadowsweet, Moonwort, Myrrh, Orris Root, Reed, Sandalwood, Skullcap, Spikenard, Star Anise, Thornapple, Vanilla, and Water Lily
Gemstones & Minerals: Alexandrite, Amethyst, Ametrine, Angelite, Aquamarine, Aragonite, Azurite, Beryl, Blue Lace Agate, Calcite, Charoite, Chrysocolla, Dioptase, Fluorite, Jade, Jasper (ocean), Jet, Kyanite, Labradorite, Lapis Lazuli, Larimar, Lepidolite, Lodestone, Moonstone, Morganite, Obsidian (gold sheen), Opal, Quartz, Rose Quartz, Sapphire, Selenite, Sodalite, Staurolite, Sugilite Topaz (blue), Tourmaline (black, blue, pink, watermelon), Tsavorite, Turquoise, and Zircon (blue)
Metals: Copper, Mercury, and Silver
From the Sea: Coral, Mother-of-Pearl, and Pearl

Water

Angels: Raphael
Goddesses: Amphitrite, Aphrodite, Bad, Boann, Brigantia, Chalchiuhtlicue, Coventina, Isis, Kupala, Ran, Sarasvati, Sedna, and Tiamat
Gods: Aegir, Belenus, Ea, Khnum, Mabon, Manannan, Mimir, Neptune, Njord, Osiris, Poseidon, and Prometheus
Magical Beings: Mermaids, Norns, and Undines
Animals: Bat, Beaver, Cattle (cow), Dog, Hare, Hippopotamus, Horse, Moose, Otter, Polar Bear, and Raccoon
Birds: Albatross, Blackbird, Cormorant, Crane, Dove, Duck, Heron, Kingfisher, Seagull, Stork, Swan, Swift, and Vulture
Reptiles: Crocodile, Frog, Salamander, Snake, and Toad
Insect/Misc.: Dragonfly
Mythical: Dragon and Selkies
Ritual Tools: Cauldron, Chalice, and Cup
Principle: To Dare
Issues, Intentions and Powers: adaptability, agriculture, balance, beginnings, change/s, clairvoyance, compassion, consecrate/bless, consciousness (subconscious), creativity, desire, divination, dream work, emotions, empathy, energy (general, psychic, receptive), fertility, friendship, grace, growth, healing, heartbreak, influence, introspection, intuition, life, magic (animal, dragon, moon), memory /memories, nurture, patience, power, pregnancy/childbirth, protection, psychic ability, purification, purity, rebirth/ renewal, reconciliation, reversal, secrets, sensitivity, sensuality, shamanic work, sleep, sorrow, spirituality, strength (inner), stress, transformation, weather (general, storms), well-being, and wisdom

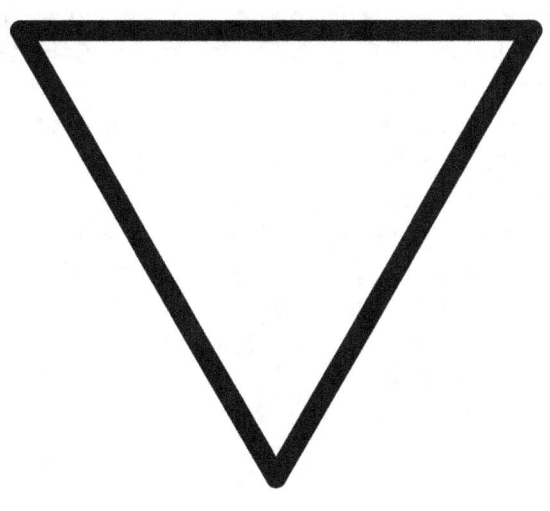

CHAPTER 18

Energy

Divination

Divination is a practice deeply rooted in human history, spanning cultures and civilizations across time. At its core, divination is the art of seeking insight and guidance from mystical or supernatural sources to understand the past, present, or future. It's a fascinating journey involving various methods, such as reading omens in nature, interpreting patterns in celestial bodies, or deciphering symbols through intricate tools like tarot cards, runes, and crystal balls. Divination offers us a unique perspective into the unknown, providing a glimpse into the threads of fate that weave through our lives.

Tarot Cards

Tarot is an intricate divination system consisting of 78 cards divided into major and minor arcana cards. Heavily relying on classical mythology and symbolism, tarot allows one to receive answers to events by interpreting messages based on how the cards are dealt. This can be done utilizing card spreads like the classic Celtic cross or a simple 3 card past, present, and future layout.

Oracle Cards

Less structured than tarot, oracle cards use a combination of artwork and written interpretations, which can sometimes include exercises. Oracle cards can be based on nearly any subject matter and are open to various styles and formats. Perfect for guiding without the intricacies associated with tarot.

Draw Your Cards

There are multiple ways to select the cards for your reading.
Cutting the deck with one hand and pulling the card on top is a simple, no-nonsense approach. Another way is to hold the deck in one hand and tilt it to reveal a gap; you can take the top card. Next, you can fan the cards out and choose the card your intuition pulls you to. Finally, draw a single card for a simple reading or several cards for what's known as a spread. Tarot spreads can speak more broadly to your situation. The more cards you use in a spread, the more in-depth the reading tends to be, but a big spread can be overwhelming for beginners.

After you choose your card(s), lay them down in your pattern for the spread. Now, you can gaze at them, pay attention to what comes immediately to mind, and then go from there.

Interpret the card(s) you draw.
Stay focused on the cards and the feelings you get, connect the cards to your senses, and write down what comes to mind. After your impressions are completely logged, look in the companion book for the general meaning of the cards you pulled. That's it. Eazy Peezey.

Manifesting with Colored Ink

Blue - clarity, creativity, faith
Pink - love, kindness, harmony
Purple - intuitive, needs, imagination
Black - protection, banishing, releasing
Silver - emotions, reflection, moon energy
Orange - joy, optimism, excitement
Brown - earthly needs, material needs, security
Red - motivation, ambition, passion
Yellow - strength, positive thought, sun energy
Green - healing, wealth, growth

Knot Your Troubles

You can use this one no matter what your problem is. If you choose a color for the yarn to suit your purpose, you can fine-tune the spell to your particular situation.

All you need for this spell is a piece of yarn in the appropriate color, at least 12 inches long.

Now hold the yarn, with one end in each hand, and pull it taut. Think about your problem (just one per spell, please).
Concentrate on your difficult situation and start tying knots in the yarn. Visualize all your troubles getting bound up in the knots and trapped there. Keep tying until you feel it's enough.

Take the knotted yarn outside and bury it to keep your problems away.

Imbolc Spread

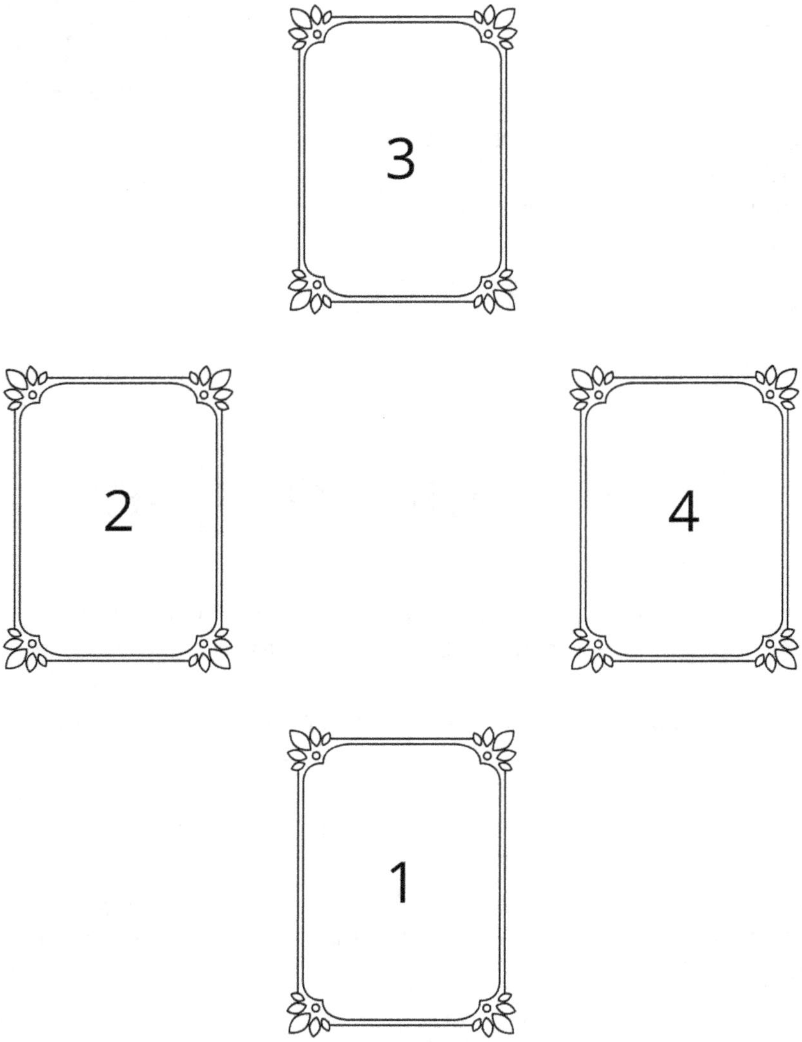

Card 1 - Offering to the goddess Brigid
Card 2 - My darkness to leave behind
Card 3 - My message from the goddess
Card 4 - Embracing my fire goddess within

Imbolc Tarot Spread

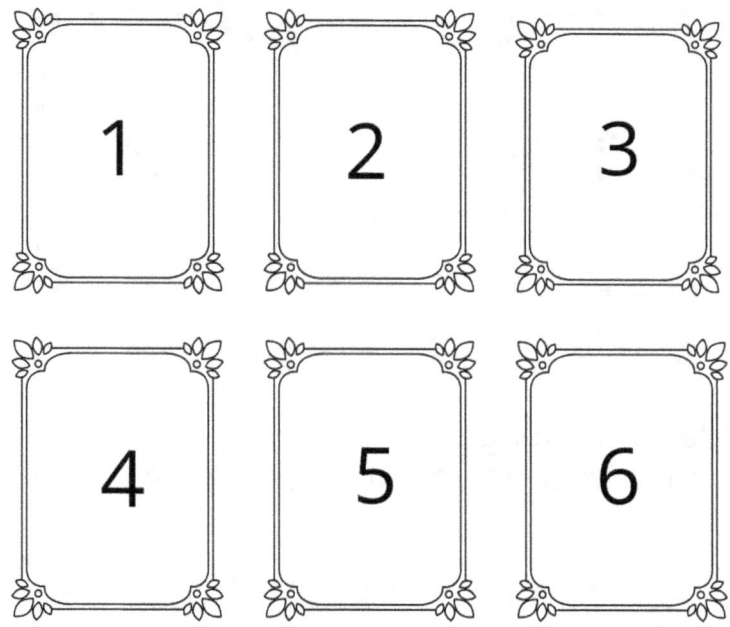

Card 1 - What is still frozen in my life
Card 2 - What will keep me warm and comfortable
Card 3 - What clutter in my life needs to be cleared
Card 4 - The first sign of growth I will see this spring
Card 5 - What project should I begin immediately
Card 6 - My message of inspiration

Everyday Tarot

Card 1 - Today's challenge
Card 2 - Solution to problems that may arise today

Imbolc Awakening

Card 1 - Planting Seeds: What do I want to cultivate in my life

Card 2 - Spring Cleaning: What needs decluttering

Card 3 - Bringing Warmth: How can I spread happiness

Card 4 - Shining a Light: What part of my life needs clarity

Card 5 - Rebirthing: Of my dormant gifts, which will be reawakened

Imbolc Self

Card 1 - Dreams
Card 2 - Fears
Card 3 - Reality

Law of Attraction

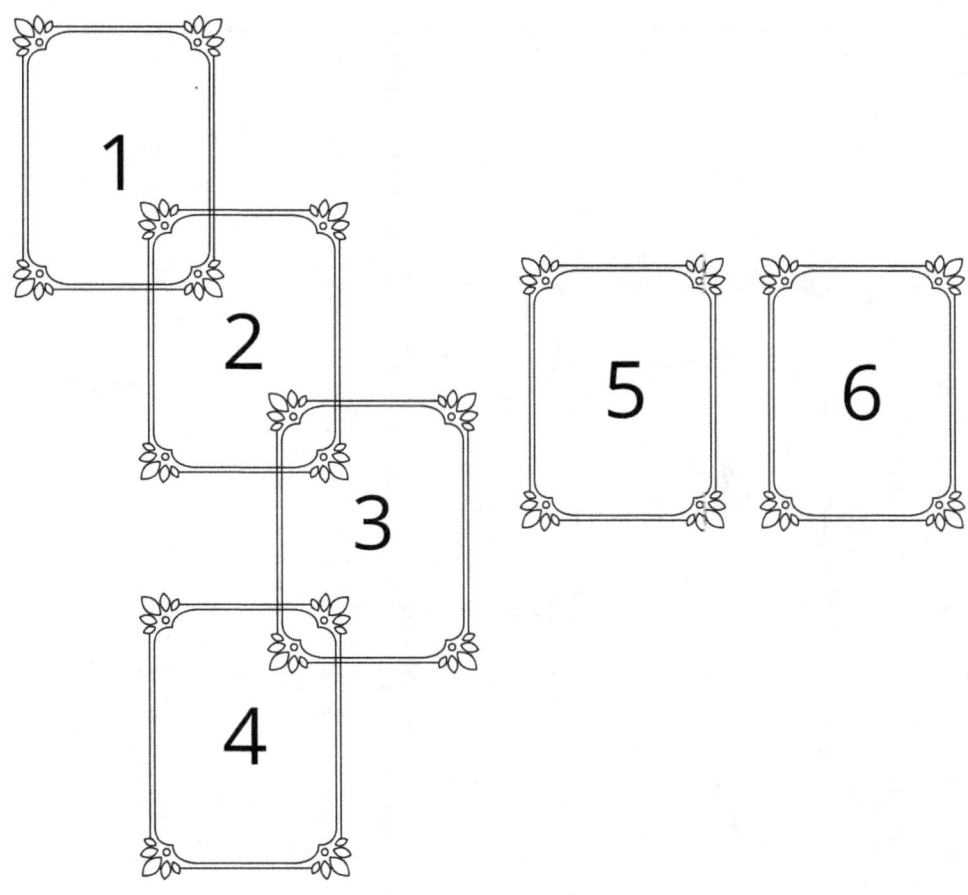

Card 1 - The vibration I'm emitting
Card 2 - What do I need to be more open about receiving
Card 3 - What will happen when I am more open to this
Card 4 - Card that represents the next step. Leap of faith
Card 5 - How can I manifest more successfully
Card 6 - Message from my higher self or source of energy

Brigid's Tarot Spread

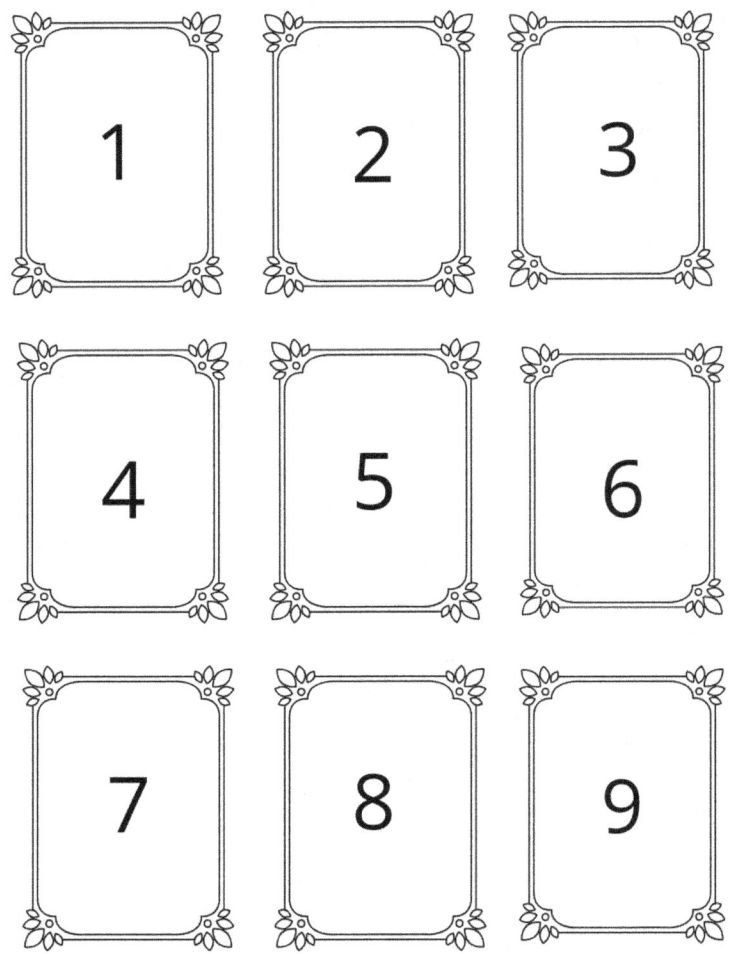

Card 1 - Healing. How can I care for myself better

Card 2 - Hearth: My Support system

Card 3 - Fertility: What will grow, develop, and bring abundance to my life

Card 4 - Warrior: How can I empower myself Be more proactive in what things

Card 5 - Smithcrafting: Where I need to work harder, a special skillset

Card 6 - Transformation: How am I currently changing

Card 7 - Fae: My connection to otherworldly things

Card 8 - What I need to explore and express. My unique art

Card 9 - Well of inspiration: My near future events and dreams that will come true

Know, Grow, & Let Go

Card 1 - What do I need to know
Card 2 - What needs to grow
Card 3 - What can I let go of

Imbolc Growth

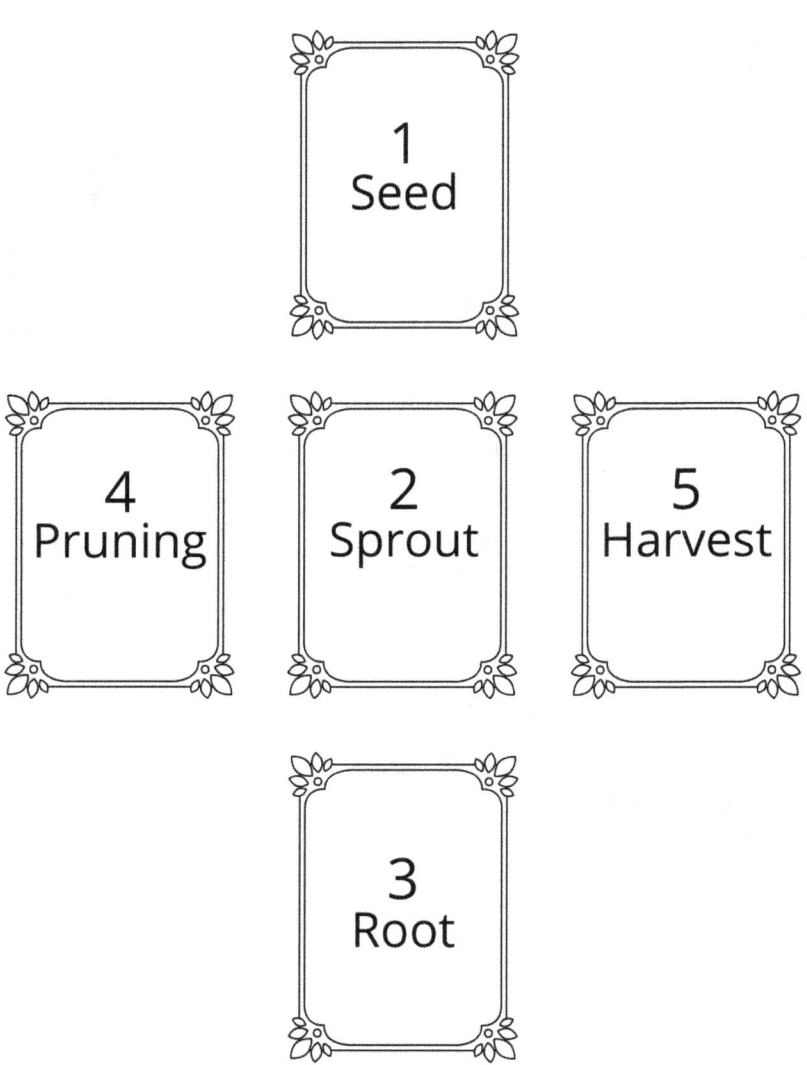

Card 1 - The Seed already stirring within you
Card 2 - What you are already beginning to see above the soil
Card 3 - What feeds this particular seed/dream/project
Card 4 - What you are ready to prune and release
Card 5 - What you will harvest from this seed

How's It Looking?

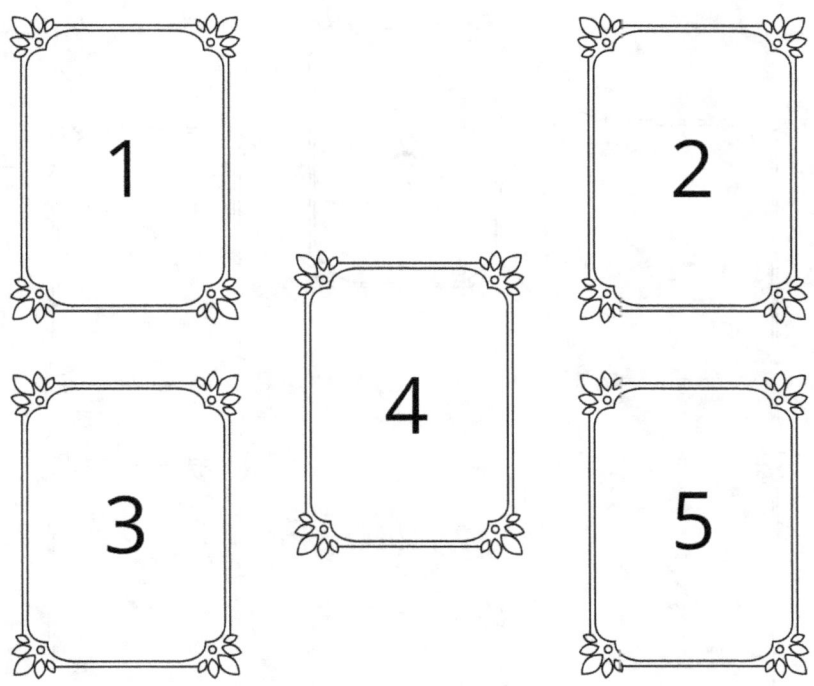

Card 1 - How I am right now
Card 2 - Am I on the correct path
Card 3 - What is my main obstacle
Card 4 - What is helping me
Card 5 - How can I make progress

Spirit Guide

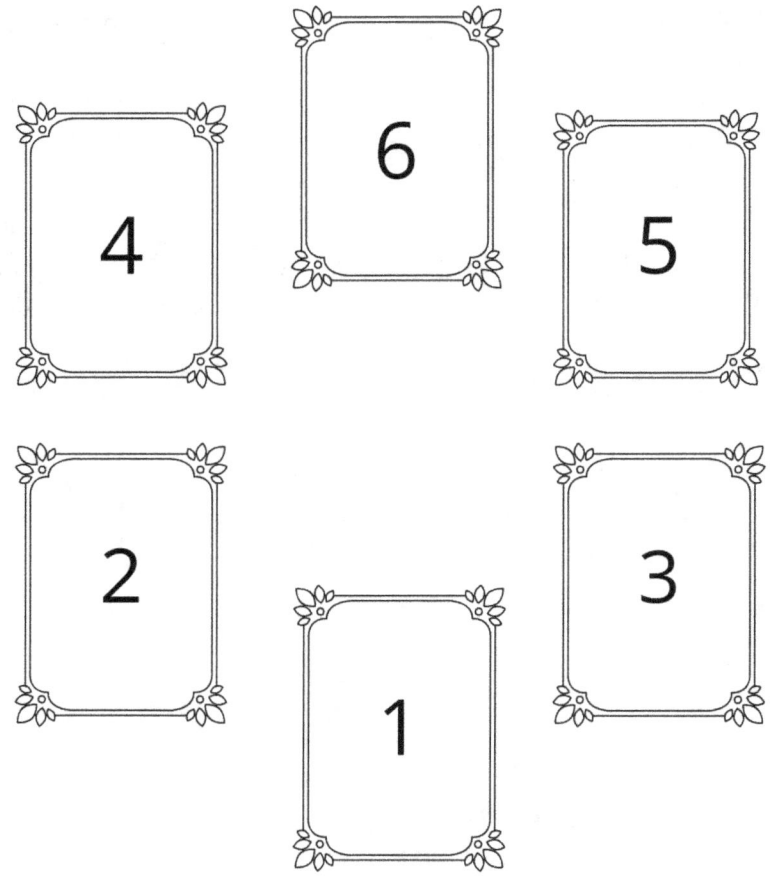

Card 1 - What's hiding in the darkness / my subconscious that I need to explore

Card 2 - What will give me strength as I face my shadow self

Card 3 - What must I work to release during this season of rest

Card 4 - What aspect of my life requires hibernation

Card 5 - How will this hibernation benefit me

Card 6 - What lessons can I learn from this season

New Season

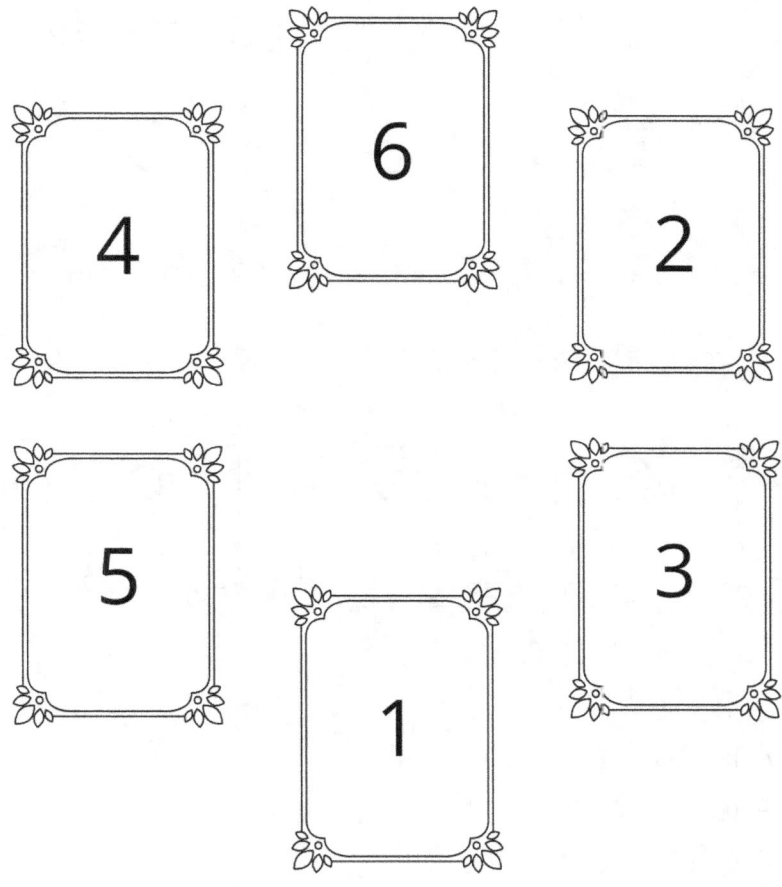

Card 1 - Card to represent the new season as a whole
Card 2 - Card to represent my love life
Card 3 - Card to represent my finances
Card 4 - Darkness: What will hinder me this season
Card 5 - Rising Sun: What will flourish this season
Card 6 - Card to represent my personal growth

Happy Dance

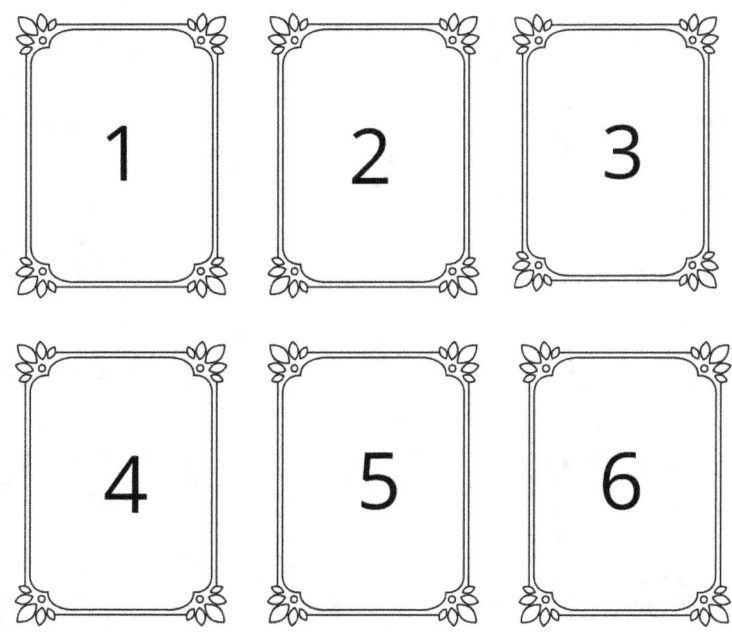

Card 1 - A lesson from the past
Card 2 - A joy in the present
Card 3 - A gift in the future
Card 4 - Something to contemplate
Card 5 - Something to activate
Card 6 - Something to celebrate

Frozen

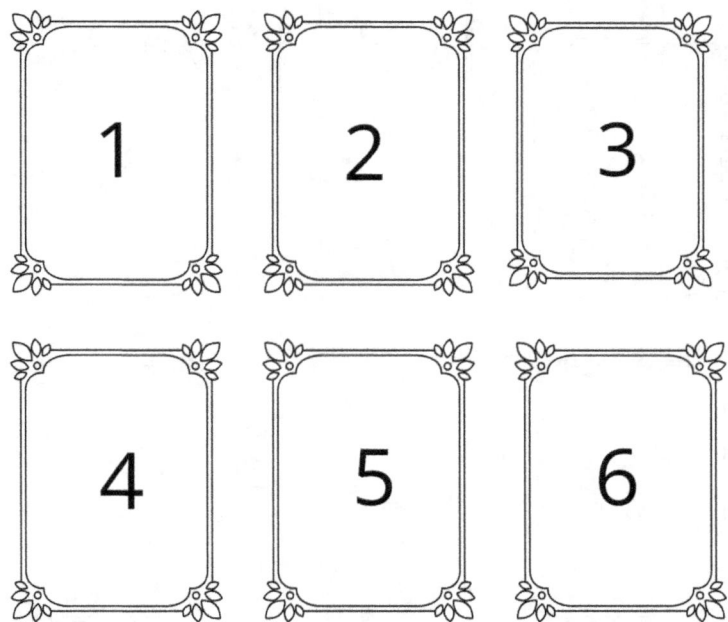

Card 1 - What is still frozen in your life
Card 2 - What will keep you warm and comfortable
Card 3 - What clutter needs to be cleared
Card 4 - The first signs of growth you'll see this spring
Card 5 - A project to begin immediately
Card 6 - A message of inspiration for you

Imbolc

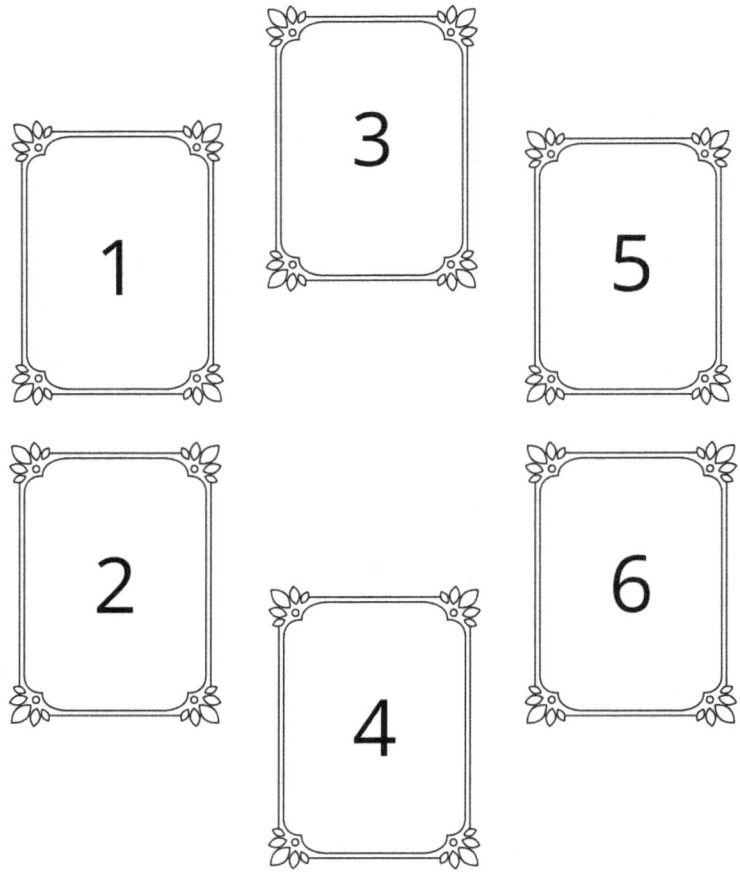

Card 1 - What needs to be started
Card 2 - What will kindle my inspiration this season
Card 3 - What will grow and bring abundance in my life
Card 4 - What needs to be let go
Card 5 - What kind of growth is needed at this time
Card 6 - Message from Brighid

Mo Money Plz

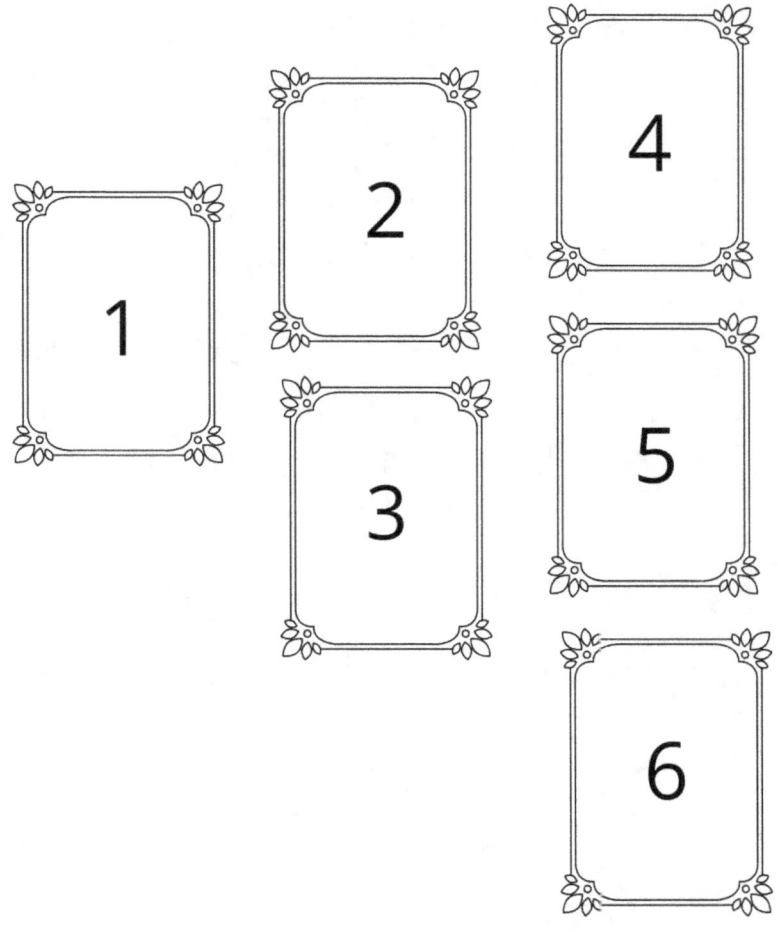

Card 1 - The main cause of my financial problem
Card 2 - How can I relieve myself of my current problem
Card 3 - What are my fears surrounding money
Card 4 - Something I can change about how I handle my money
Card 5 - A sacrifice I may need to make
Card 6 - Opportunities to consider

Spring Cleaning

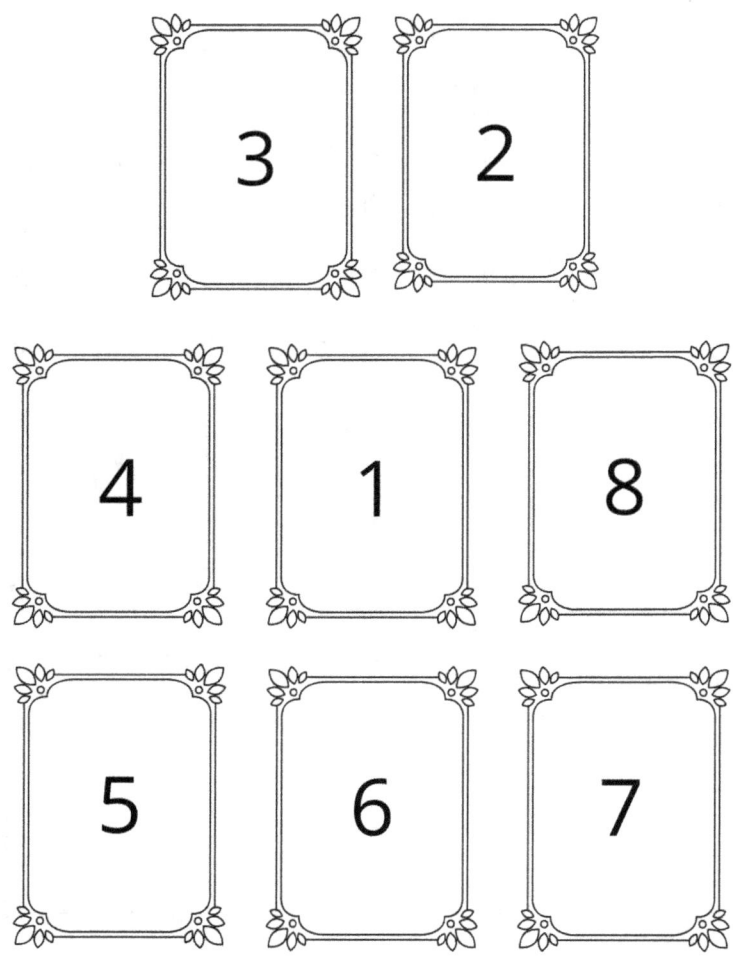

Card 1 - Me right now
Card 2 - Intention for spring
Card 3 - What is an area of my life that needs decluttering
Card 4 - What's hidden in the closet
Card 5 - What am I ready to give away
Card 6 - What brings joy
Card 7 - What can I keep
Card 8 - Outcome

Runes

The Germanic tribes of Northern Europe used runes for religious and secular purposes—the earliest examples of runes phonetically representing language date back to the second century BCE. The development of the rune alphabet was spurred by increased trade activity with Mediterranean cultures that already had a fully developed alphabet.

Before, the runes were primarily used as a magical system of pictographs representing natural forces and objects. People believed that invoking the appropriate rune could contact the corresponding force in nature.

There were several different runic alphabets throughout Northern Europe over the centuries, but the most common is the Germanic alphabet.

Tyr / Thorn
Tyr represents the powerful god of warriors, known for his fierce determination.

Beorc / Berkana / Berkano
Beorc represents the birch tree and new beginnings.

Ehwaz / EH
Ehwaz represents the noble and powerful horse.

Man / Mannaz / Mann
Mannaz represents the concept of humanity.

Lagu / Laguz /Logr / Laf
Laguz represents the raw and untamed energy of water.

Ing / Inguz / Ingwaz
Inguz represents the god Ing and symbolizes the abundance of fertility.

Dag / Dagaz / Daeg
Daeg represents the end of one cycle and start of a new one.

Odal / Othila / Othala / Ethel
Othala represents home and family, symbolizing those around us.

Feoh / Fehu / FE / FA
Fehu, a rune that translates to "cattle," denotes abundance and fertility.

UR / Uruz
Uruz, a rune that translates to "wild ox," represents determination, courage.

Thorn / Thurisaz
Thurisaz is a complex symbol that has a few different translations..

AS / Ansur / Ansuz / OS
Ansuz symbolizes the breath of Odin and can represent the concept of a god.

Runes

Rad / Raido / Reidh / Raidho
Raido represents the concept of a journey, both literally and spiritually.

Ken / Kenaz / Kano
Kenaz represents the concept of a torch, which symbolizes illumination.

Gyfu / Gebo
Gifu represents the gift or exchange.

Wyn / Wunjo / Wynn
Wunjo brings the concept of joy.

Hagal / Hagalaz / Haegl / Hagal
Hagalaz represents hail, symbolizing the destructive power of nature.

NYD / Nauthiz / Naudhr
Nauthiz represents necessity and the struggle that comes with it.

IS / Isa / ISS
Isa symbolizes the concept of ice or being frozen.

Jera / Ger
Jera signifies the idea of reaping the rewards of one's labor.

elhaz / Algiz / Eolh
Eihwaz is a rune that represents the ash or yew tree.

Peorth / Perth / Perthro
Perthro represents the concept of fortune.

Eoh / Eihwaz
Eolh represents the concept of the elk, but in the context of protection.

Sigel / Sowelu / Sowilo
Sigel represents the life-giving energy of the sun and the illumination it brings.

Rune Castings

 Odin- a one rune draw is perfect for an immediate response. This is a simple, straightforward reading. The rune represents the critical factor in the issue at hand.

Nom- a three-rune spread enables you to deal with the subject as it presents itself at this moment in time.

1 - The left rune represents an important element of the past.
2 - The middle rune represents a deciding element of the present.
3 - The right rune represents the critical element of the future.

Rune Cross

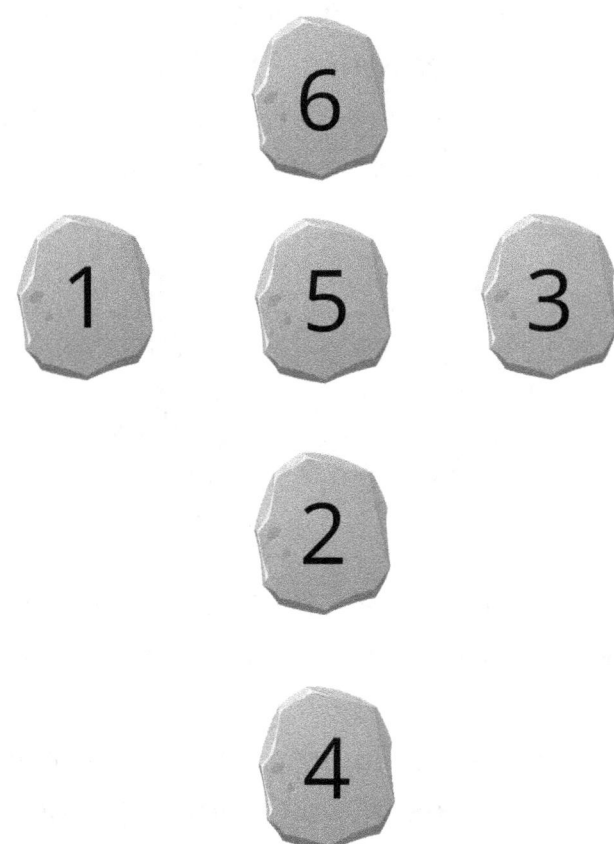

1 - Past situations
2 - Present situation
3 - Future situations
4 - Influences on question
5 - What influences have a positive outcome
6 - Most likely outcome

Rune Casting

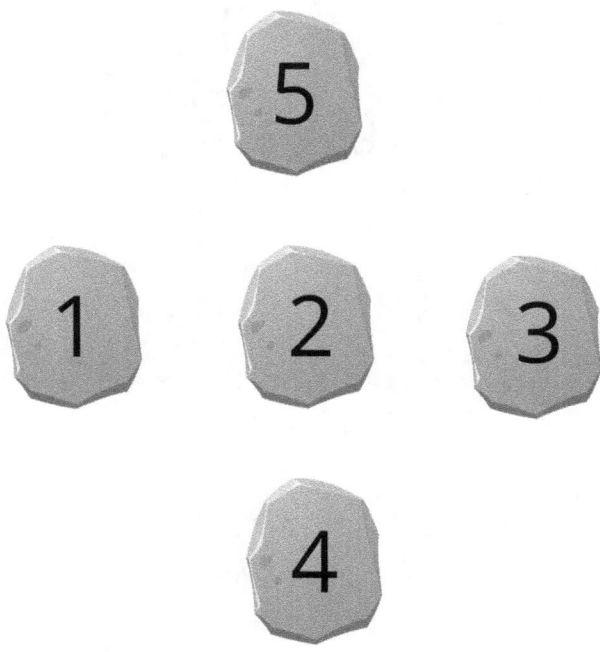

1 - Problems that may influence
2 - Future influences
3 - Immediate answer
4 - Basic influences that impact answer
5 - Positives that may influence

Rune Casting

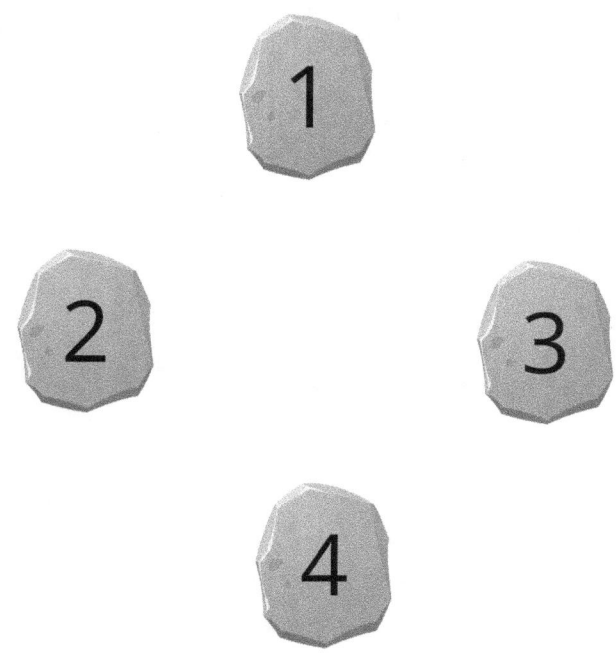

1 - Past desires that relate to the question
2 - Desire of others
3 - Present desires
4 - Represents heart's innermost desire if positive,
desire will manifest

CHAPTER 19

Beliefs and Practices

Witchcraft

Witchcraft is a broad term that encompasses a diverse range of practices, beliefs, and traditions. It is often associated with magical or supernatural powers in various cultures and historical periods.

Magical Practices:
Witchcraft involves using magical techniques, rituals, and spells to bring about specific outcomes or influence events. This may include spellcasting, divination, herbalism, and other esoteric practices.

Nature-Based Spirituality:
Many forms of Witchcraft are grounded in a deep connection to nature. Practitioners may view the natural world as sacred and draw inspiration from its cycles, elements, and energies.

Worship of Deities:
Some witches engage in the worship or acknowledgment of deities, spirits, or entities. The nature and number of these beings vary widely based on the specific tradition or personal belief system.

Pagan and Folk Traditions:
Witchcraft is often associated with pagan and folk traditions. It has roots in historical practices, such as folk magic, herbalism, and the worship of pre-Christian Witchcraft; each has its own beliefs, rituals, and codes of conduct.

Stigmatization and Misconceptions:
Throughout history, Witchcraft has often been stigmatized, leading to persecution of those accused of practicing it. This is notably seen in the historical witch trials. In modern times, ongoing efforts are to dispel misconceptions and promote understanding.

It's important to recognize that the term "witchcraft" is multifaceted, and its meaning can vary widely depending on cultural, historical, and individual perspectives. While some practitioners identify as witches within specific spiritual frameworks, others may use the term more broadly to describe their magical or esoteric practices.

Pagan

"Pagan" is a term with broad and varied historical and contemporary usage. In its most general sense, "pagan" originally referred to individuals or communities practicing polytheistic, pre-Christian religions, particularly in the context of ancient civilizations. However, its meaning has evolved and diversified over time.

Historical Usage:
In ancient times, especially during the spread of Christianity, "pagan" was used to describe non-Christians or those following indigenous, polytheistic belief systems. It often carried a connotation of being outside the major monotheistic religions.

Contemporary Religious Usage:
Many Pagans emphasize a connection to the natural world, celebrating the changing seasons, the cycles of the moon, and the elements. Rituals and practices often involve outdoor ceremonies, symbolic tools, and a recognition of the sacred in the world around them.

Polytheism and Pantheism:
While not universally true, many Pagan traditions involve worshipping or acknowledging multiple deities, spirits, or forces. Polytheism and pantheism are common themes within Pagan belief systems.

Wicca:
Wicca is one of the most well-known and widely practiced modern Pagan traditions. It emerged in the mid-20th century and is characterized by worshiping a God and Goddess, rituals, and a code of ethics known as the Wiccan Rede.

Inclusivity:
Modern Paganism is highly diverse and inclusive, encompassing many beliefs, practices, and traditions. It welcomes practitioners from various backgrounds, and individuals may identify as Wiccans, Druids, Heathens, eclectic Pagans, and more.

It's important to recognize that the term "pagan" is a broad umbrella that covers a rich tapestry of beliefs and practices. Individuals who identify as Pagans may have very different spiritual paths, rituals, and beliefs, and the term is often used for rituals and beliefs. The term is often an umbrella for many nature-based and polytheistic spiritual practices.

Hoodoo

Hoodoo is a folk magic system with roots in African American culture, particularly among communities in the Southern United States. It is distinct from other magical traditions like Wicca or European witchcraft and draws upon a combination of African, Native American, and European folk practices. Hoodoo is often characterized by its practical and pragmatic approach to magic.

Historical Background:
Hoodoo originates in the African diaspora, evolving through blending various cultural and magical practices over time. It incorporates elements from African traditional religions, Native American herbalism, and European folk magic.

Rootwork and Conjure:
Hoodoo is sometimes referred to as "rootwork" or "conjure." The term "rootwork" reflects using roots, herbs, and botanical ingredients in magical practices, while "conjure" emphasizes calling upon spiritual forces for assistance.

Practical Magic:
Hoodoo is known for its emphasis on practical magic to address specific needs, such as protection, love, prosperity, or healing. It often involves using charms, talismans, and rituals to achieve these goals.

Use of Natural Ingredients:
Hoodoo practitioners often work with various natural materials, including herbs, roots, minerals, and animal parts. These ingredients are believed to have specific magical properties and are incorporated into spells, mojo bags, or other ritual tools.

Candle Magic:
Candle magic is a common practice in Hoodoo. Different colored candles represent various intentions, and they may be anointed with oils, inscribed with symbols, or used in conjunction with specific prayers or chants.

Mojo Bags and Gris-Gris Bags:
Hoodoo practitioners often create small pouches called mojo bags or gris-gris bags filled with specific herbs, roots, and other items tailored to a particular magical goal.

These bags are typically carried or placed in specific locations for their magical influence.

Spiritual Practices:
Hoodoo may incorporate elements of ancestor veneration, spirit work, and the invocation of spiritual forces. Practitioners may work with spirits, saints, or deities, depending on their personal beliefs.

Protection and Cleansing:
Hoodoo includes various practices for protection and spiritual cleansing. This can be protection and spiritual cleansing. This can involve the use of rituals, baths, smudging, or the creation of protective talismans.

Crossroads Magic:
The crossroads are considered potent places in Hoodoo, symbolizing the intersection of different spiritual forces. Crossroads magic may involve burying or leaving offerings at crossroads to gain magical assistance or make pacts.

It's important to note that Hoodoo is a diverse and evolving tradition with regional variations and personal adaptations. While some practitioners may incorporate elements of Hoodoo into their magical practices, others may follow it as a distinct and specific tradition. Additionally, respect for cultural context and sensitivity to the origins of Hoodoo are important considerations for those exploring or incorporating its practices.

Voodoo

Voodoo, also spelled Vodou or Vodun, is a spiritual and religious tradition with roots in West African animist beliefs. It developed in the African diaspora, particularly in Haiti, where it merged with elements of Catholicism and indigenous Caribbean spirituality. Voodoo is known for its diverse pantheon of spirits, rituals, and magical practices.

Spiritual Pantheon:
Voodoo involves the veneration of a diverse array of spirits or deities, often called "lwa" or "loa." These spirits are associated with various aspects of life, nature, and human experience. The pantheon includes powerful, ancestral, and spirits linked to specific elements or forces.

Ancestor Veneration:
Ancestor worship is a significant aspect of Voodoo. Ancestors are believed to continue influencing the lives of their descendants, and rituals involving offerings and prayers are conducted to honor and seek guidance from them.

Ceremonial Rituals:
Voodoo ceremonies, or "séances," involve music, dance, chanting, and offerings to invoke the spirits. These rituals are led by a Voodoo priest or priestess, often called a "houngan" or "mambo."

Possession Trance:
During Voodoo rituals, participants may experience possession by the spirits. This involves a temporary merging of the individual's consciousness with that of a spirit, allowing the spirit to communicate, provide guidance, or address specific concerns.

Magical Practices:
Voodoo incorporates magical practices for various purposes, including healing, protection, love, and divination. Ritual tools such as candles, herbs, charms, and baths harness spiritual energies and invoke specific lwa.

Voodoo Dolls:
Contrary to popular misconceptions, Voodoo dolls are not inherently associated with focus intentions, healing, or seeking assistance from the spirits.

Hoodoo Influence:
Hoodoo, mentioned in a previous response, is a distinct magical tradition, but its practices have influenced some aspects of Voodoo, particularly in the United States. Hoodoo elements like herbs, candles, and charms may be incorporated into Voodoo's magical practices.

Syncretism with Catholicism:

Voodoo in Haiti often displays a syncretic relationship with Catholicism. Saints from the Catholic tradition are sometimes equated with or incorporated into the Voodoo pantheon.

This syncretism allowed practitioners to maintain their spiritual practices despite historical suppression.

Community and Social Functions:

Voodoo serves not only as a spiritual practice but also as a community-oriented tradition. It plays a role in social events, rites of passage, and addressing community issues. The sense of community is integral to the practice of Voodoo.

It's important to approach discussions about Voodoo with cultural sensitivity and respect.

Voodoo has been historically stigmatized and misunderstood due to stereotypes and sensationalism. Understanding Voodoo's cultural and historical context is important for appreciating its significance as a rich and diverse spiritual tradition.

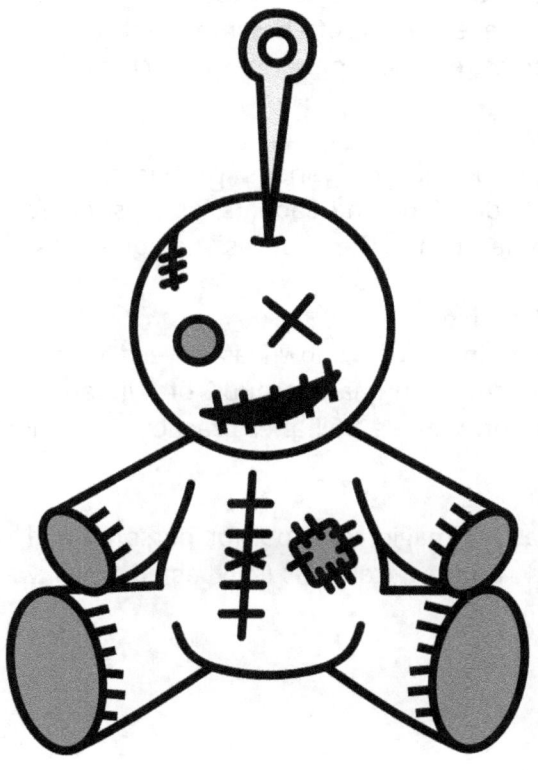

Wicca

Wicca is a contemporary pagan religious movement that emerged in the mid-20th century. It is characterized by its reverence for nature, worship of a dual deity (often represented as the God and Goddess), and the practice of rituals and magic. Wicca is considered a modern witchcraft tradition, and its practitioners are commonly referred to as Wiccans.

Founding and Development:
Wicca was popularized by Gerald Gardner, a British civil servant, in the mid-20th century. Gardner claimed Wicca was based on ancient pagan traditions, but its origins are more closely linked to esoteric and occult influences of the time.

Nature-Centric Beliefs:
Wicca strongly emphasizes nature, viewing it as sacred and imbued with spiritual energy. Practitioners often celebrate the changing seasons, lunar phases, and the cycles of nature.

Duotheistic Worship:
Wiccans typically worship a duotheistic pair— a God and a Goddess. The God is associated with masculine energies, often symbolizing the Sun, while the Goddess is associated with feminine energies, often symbolizing the Moon. These deities are sometimes understood as representing various aspects of divinity.

Rituals and Sabbats:
Wiccan rituals are performed for various purposes, including worship, magical workings, and personal development. Sabbats, or seasonal festivals, mark significant points in the annual cycle, such as the solstices and equinoxes.

Coven and Solitary Practices:
Wicca can be practiced in groups known as covens or by individuals working as solitaries. Covens are small, intimate groups of Wiccans who come together to worship, learn, and perform rituals. Solitaries practice Wicca independently.

Magical Practices:
Wicca strongly emphasizes magic as a tool for personal and spiritual development. Ritual magic, spellwork, and magical tools (such as athames, wands, and chalices) are common in Wiccan practices.

Ethical Guidelines:
Wiccans often adhere to an ethical code known as the "Wiccan Rede," which emphasizes harmlessness and the principle, "An it harm none, do what ye will." This encourages practitioners to consider the ethical implications of their actions.

Initiation and Degrees:
Some Wiccans follow an initiatory tradition where individuals progress through different degrees of initiation, each marked by specific teachings and experiences. Others may follow eclectic or non-initiatory paths.

Book of Shadows:
Wiccans often maintain a personal book, known as a "Book of Shadows," where they record rituals, spells, and personal reflections. This book is considered a sacred and personal document.

Inclusivity:
Wicca is diverse, and practitioners may interpret and practice its principles differently. Some Wiccans emphasize its religious and spiritual aspects, while others focus more on magical practices.

Wicca has grown and diversified since its inception, and there are many different traditions and approaches within the broader Wiccan movement. It is recognized as one of the fastest-growing pagan religions, and its influence extends beyond religious circles into popular culture and contemporary discussions about witchcraft and spirituality.

The world is home to a vast array of religions, each with its own unique beliefs, practices, and cultural contexts. Here, I'll provide an overview of some major world religions, highlighting key aspects of each.

Christianity:
Founder: Jesus Christ
Sacred Texts: The Bible (Old and New Testaments)
Beliefs:
Monotheistic belief in one God.
Jesus Christ is considered the Messiah and the Son of God.
Salvation through faith in Jesus Christ.
The Holy Trinity: Father, Son, and Holy Spirit.
Denominations: Various denominations, including Catholicism, Protestantism, and Eastern Orthodoxy.

Islam:
Founder: Prophet Muhammad
Sacred Texts: The Quran
Beliefs:
Monotheistic belief in one God (Allah).
Prophet Muhammad is the final messenger.
Five Pillars of Islam: Shahada (faith), Salah (prayer), Zakat (charity), Sawm (fasting during Ramadan), and Hajj (pilgrimage to Mecca).
Denominations: Main branches include Sunni and Shia.

Hinduism:
Origins: Evolved over thousands of years, with no single founder.
Sacred Texts: Vedas, Upanishads, Bhagavad Gita
Beliefs:
A diverse range of beliefs and practices.
Concepts of karma (actions and consequences) and dharma (righteous duty).
Reincarnation and the pursuit of moksha (liberation from the cycle of rebirth).
Polytheistic with a focus on major deities such as Brahma, Vishnu, Shiva, and Devi.

Buddhism:
Founder: Siddhartha Gautama (Buddha)
Sacred Texts: Tripitaka (Pali Canon)
Beliefs:
Four Noble Truths: Existence of suffering, its cause, its end, and the path to its end (Eightfold Path).
Nirvana is the ultimate goal: liberation from the cycle of reincarnation.
Middle Way: Avoidance of extremes in life.
Denominations: Theravada, Mahayana, Vajrayana.

Judaism:
Founders: Abraham, Moses
Sacred Texts: Tanakh (Hebrew Bible), including Torah, Prophets, and Writings.
Beliefs:
The covenant between God and the Jewish people.
Monotheism.
Ten Commandments as moral and ethical guidelines.
Messianic belief in the coming of a future Messiah.
Denominations: Orthodox, Conservative, Reform, and others.

Sikhism:
Founder: Guru Nanak
Sacred Texts: Guru Granth Sahib
Beliefs:
Monotheistic belief in one God.
Equality of all humans.
Devotion to God, honest living, and community service.
Rejection of caste system and rituals.
Distinct Practices: Wearing of the Five Ks (articles of faith), including the uncut hair and a ceremonial sword.

Jainism:
Founder: Mahavira
Sacred Texts: Agamas
Beliefs:
Non-violence (ahimsa) is a core principle.
Belief in karma and reincarnation.
Ascetic lifestyle for spiritual purification.
Pursuit of liberation (moksha) through self-discipline.

Bahá'í Faith:
Founder: Bahá'u'lláh
Sacred Texts: Bahá'í writings
Beliefs:
Oneness of God, humanity, and religion.
Progressive revelation through successive prophets, including Abraham, Moses, Buddha, Jesus, Muhammad, and Bahá'u'lláh.
Emphasis on unity, justice, and equality.
Advocacy for the elimination of prejudices and the establishment of world peace.

Confucianism
Founder: Confucius (Kong Fuzi)
Texts: Analects
Beliefs:
Emphasis on moral and ethical conduct, filial piety, and social harmony.
Respect for tradition and the importance of education.
The concept of ren (benevolence) and li (rituals).

Shinto
Origin: Indigenous to Japan
Beliefs:
Reverence for kami (spiritual beings) and natural elements.
Rituals and ceremonies at shrines.
Connection to nature and ancestral spirits.
Emphasis on purification and harmony.

These brief overviews highlight the diversity of world religions, showcasing their unique beliefs, practices, and cultural influences. It's important to note that within each religion, there can be significant variations and interpretations based on different traditions, sects, and individual perspectives. Additionally, many people may identify with multiple aspects of different religious or spiritual traditions, contributing to the richness of the global religious tapestry. So, in other words, You Do You!

The Golden Rule

Yoruba Traditions
"One who does evil to another does so to himself." - proverb

Atheism
"Treat others as you would want them to treat you and can reasonably expect them to want to be treated. Think about their perspective."
-The 10 Non-Commandments

Christianity
"Do unto others as you would have them do unto you."
-Matthew 7:12

Zoroastrianism
"Whatever is disagreeable to yourself, do not do unto others.
-Shayast-na-Shayast 13:29

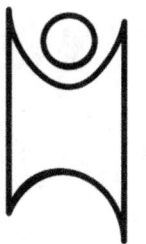

Humanism
"Before performing an action which might harm another person, try to imagine yourself in their position, and consider whether you would want to be the recipient of that action. If you would not want to be in such a position, the other person probably would not either, and so you should not do it."
-Adam Lee

Bahá'í Faith
"And if thine eyes be turned towards justice, choose thou for thy neighbour that which thou choosest for thyself."
-Tablets of Bahá'u'lláh

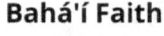

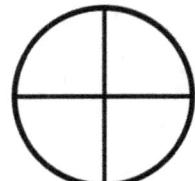

First Peoples
"Even though you and I are in diferent boats, you in your boat and we our canoe, we share the same river of life. What befalls me befalls you." -Oren Lyons, Turtle Clan, Seneca Nation

Jainism
"A man should wander about treating all creatures as he himself would be treated."
-Sutrakritanga 1.11.33

Islam
"By no means shall you attain righteousness unless you give freely to others of that which you love; and whatever you give, of a truth Allah knows it well."
-Qur'an 3:92

Wicca
"And it harm none, do
what thou wilt." - Wiccan Rede

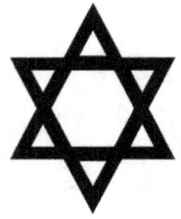

Judaism
"What is hateful to you, do not do to your fellow: this is the whole Torah; the rest is commentary; go and learn."
-Babylonian Talmud

Sikhism
"As you see yourself, see others as well; only then will you become a partner in heaven."
-Sri Guru Granth Sahib Ji, 480

Hinduism

"This is the sum of Dharma
-duty: Do nothing unto others which would cause
you pain if done to you."
-Mahabharata 5:1517

Shinto

The heart of the person before you is a mirror. See there your
own form."

Confucianism

"Tse-kung asked, 'Is there one word that can serve as a
principle of conduct for life?' Confucius
-Doctrine of the Mean 13.3

Taoism

"Regard your neighbor's gain as your gain, and
your neighbor's loss as your own loss."

Buddhism

"All are afraid of the stick, all
fear death. Putting oneself in another's place, one should not hurt or
kill others."
-Dhammapada, verse 129

Unitarianism

"We affirm and promote respect for the interdependent web of all
existence of which we are a part."
-7th Principle

CHAPTER 20

Types of Practitioners

Practitioners

Alexandrian
American Folk Magic
Ancestral/Hereditary
Appalachian
Art
Astronomy
Augury
Baby
Blood
Celtic
Ceremonial
Chaos
Christian
Correllian
Cosmic
Cottage/Hearth
Coven
Crystal

Death
Desert
Dianic
Divination
Druid
Eclectic
Elemental
Elf
Enchanter
Energy
Faerie
Fire
Folk
Forest
Garden
Gardnerian
Gothic

Green
Grey
Hedge
Hellenic
Hermit
Hoodoo
Kitchen
Lunar
Music
Natural
Nature
Nocturnal
Norse
Ozarks
Pagan
Pow-Wow
Religious
Santeria

Satanic
Sea
Seasonal
Secular
Shadow
Shamanic
Sun/Solar
Storm
Swamp
Tech
Thelma
Thunder
Traditional
Urban
Voodoo
Wiccan
White

The Gardnerian Witch follows the traditions of Gardnerian Wicca, which Gerald Garner created in the 1950s. This type of witchcraft has a hierarchical system with a high priest and priestess; these witches often practice in covens. To become a Gardnerian Witch, you must go through various initiations. You must learn the traditions and culture of that branch of witchery and complete initiation into a coven to be considered a true witch.

The Alexandrian Witch is similar to the Gardnerian Witch in that they both follow some of the same traditions and are based on Wicca belief systems. However, Alexandrian witchcraft has its own unique traditions and initiation processes. The Alexandrian Witches also practice more ceremonial magic than the Gardnerians, and many Alexandrians also practice Oabalah.

Which witch are you? Sorry for the pun. Are you more confused now than you were before? Me too, but what is a name? You know who and what you are,

OK, so, which witch are you? Sorry for the pun. Are you more confused now than you were before? I am, too, but what is a name? You know who and what you are; that is all you need.

"A rose by any other name would smell as sweet" - Williams Shakespeare.

Simplified Psychic Abilities

Clairvoyance - When you see stuff (clear vision)

Clairaudience - When you hear stuff (clear hearing)

Clairsentience - When you feel stuff (clear sensing and feeling)

Clairempathy - When you feel other people's stuff

Claircognizance - When you just know stuff (clear knowing)

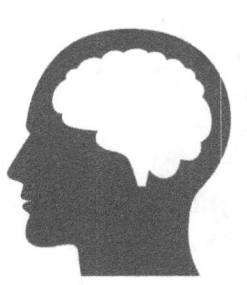

Clairsgustance - When you taste stuff (clear taste)

Clairalience or Clairscent - When you smell stuff (clear smell)

Clairtangency /Pyschometry - When you get touched and stuff (clear touch)

Telepathy - When you can communicate through thoughts and stuff

Telekenisis - When you can move things with your mind and stuff

CHAPTER 21

Symbols

Symbols have played a significant role throughout history, serving as a means of communication, expression, and identity. From ancient to modern times, symbols have been used to represent abstract concepts, convey religious beliefs, and create social cohesion. They have been etched into cave walls, inscribed on tablets, and emblazoned on flags. The power of symbols lies in their ability to capture the essence of an idea in a single image. They can evoke strong emotions, inspire action, and unite people across cultures and languages. The cross, for example, represents both religious devotion and colonial domination. Symbols are not static; they evolve with society, and their meanings can change. Symbols remain a crucial aspect of communication, and understanding their meaning and context is essential for comprehending the complex ways in which humans communicate.

Pentagram

Pentagram is from two Greek words, "penta-" meaning five, and "-grammon" meaning line.

In Neoplatonism, the pentagram was said to have been used as a symbol or sign of recognition by Pythagoreans, who called the pentagram υγεια "health."

Pentacle

From pentagram + circle.
Agrippa attributed the five Neoplatonic elements (Air, Water, Fire, Earth, and Spirit) to each of the pentacle's five points, uniting them in perfect balance.

Inverted Pentagram

Also known as Material Pentagram. "It is a symbol of evil because it overturns the proper order of things and demonstrates the triumph of matter over spirit" - Elisha's Levi

The Church of Satan embraced an inverted pentagram and a goat's head as its symbol in 1966.

Spirit

Air

Water

Earth

Fire

The pentagram was used in ancient times as a Christian symbol for the five senses or Christ's five wounds. A Christian use of the pentangle occurs in the 14th-century English poem Sir Gawain and the Green Knight, in which the symbol decorates the shield of the hero, Gawain. The unnamed poet credits the symbol's origin to King Solomon and says the symbol is key to understanding the work. The poet explains that each of the five interconnected points represents a virtue tied to a group of five.

Gawain is 'keen in his five senses, dextrous in his five fingers, faithful to the salvation provided through the Five Wounds of Christ, takes courage from the five joys Mary had of Jesus, and exemplifies the five virtues of knighthood.'

Brigid Cross

The Irish tradition of making crosses on Imbolc or "Lá Fhéile Bhríde" (St. Brigid's Day) is a Christian ritual that most Irish people remember.

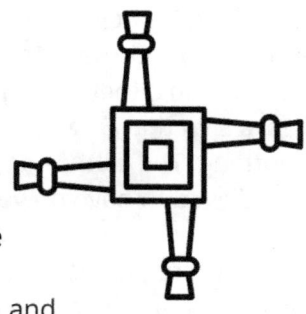

The spiral of the Brigid Cross invokes the North Star and the pattern that the Big Dipper makes in the sky over the course of a year. As the night sky turns around, the North Star, the Big Dipper, turns through the seasonal year like the hand of a clock, symbolizing the cycles of life, death, and rebirth.

Brigid symbolizes the flame of life that mothers tend so that their families don't die in the winter months. In the winter, Brigid becomes the Cailleach, the woman in agedness, and on Imbolc, she collects the kindling of the fires that will get her to the spring of regeneration.

In Ireland, Christians interpret Brigid as a nun. Children take bits of straw and weave them into spiraling Brigid's crosses.

The origins of the St. Brigid's Cross date back to the saint herself, who is said to have invented it while attending to a sick person. Making this cross has become a symbol of hope and renewal and is often seen as a way to connect with the natural world and the cycle of the seasons.

P.S. Remember, in my "Yule" book, Cailleach was one of the Christmas witches!

Imbolc is also the day the Cailleach gathers her firewood for the rest of the winter. Legend has it that if she intends to make the winter last a good while longer, she will make sure the weather on Imbolc is bright and sunny so she can gather plenty of firewood to keep herself warm in the coming months. As a result, people are generally relieved if it is a day of foul weather, as it means the Cailleach is asleep, meaning she will soon run out of firewood, and that, therefore, winter is almost over.

The Brideog

The Brideog Night was celebrated on January 31st.
The next day, February 1st, was St. Bridgid's feast day.
In the morning, they look for a mark on the
ashes, a sign that Brigid has passed that way in the night
or morning. The clothes or strips of cloth are brought inside
and believed to have powers of healing and protection now.

Brigid is a very important saint/goddess at this
time of year, as she represents the light half of the
year and the power that will bring people from the dark
season of winter into spring. The following day,
girls carry the Brideog (a representation of
Brigid) through the village or neighborhood, from
house to house. Adult women – those who are
married or who run a household – stay home to
welcome the Brigid procession, perhaps with an
the offering of coins or a snack.

CHAPTER 22

Spirit Guides

Spirit guide Introduction

Spirit guides are nonhuman or human entities that reside in the spiritual realm and make their wisdom available to the living. They take various forms, including guardian angels, animal or nature spirits, elves and fairies, saints or ascended masters, and ancestors or descendants who have crossed the spiritual realm. According to believers, spiritual guides assist humans in their daily lives even though they are unaware of the guides' presence. Those interested are encouraged to seek out their guides to gain practical and mystical information, healing abilities, and protection from harm.

So here are my thoughts:
If you take comfort in believing in spirit guides, go right ahead and do it. Once again:

Live your life!
You Do You, Boo!

Types of Spirit Guides

Ascended Masters
Humans like us but who have transcended the spiritual plane (ex: Buddha)

Star Beings
Star beings are galactic entities whom you may have already known from the past.

Animal Spirit Guides
Totems or Power Animals that provide healing and support during tough times

Nature Spirits
Ethereal personifications of nature who have come since the beginning of time

Ancestral Guides
They are spirit guides coming directly from our genetic lineage.

Angelic Spirit Guides
More commonly known as your guardian angel.

Elementals
Spirits who possess earthly elements, such as Earth, water, fire, and air

Ascended Masters

Ascended Masters are spiritual beings who have lived earthly lives and mastered their paths of spiritual transformation to ascend. They can be powerful teacher guides for us on our personal ascension paths, and their goal is our enlightenment.

Ascended Masters have been down in the trenches, so to speak. So, they deeply understand our emotional and physical challenges and can offer powerful guidance to help us learn our lessons and more vibrantly thrive in our lives. Some ascended masters are Jesus, Buddha, Quan Yin, Merlin, Sai Baba, Sanat Kumara, and Saint Germain.

Star Beings

Star Beings Benevolent star beings can act as spirit guides for members of humanity, especially Starseed souls. A Star being or spirit guide may be a being who you have known in past or future life incarnations in some other star system like the Pleiades, Arcturian, Andromedon, Lyrian, Sirian, Orion Star System, and many others.

Star Being guides are most often present to help us as humanity and individuals to evolve, grow as souls, and progress on the ascension path. The most helpful star-being guides are those who have been through the ascension process and can now help us to navigate the present ascension journey we as humanity are undergoing.

Angels

Angels are spiritual beings from the angelic hierarchy who can act as Divine messengers and spiritual guides for humanity. Angels, Archangels and Guardian Angels are the types of angelic beings that most often work with humans directly.

Angels work with people by communicating messages, transmitting uplifting and inspiring energies, as well as triggering your intuition and offering nudges of guidance to keep you moving in the right direction throughout your incarnation. Your guardian angel knows your unique soul purpose, mission, and also strengths and can guide and support you in coming into your highest truth and vibrantly thriving in your life.

Animal Spirits

Animal Spirit Guides, also known as Power Animals or Totems, are types of spirit guides that show up in animal form. They guide us in our lives through relaying inspiration, offering healing, and even lending direct support in challenging times.

Animal Guide's spiritual focus is on helping you to thrive as a physical being, which includes staying grounded, centered, and in tune with the earth. This does not mean that they don't have powerful spiritual wisdom, magic, and power to relay, though.

Certain animal spirit guides like Jaguar, Vulture, or Snakes are well known for traveling through the veil between the physical and spirit world, and when they show up in your life, they may help you to the same.

Familiar Spirit

A non-corporeal entity that is known (familiar) to a witch. This can be the spirit of a deceased person or animal (common) or a spirit that has always existed as a non-corporeal entity (rare) and can take any form they choose. These spirits can help the practitioner with their magical workings, serve as a guide, or even protect from magical attacks. This is the traditional definition and usage in the practices of witchcraft.

Familiar Pet

Familiar (pet): A corporeal pet animal belonging to a witch. It can be any living animal the owner must care for by feeding, grooming—and cleaning up after. 14th - 17th century witch hunters created this usage as a means to manufacture 'evidence' against a person accused of witchcraft by the Christian church.

This usage has also been popularized by fairytales, Hollywood, and other pop culture, further distorting the definition.

Who's Who

Spirit Companion
These spirits have chosen to form a close relationship with a human friend. They generally seek a practitioner they feel can form a bond or companionship. They are not guides or teachers; however, they may fill those roles for their practitioners if they choose to do so. Most companions are found during the natural course of a spirit worker's spiritual journey or even through spirit adoption.

Spirit Guardians
These spirits choose to protect a person, place, or item. Guardians may be assigned to an individual at birth or during different times in their life. An individual may also seek them out. In times of danger, a guardian may be called upon to help keep their practitioner safe.

Spirit Guides
There are a few different types of spirit guides. Lifetime guides are those an individual will have with them their entire lives. These guides generally appear and are assigned at birth. Depending on several factors, they may choose to leave when death occurs or continue with the individual. Temporary or short-term guides will show up from time to time in an individual's life.

Spirit Familiars
Familiar spirits have a special connection with a practitioner. They can take on one or many different forms and aid the practitioner. They share a bond regarding their craft. They also can provide companionship and protection.

Your spirit guides communicate with you using your clair abilities.
For example, clairsentience (gut feeling), clairvoyance (clear seeing), clairaudience (clear hearing), etc. Or through Synchronicities, downloads, and dreams.

You can communicate with your spirit guides by...
Talking to them out loud or in your head/ thoughts.
Asking for answers in dreams or through signs.
Use divination tools like tarot cards and pendulum, or leave a cup/bowl of water with questions/intentions on paper. Don't drink water since it absorbs energy.

Your spirit guides always have your best interest; if it doesn't feel right to you, stop contacting said 'spirit guide.' Cleanse and protect/banish entities from your environment.

Elemental Guides

An Elemental is a spirit that inhabits one of the Earth's elements, such as Earth, fire, air, or water. Elementals are not all benevolent allies for humanity, but one that could be seen as an Elemental Spirit Guide. Gnomes are the elemental beings connected to the Earth element. Undines are connected to water. Sylphs are connected to the element of air, and Pyraustas (sometimes called Salamanders) are the elemental beings connected to the ether's warmth and fire.

Besides the 4 types of elemental beings, many kinds dwell in the etheric and astral levels of the Earth and sustain nature and humankind. Flower faeries, tree elves, and nature sprites are some of these additional types of beings.

Ancestor Guide

An ancestor spirit guide is a spiritual guide connected to you through your genetic or spiritual lineage. They may be deceased loved ones you knew in your lifetime who now guide you from the realms of spirit. But more often, ancestor guides come from further back in your lineage. This could be a great, great, great grandmother. Or someone like an ancient Yogi Guru you followed in a past incarnation. Ancestor spirits guide and support you in many ways. They may step forward as guides to help you heal, wound, limit beliefs or traumas passed down through generations, or the practical day-to-day guides.

Gods and Goddesses

Gods and Goddesses are spiritual beings who, in certain cultures or spiritual traditions, are honored as being Divine. Goddesses and gods are vehicles for Divine energy, and they often have vibrant stories, personalities, and character traits that give a face to the Divine Life Force.

They are typically beings who have gone through a physical incarnation journey in another cycle, another epoch of time, and they now live in the spirit world and act as allies and often teacher guides for those still on physical incarnation journeys.

As spirit guides, they offer an example or template for how certain Divine qualities manifest

Quicky Animal Spirit Guide

Wolf
Meaning: Instinct, freedom, and social connections. Wolves are often seen as guides in matters of intuition and self-discovery.

Owl
Meaning: Wisdom, intuition, and mystery.
Owls are associated with the unseen and are often seen as symbols of transformation.

Raven
Meaning: Magic, transformation, and messenger between realms. Ravens are often linked to the mystical and the unknown.

Hawk:
Meaning: Vision, insight, and protection.
Hawks are seen as guardians and symbols of heightened perception.

Butterfly
Meaning: Transformation, renewal, and spiritual growth. Butterflies symbolize the journey of the soul.

Snake
Meaning: Transformation, rebirth, and healing. Snakes are often associated with shedding old habits and embracing change.

Bear
Meaning: Strength, introspection, and healing. Bears are seen as guides through introspective journeys.

Dragonfly
Meaning: Change, adaptability, and self-realization. Dragonflies are seen as symbols of transformation and adaptability.

Fox
Meaning: Cleverness, adaptability, and quick thinking. Foxes are often seen as guides in navigating tricky situations.

Deer
Meaning: Gentleness, grace, and intuition. Deer are associated with sensitivity and awareness.

Eagle
Meaning: Spiritual insight, vision, and freedom. Eagles are symbols of divine connection and inspiration.

Dolphin
Meaning: Harmony, playfulness, and communication. Dolphins are seen as guides in social and emotional balance.

Tiger
Meaning: Power, strength, and courage.
Tigers symbolize both physical and spiritual strength.

Hummingbird

Meaning: Joy, love, and agility.

Hummingbirds are associated with the sweetness of life and quick, decisive action.

Elephant

Meaning: Wisdom, loyalty, and strength.

Elephants are seen as symbols of patience and resilience.

Cat

Meaning: Independence, mystery, and magic. Cats are often associated with psychic abilities and intuition.

Spider

Meaning: Creativity, manifestation, and connection to past and future.

Spiders are often seen as weavers of fate.

Crow

Meaning: Transformation, change, and magical abilities. Crows are often associated with shape-shifting and spiritual insight.

Buffalo

Meaning: Abundance, strength, and gratitude. Buffalos are seen as symbols of the earth and its resources.

Horse

Meaning: Freedom, strength, and power.

Horses symbolize the journey of the soul and personal drive.

Swan

Meaning: Beauty, transformation, and grace. Swans are often associated with the journey of the soul and inner transformation.

Peacock

Meaning: Beauty, confidence, and self-expression. Peacocks symbolize the importance of embracing one's true colors.

Frog

Meaning: Transition, cleansing, and fertility. Frogs are seen as symbols of transformation ~ renewal.

Lion

Meaning: Strength, courage, and leadership. Lions symbolize the power of overcoming challenges with dignity.

Giraffe

Meaning: Vision, intuition, and foresight.

Giraffes are associated with gaining a higher perspective in life.

Leopard

Meaning: Stealth, adaptability, and sensuality. Leopards symbolize the importance of blending in and using one's intuition.

Raccoon
Meaning: Resourcefulness, dexterity, and adaptability. Raccoons are seen as guides in navigating life's challenges.

Penguin
Meaning: Community, cooperation, and resilience. Penguins symbolize the strength found in unity and working together.

Wombat
Meaning: Groundedness, protection, and persistence. Wombats are associated with maintaining a strong foundation.

Kangaroo
Meaning: Balance, agility, and family.
Kangaroos symbolize the importance of maintaining a strong family bond.

Shark
Meaning: Authority, survival, and adaptability. Sharks are seen as symbols of authority and effective navigation.

Ant
Meaning: Diligence, teamwork, and patience. Ants symbolize the strength found in cooperation and hard work.

Coyote
Meaning: Trickster energy, adaptability, and intelligence. Coyotes are often associated with lessons learned through playfulness and cunning.

Squirrel
Meaning: Preparedness, resourcefulness, and balance. Squirrels are associated with planning for the future and adaptability.

Crane
Meaning: Focus, longevity, and balance.

Bat
Meaning: Rebirth, intuition, and transformation. Bats are often associated with navigating the unseen realms.

Star Beings

Star beings are galactic entities whom you may have already known from the past.

The Pleiadian Starseed
The Andromedan Starseed
The Lyran Starseed
The Sirian Starseed
The Orion Starseed
The Arcturian Starseed
The Mintaka Starseed
The Venusian Starseed
The Reptilian Starseed
The Martian Starseed
The Avian Starseed
The Polarian Starseed

While there are Angels beyond count, we commonly work with the most well-known 15

Archangels are named throughout many religions and spiritual practices throughout the world - though they are non-denominational. They are neither male nor female but do hold more traditionally masculine or feminine energetic qualities and are sometimes referred to as "he" or "she." However, this distinction does not matter to the Archangels; therefore, call them whatever feels right to you.

Remember, it's about energy, not a physical body or attribute. The Archangels desire to create peace and love. They were created specifically to assist humans with their journey on Earth. Call on the Archangels when you feel afraid or unsure. They will bless you with what you need. Take the time to thank the Archangels for all the love and light they create in your life.

Ariel

Azrael

Chamuel

Gabriel

Haniel

Jeremiel

Jophiel

Metatron

Michael

Raguel

Raphael

Raziel

Sandalphon

Uriel

Zadkiel

CHAPTER 23

Element Spell Jars

Air
Star Anise
Mint
Lavender
Lemongrass
Salt
Flourite
Amethyst

Earth
Mugwort
Patchouli
Corn Kernels
Primrose
Some dirt
Unakite
Tiger's Eye

Fire
Cloves
Rosemary
Pepper Flakes
Calendula
Red Salt
Garnet
Carnelian

Water
Chamomile
Roses
Eucalyptus
Sea Salt
Aquamarine
Lapis Lazuli

How to personalize your spell jar

Include handwritten intentions, sigils, or doodles.
Add an inspiring quote or poetry.
Use several items that resonate with you.
Use locally grown herbs and flowers that you have foraged.
Personal things related to your desired outcome.

Scrying Mirror

Scrying is a technique to obtain insights from images perceived in reflective, translucent, or luminescent surfaces. However, this is not simply observing one's reflection in a bathroom mirror; the images obtained during scrying represent inner spiritual visions. Various materials, including crystals, glass, or water, can create a scrying mirror. The term "scry" is derived from the word "descry," which means to catch sight of or detect something. The origin of "descry" can be traced back to the Old French term "descrier," meaning "to call out."

History: In modern times, scrying is believed to reveal visions from one's subconscious or inner spirit, whereas, in the past, it was attributed to gods, spirits, or other divine influences. Persian mythology tells the tale of the famous Cup of Jamshid, a scrying mirror said to contain an elixir of immortality that reflected the entire world. Nostradamus, a renowned French apothecary and seer from the 16th century used a bowl of clear water for scrying and documented his visions. Joseph Smith Jr., who lived from 1805 to 1844, founded the Mormon religion based on insights from seer stones.

Uses: Despite the belief held by some that scrying abilities are reserved only for a special few, it is widely accepted that anyone can attain proficiency in this ancient practice through dedication and practice. To commence your journey, acquire a scrying mirror, which can be purchased or crafted using various materials and designs. Stones such as malachite, obsidian, and tourmaline are particularly suited for scrying purposes. Alternatively, you may explore Nostradamus's technique involving a bowl of water. Additionally, achieving a state of deep inner focus and exploration through meditation or trance is essential. With continuous practice, vivid visions will manifest themselves before you. Countless resources, including books, websites, and organizations, provide specific methods to learn from and offer guidance on interpreting the visions that unfold during your scrying endeavors.

Worry Water
Water is the element of the ocean. It will absorb the feelings and emotions you release into it. Use this energy transmutation ritual to help release stress and anxiety from inside the body into a pool of water and then disperse it to newer, neutral energy. Tell your secrets, fears, and worries to the water, open up, don't hold back and then pour the water out, either down the drain or into the Earth, not directly onto plants, though perhaps for the concert; trade it, or I'll pour worry water on undesirable weeds in my garden.

Warding

Warding is a form of defensive magic that offers a gentle approach to protection. Its purpose is to safeguard against negative energies, redirecting them away from you or your surroundings in a general sense.

Methods
Guardians
Create a guardian to guard your home or space against negative energies.

Crystals
Corresponding crystals can be worn on jewelry to protect against negative energy. Place crystals in a room or around your house to create a protective barrier.

Salt
Black salt can be used in rituals or just used alone. Sprinkle salt around your doors and windows, or make protection jars with it.

Herbs
Burn protective herbs and pass the smoke through your space or tools. Sprinkle herbal oils and tinctures on yourself and your space for protective barriers.

Visualization
Use your intention and energy to visualize a powerful barrier of protecting light around yourself or your space.

Trust your instincts and rely on methods that resonate with you. Avoid using techniques that don't feel right or that you haven't thoroughly researched.

Spell for Warding

Ingredients:
Small white candle
Protection herbs (e.g., rosemary, basil, sage)
Protective crystals (e.g., black tourmaline, obsidian, clear quartz)
Sea salt
Anointing oil (e.g., olive or coconut oil)
Fire-safe bowl or cauldron

Instructions:
Clear and prepare your sacred space. Light a white candle.
Crush protection herbs and roll the white candle in anointing oil. Coat the candle in crushed herbs.
Place a circle of protective crystals around the candle and sprinkle sea salt in a circle around them.
Light the white candle and state your warding intention.
Visualize a protective shield forming around you and your space.
Let the candle burn down completely in a safe manner.
Express gratitude and close your sacred space.

Banishing

Regarding defensive magic, banishing is a much more targeted and forceful approach than warding. Its purpose is to eliminate a specific energy, spirit, or individual. However, it's essential to carefully consider the consequences before resorting to banishing.

Methods
Use the Elements
Burn a slip of paper with your target's name on it or throw a leaf with your target's name on it in a running river/stream. Burn corresponding herbs and pass the smoke through your space.

Candles
Anoint your candle with corresponding herbs and oils, then burn it when the candle has burnt out; the banishing is complete.

Sigils
Make your own banishing sigil, or find one that resonates with you; place it in the space or on the item you are banishing energy from.

Herbs & Tinctures
Use herbal smoke to force energy out of a space or object; make a spray or herbal tincture to sprinkle around your home.

Trust your instincts and rely on methods that resonate with you. Avoid using techniques that don't feel right or that you haven't thoroughly researched.

CHAPTER 24

Dressing Candles

Preparing candles can be as simple or intricate as you desire. Dressing a candle is a way to make herbs adhere to it so they burn as it melts.

Using Oil:
For a decreased spell, rub the oil anti-clockwise.

Sprinkle your herbs on a plate and roll your oiled candle in them to make them stick.

Using Candle Wax:
To use candle wax to dress your candle, choose a candle and light it. Allow the wax to melt for a few minutes. Once it starts melting, drip the melted wax onto the candle that you want to dress. Then, use the melted wax to stick the herbs to the candle. You can do this by hand or place the herbs on a plate and roll the candle in the herbs so that they stick to the melted wax.

Colors at First Glance

Bringing balance to our lives with color energy is easy. We can do it by wearing our favorite colors, painting rooms in calming colors, or adding different colors to our decor. If we pay attention to the colors around us and how they make us feel, we can use them to improve our lives and increase our vibrations.

Black for banishing, protection, binding, releasing, and defense.

Green for money, prosperity, employment, fertility, growth, luck, abundance, and your Heart Chakra.

Red for strength, passion, courage, action, survival, love, and your Root Chakra.

Yellow for intellect, confidence, travel, movement, joy, imagination, productivity, willpower, and your Solar Plexus Chakra.

Orange for attraction, energy, legal matters, ambition, vitality, opportunity, creativity, inspiration, and your Sacral Chakra.

White for protection, purification, peace, purity, tranquility, and balance.

Blue for healing, peace, forgiveness, communication, truth, calming, focus, memory, and your Throat Chakra.

Purple for spirituality, wisdom, peace, harmony, intuition, psychic abilities, divination, dreams, and your Third Eye Chakra.

But remember to do what feels right to you.
As always: You Do You, Boo!

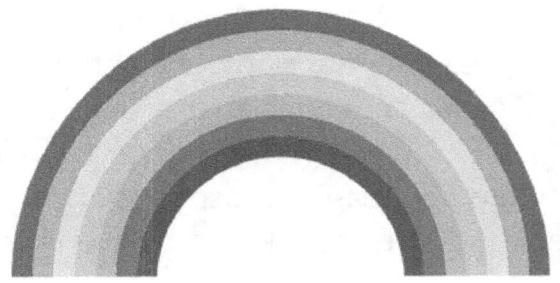

Spell Candle Color

Orange: Courage, creativity, joy, and success. Sunday is associated with orange candles, so burn on that day.

Brown: Grounding, earth element, stability, practicality and focus Tuesday is associated with brown candles, so burn on that day.

White: Peace, healing, protection, divination and purity. Monday is associated with white candles, so burn on that day.

Blue: Protection, creativity, spirituality, harmony, and divine guidance. Thursday is associated with blue candles, so burn on that day.

Yellow: Communication, focus, intuition, and inspiration. Wednesday is associated with Yellow candles, so burn them on that day.

Black: Absorbing negativity, protection, breaking bad habits, breaking hexes and curses, clearing obstacles, and banishing evil. Saturday is associated with black candles, so burn on that day.

Purple: Psychic abilities, divination, clairvoyance, spirit guides, and manifestation. Thursday is associated with purple candles, so burn them on that day.

Pink: Love, romance, self-love, harmony, and compassion. Friday is associated with bink candles, so burn on that day.

Green: Fertility, money, abundance, prosperity, and luck. Friday is associated with Green candles, so burn on that day.

Red: Passion, power, sex, vitality, and desire. Tuesday is associated with Red candles, so burn on that day.

Candle Observance

Flickering Flame

A flickering candle flame often indicates the presence of a spirit, and your request was understood.

Jumping Candle Flame

A lot of energy surrounds your spell; this is typically a good sign and indicates your magic or intention will manifest quickly.

Dancing Flame

Suggests success, but it is likely to coincide with complications. The taller the flame jumps, the more resistance and obstacles you'll likely encounter.

Candle Popping

It signifies that a spirit or ancestor is trying to communicate with you by using candle crackles, sizzles, and pops.

Self- Extinguishes

Indicates your intention or spell has been resolved. Your candle will sometimes self-extinguish if the outcome has already happened before the candle is completely burned out.

Weak Flame

A weak flame will deliver inefficient outcomes, and your intention is up against various complexities.

Types of Candles and Usage

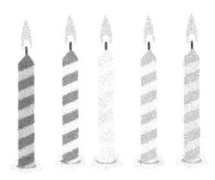 Fast Spells: Birthday Candles

Small Spells: Chime & Tealight Candles
Burn Time: 2-4 hours

Medium Spells: Votive & Taper Candles
Burn Time: 6-10 hours

Big Spells: Pillar & 7-day Jar Candles
Burn Time: 12 hours to several Days

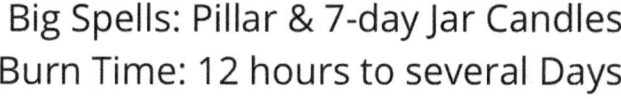

CHAPTER 25

Build up your Altar

Designing an Imbolc Altar: A Guide to Celebrating the Winter-Spring Transition

Imbolc is a fire festival marking the transition from winter to spring and a time to honor the Goddess Brigit and other gods and goddesses associated with Imbolc. One way to celebrate this Sabbat is to create a special altar. Here's what you need to know:

Choosing Decorations
When creating an Imbolc altar, select items that represent the Sabbat. Popular items include candles, images of Brigit, snow, and plants in pots. Colored cloths and fabrics in shades of white, yellow, and green are also often seen on Imbolc altars. You can also add items that are personally meaningful to you, such as crystals, herbs, and other symbols of your spiritual path.

Finding the Perfect Location
Deciding where to place your Imbolc altar is an important decision. It is best to find a place that feels special and sacred to you. Some people prefer to create a shrine in their bedroom or living room, while others like to set up a permanent altar in a quiet corner of their home. Remember, there is no right or wrong place to put an Imbolc altar, so just use your intuition and choose a spot that feels right to you.

Honoring the Sabbat
Designing an Imbolc altar can be a beautiful and powerful way to honor the Sabbat and bring its energy into your home. Take time to think about the meaning of Imbolc and what it represents to you. Select items that reflect your spiritual journey and that help you connect with the energy of this special day.

Altar

An altar is any structure on which offerings, prayers, or rituals are made. This space can be used for meditation, ritual, and showing gratitude. Establish a sacred space in your home by setting up an altar. You can decorate your altar according to each season with the flora/fauna or symbolize an element (Air, Earth, Water, Fire).

Candles: Represent the illumination of personal truths, warmth, hope, light, and the element of fire.

Flowers: Represent feminine energy, growth, beauty, pleasure, evolution, and the Earth element.

Artwork and Imagery: Represent creativity, expression, emotion, communication, ancestors, deities, and guides.

Crystals: Are powerful transmitters of vibration- each has a unique energy and purpose.

Other Things You Might Add:
Cauldon
Dagger
Feathers
Water
Chalice ~ Cup
Candles
Besom
Matches
Divination Tools
Crystals
Athame
Boline
Compass
Mirror
Wand
Spell Jars
Herbs
Book of Shadows
Mortar and Pestle
Grimoire
Offering Plate ~ Dish
Pentagram
Incense
Bell

North Earth

West Water

East Air

South Fire

CHAPTER 26

Sigils

Sigils in Witchcraft
Sigils are magical symbols that have a specific purpose. They have the power to attract, repel, and charge. Use sigils for easy on-the-go magic!

Activation
When using sigils to repel or banish, the original intention of the sigil must be forgotten or released. This is so the symbol itself becomes charged with the intention, allowing it to manifest. The best way to do this is to have faith in your sigil and intention, to let go of it or destroy/hide it.

Enchanting and Charging
You can enchant objects, people, places, and tools by writing sigils on them. With this method of sigil magic, you don't need to destroy or release the sigil to activate it. By writing, carving, or painting the sigil onto an object, you are giving it a task - therefore activating its magical purpose.

Destructible Sigils
These are activated by being destroyed.
This means you'll draw the Sigil, charge it with intention, and destroy it. You can burn it or tear it apart.

Temporary Sigils
You have to draw the Sigil, charge it with intention, and then leave it on your skin.
You can also carve the Sigil onto a candle and light the candle.

Permanent Sigils
They are made to last. So, draw them into a piece of paper that you can place anywhere you like or create a piece of jewelry.

Personal or Premade
When you make a sigil with your own energy, it responds best to you. You can tailor personal sigils to your exact needs.

Sigils made by someone other than yourself can hold a lot of power. When many people use the same sigil or spell, it often becomes charged with the energy and faith of those people.

Tip: Keep track of the creation of your sigils and your failed attempts.
Use your designs for inspiration for new sigils! Be sure to write the meaning of your sigils next to them in your grimoire or book of shadows as well, for referencing later.

Sigil Making

Adding Your Personal Touch to Sigils

When creating sigils, it's important to add your own unique touch – especially when making them yourself. Take the time to include any signature doodles or markings that represent you. This acts as a calling card to the universe, signaling that this intention belongs to you. Don't hesitate to experiment and revise your sigils as needed. It may take a few attempts before you find the design that resonates with you.

Establishing Your Intention

To set a clear and concise intention, write it down. Use the present tense to make it feel like it has already come to fruition. While you work, visualize your goal becoming a reality.

Cross Letters Out

Now cross out vowels and repeating letters.

Basic Shapes

Break the remaining letters down into their basic shapes and lines.

Create Your Own Sigil

To make a symbol unique to you, use any of the remaining shapes. While you don't have to use repeating shapes, you have the freedom to do so. Add dots, squiggles, arrows, or any other element that feels right. Remember, this is your own creation, so be imaginative and make it your own.

Helpful Tip for Sigil Creation

Keep track of the process of creating your sigils, including failed attempts. Use these designs as inspiration for future sigils! It's also important to record the meanings of your sigils alongside them in your grimoire or book of shadows for future reference.

Sigil Making

Creating Shapes for the Creatively Challenged

For those who struggle with artistic expression, this method is perfect for creating shapes. You can also use the shapes you create as a jumping-off point and add your own symbols or rearrange them completely to suit your needs.

Set Your Attention:

Just like the first method, write out your intention

Cross Out Letters:

Now cross out vowels and repeating letters.

Convert To Numbers:

Use a chart to convert letters to numbers. Cross out any repeating numbers.

Make A Chart:

Create a shape with designated spots for numbers 1-9. A grid is a simple place to start. Get creative with your grid shape!

Make Your Sigil:

Connect your numbers together to make a unique shape. Add extra lines if you want to. Then add any personal flare that you'd like!

Making Sigils Using Charts

If you're creatively challenged, this method allows you to make shapes without the need for artistic expression. You can also use the shapes you make as a starting point, and add your own shapes and symbols to it or rearrange it entirely.

Set your intention.
Just like the first method, write
out
your intention.

I AM PEACEFUL

Cross letter out.
Now cross out vowels and
repeating letters.

~~I~~ AM P~~E~~AC~~E~~F~~U~~L
M PCFL

Convert to numbers.
Use a chart to convert letters to
numbers. Cross out any
repeating numbers.

	1	2	3	4	5	6	7	8	9
	A	B	C	D	E	F	G	H	I
	J	K	L	M	N	O	P	Q	R
	S	T	U	V	W	X	Y	Z	

4 7 3 6 3
4 7 ~~3~~ 6 ~~3~~
4 7 6

Make a Chart
Create a shape with designated spots for numbers 1-9. A grid is a
simple place to start. Get creative with your grid shape!

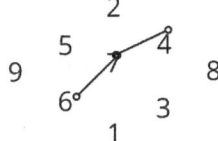
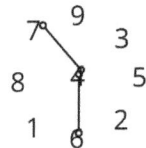

Make your Sigil
Connect your numbers to make a unique shape. Add extra lines if
you want to. Then add any personal flare that you'd like!

Sigil Making

Write your intention. Be clear, concise, and write in present tense.

Cross out all vowels and repeating letters.

Use the chart to convert the remaining letters to numbers. Cross out any repeating numbers.

1	2	3	4	5	6	7	8	9
A	B	C	D	E	F	G	H	I
J	K	L	M	N	O	P	Q	R
S	T	U	V	W	X	Y	Z	

Numbers Left:

Create a unique shape by connecting your numbers in one of the charts or make one of your own. Get creative.

Final Sigil:

CHAPTER 27

Correspondence
Flowers and Herbs

I have included worksheets to familiarize you with some correspondence associated with this season. Feel free to add others to personalize your unique way of celebrating this sabbat. In addition, I have included how to dry herbs and how to make an infusion oil.

Foraging Calendar

January, February, and March
Chickweed, Common Mallow Leaves, Common Sorrel, Cowberry. Crow Garlic. Dandelion Root. Garlic Mustard, Ground Elder, Hairy Bittercress, Nettles, Pignut, Sheep's Sorrel, Silver Birch Sap, Wild Garlic, Winter Cress, Wood Sorrel

April, May, and June
Beech Leaves, Borage, Broom, Chickweed, Cleavers, Common Poppy, Dandelion Leaves and Roots, Dog Rose Flowers, Elderflower, Garlic Mustard, Ground Elder. Hawthorn Blossom, Hops, Nettles, Pignuts, Sheep's Sorrel, Spearmint, Sweet Cicely, Watercress, Wild Garlic. Wild Thyme, Wood Sorrel, Yarrow

July, August, and September
Acorns, Apples, Beech Nuts, Bilberries, Blackberries, Burdock, Chamomile, Chickweed, Chicory, Cleavers, Common Mallow, Dandelion Leaves and Flowers, Elderberry, Fat Hen, Garlic Mustard, Gooseberries, Hawthorn Berries, Hazelnuts, Horseradish, Juniper Berries, Nettle, Plums, Rowan Berries, Sheep's Sorrel, Spearmint, Sweet Chestnuts, Sweet Cicely, Walnuts, Wild Cherries, Wild Strawberries, Wild Thyme, Wood Sorrel, Yarrow

October, November, and December
Chestnuts, Chickweed, Crab Apples, Hawthorn Berries, Horseradish, Nettles, Rosehips, Sheep's Sorrel, Sloes, Spearmint, Sweet Chestnuts, Walnuts

I live in the North Eastern United States; you may find different species depending on where you live.

Companion Planting

Swiss Chard: Onions, Cabbages, Beetroot.

Cabbage: Brussel Sprouts, Tomatoes, Broccoli, Spinach, Swiss Chard, Kale.

Carrots: Cabbages, Leek, Radishes, Peas. Onions, Lettuce.

Onion: Lettuce, Beetroot, Cabbages, Carrots, Parsnip,

Potatoes: Cabbages, Peas, Squash, Beans, Corn.

Beets: Broccoli, Onions, Swiss Chard, Cabbage, Brussel Sprouts.

Cucumber: Corn, Cabbages, Radishes, Beans.

Radish: Peas, Carrots, Parsnip, Lettuce, Cucumber, Spinach.

Tomatoes: Onions, Carrots, Cabbages.

Dehydrating Herbs

When you have more than enough fresh herbs for cooking, the BEST way to keep them is in their dehydrated form.

Sun Dry
It's called sun-dry, but do NOT dry herbs under the sun. Place in a warm spot, but avoid direct sunlight.

Air Dry
A very common method to dry herbs. It is the cheapest and most natural way of preserving your fresh herbs.

Microwave Dry
This is the fastest way, and it keeps your herbs greener.

Oven Dry
It is quicker than air and sundry, but herbs will cook a little, removing some of the potency and flavor.

Food Dehydrator
An efficient way to quickly dry and preserve the flavor and medicinal value of fresh herbs.

Infusions

Infusion is a widely-used term referring to the process of soaking plant material in liquid to infuse flavor. The ingredients used for infusions can vary, including leaves, stems, bark, berries, fruits, and vegetables. Additionally, there are different liquids used for infusions, such as water, alcohol, oil, and sweet solutions made from sugar, honey, and glycerin. These various methods are used to create beverages, medicines, and flavorings.

Cold Infusions vs. Hot Infusions

Cold infusions are created by steeping the plant material in liquid for an extended period of time, allowing time to release the flavor slowly. This process releases fewer tannins than hot infusions, which often results in less bitter flavors. Cold infusions retain more of the taste of the plant being infused, making them ideal for delicate herbs and fruits. Examples of cold infusions include cold-brewed coffee and tea.

Hot infusions, on the other hand, are made by heating the infusing liquid before introducing the flavoring agents. This process releases more of the plant's volatile oils, often resulting in a pleasingly bitter note from the tannins that have been unlocked. Hot infusions are ideal when you want faster results, working within minutes rather than the hours or days needed for cold infusions. Hot infusions are also better at releasing flavors that cold water cannot.

Flavored Oils

Flavored oils are often made through hot infusion, starting with a mild-flavored or neutral oil like organic canola or safflower oil, which is then gently heated. Garlic or herbs are added to the oil, allowing the flavors to steep before straining out the plant material. Scented oils from fragrant plants such as lavender, rosemary, thyme, and citrus peel can also be made using the hot infusion method.

It's important to refrigerate flavored oils and use them within several weeks. Even though the oil has been strained, tiny particles of food material can remain suspended in the liquid and act as a vector for contamination.

Vodka ~ Vinegar ~ Water

Infused Vodka
Avoid heating alcohol at all costs, as the flame can quickly ignite and cause a fire. Instead, take a clean jar or bottle, add some flavoring agents, like berries or vanilla bean husks, and cover them with vodka. Place the container in a cool, dark place for a few days or up to a few weeks, shaking or turning it occasionally to distribute the liquid and allow the flavor to develop. Once satisfied with the flavor, strain out the solids and pour the vodka back into the container. You can use berries, vanilla beans, ginger root, or chili peppers to make delicious infused vodkas. Remember, you can substitute vodka with any liquor at least 80 proof to infuse the ingredients. Don't toss out the solids; use them to enhance adult beverages, desserts, or cooked foods.

Infused Vinegar
The method for infusing vinegar is similar to that used for vodka. Infused vinegar can be used for making vinaigrettes or as a diluted drink called a "shrub" by mixing the vinegar with water or seltzer at a 1:8 ratio. Infused vinegar can also be found in gourmet shops, often with added sugar or fruit purees. Making your own shrubs at home is more economical and straightforward. You can get 64 ounces of vinegar by infusing a few berries with eight ounces of the delicious shrub.

Infused Water
Slice up your favorite flavorful ingredients and add them to your water jug, glass, or bottle. Cucumbers, citrus segments (or just their peels), and chunks of melon or pineapple are all great choices. Enjoy a refreshing and celicious drink without any added sugar or calories.

Extracts ~ Tinctures ~ Decoctions ~ Tisanes

Extracts - are highly concentrated cold infusions made using alcohol as the menstruum. A 1:1 ratio of herb to alcohol is recommended. A smaller amount is sufficient for non-vegetal items such as nuts and spices. Citrus is another excellent option. Allow your extracts to diffuse for two to three months before straining and storing them in a dark location.

Tinctures - are the most potent infusions and are often used for medicinal purposes. Dried or fresh herbs and flowers such as mint, calendula, or rosemary are infused to extract their oils and leave the plant material behind. Alcohol is also the most popular menstruum to make tinctures. The ratio of plant material to alcohol is about 3:1 for most recipes. Tinctures can be stored for up to five years.

Glycerine - Vegetable glycerin is often used as a substitution for alcohol in tinctures—dilute culinary-grade glycerin 75/25 with water. Then, 1:2 dried plant matter was added to the glycerin mixture. Crush the herbs first to encourage infusion. Remove to a cool, dark place for four to six weeks, then strain. You can store the infused glycerin in a cool, dark place for six to twelve months.

Decoctions - involve simmering plant material like barks, roots, and berries in water for an extended time. This method is helpful for barks, such as cinnamon, and dried hard herbs and berries, such as elderberry.

Tisanes - Hot herbal infusions and decoctions are sometimes called "tisanes." This term differentiates such beverages from teas, which can only be made with leaves from the Camellia sinensis plant. Herbal "teas" are tisanes, not teas, unless they contain the leaves of the tea plant.

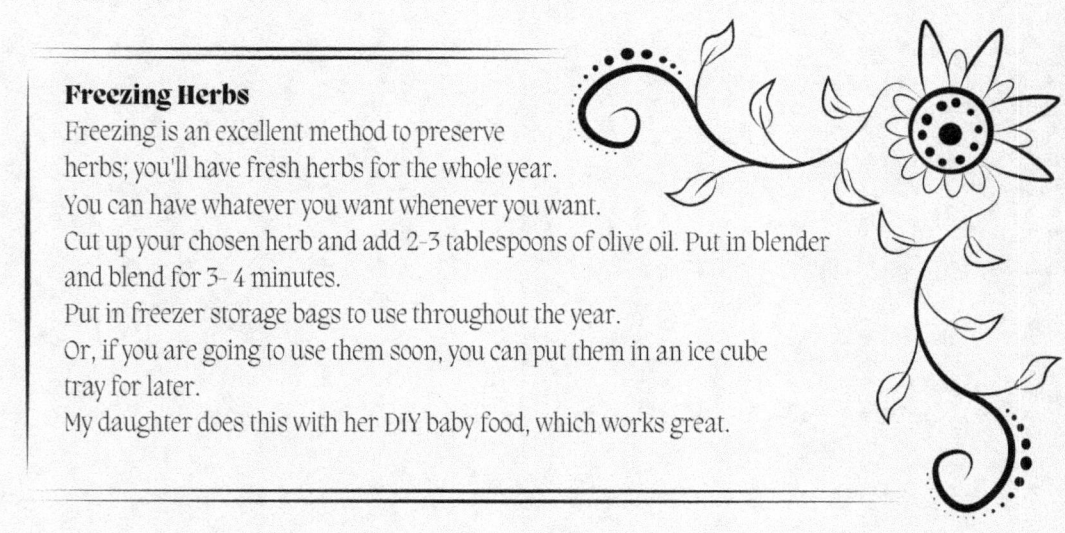

Freezing Herbs

Freezing is an excellent method to preserve herbs; you'll have fresh herbs for the whole year.

You can have whatever you want whenever you want.

Cut up your chosen herb and add 2-3 tablespoons of olive oil. Put in blender and blend for 3-4 minutes.

Put in freezer storage bags to use throughout the year.

Or, if you are going to use them soon, you can put them in an ice cube tray for later.

My daughter does this with her DIY baby food, which works great.

Florida Water Recipe

Ingredients:
16 oz of vodka
3-5 tablespoons of floral water (orange, rose, lavender, etc.)
8 drops of Lavender EO
10 drops of Lemon EO
10 drops of Orange EO
5 drops of Bergamot EO
5 drops of Cinnamon EO
5 drops of Clove EO
3 drops of Benzoin EO
Fresh rose petals & fresh rosemary (optional)

Add your vodka and floral water to a bowl and smell each EO before adding it to your bowl. Let your nose and spirit tell you if you should add more or less than what's in the recipe.

Combine all ingredients in a spray bottle

Shake well before each use

Remove rose petals and rosemary if you wish

Keep your customized Florida Water on hand to energetically cleanse your aura, car, home, workspace, altar, etc.

I like using it on my floors, windows, and doors. But you can use it in your bath or laundry to clean your tools and crystals or make it into a spray.

Cascarilla Powder

Cascarilla powder is an easy-to-make essential ingredient for protective magic Cascarilla.
(as-ka-ree-ah) is made of powdered eggshell and used primarily for protection and spiritual cleansing. It originates from hoodoo and Santeria but has become popular throughout America due to its accessibility. Cascarilla powder can also help create spiritual barriers (similar to salt), add blessings, aid in protection, and is a great nutritional addition for plants in the garden!

Florida water also has protective qualities and complements the Cascarilla very well.

Tip: When you crack an egg, run the shell under the kitchen faucet to separate the membrane from the body. Removing the membrane makes a higher-quality powder.

Ingredients:
2 dozen eggshells, dried
Food processor or mortar and pestle
½ teaspoon of Florida water (see recipe)
Small glass jar / sealable container

Directions:
Bake the eggshells at 200* for approximately 30 minutes to further dry them out. This step allows excess moisture to cook off, making a more delicate powder. This step is significant if you plan to grind the shells by hand using a mortar and pesto! You might notice the color change slightly if you're using white eggshells. Don't' worry-your powder will still come out white.

When the egg shells are dry, grind them into a fine powder using a mortar, pestle, or food processor. Add about 1/2 teaspoon of Florida water and process until you have a fine, sand-like consistency. Store the cascarilla powder in a jar or pack it into chalk.

For Cascarilla chalk, mix 1 tablespoon of flour with 1 tablespoon of loose cascarilla powder and mix thoroughly. Add a tablespoon of warm water and mix until the ingredients have combined just enough to form a ball in your hands. Roll the mixture into sticks about 1/2 to 1 inch in diameter and let them dry for 3 to 5 days. Alternately, you can roll the mixture into balls and place them in a small-pack paper condiment cup (this is the easiest method). Store the chalk in a glass, plastic, or metal container to protect it from breaking, and keep it in a cool dark place.

Note: You can enhance the magical properties of your cascarilla powder by adding additional or specific herbs. Use caution when adding; too much of these and the mixture will not stick together and form chalk.

You can use it in spells and in making sigils and magical symbols.

Quicky Herbs

Agrimony — ancient herb of healing, restoration, and benevolent protection

Alfalfa - good fortune, money magick, healing and cleansing infusions (full article)

Angelica - warding and banishing, angelic magick, summoning strength (full article)

Astragalus - vital energy, protection (shielding), promoting health, mental clarity, concentration

Basil - blessings, love, money, and happiness

Bay Leaf - confers wisdom, strength, and visions, a sacred herb of Apollo

Bearberry - psychic awareness, dreams, courage, smudging, and offerings

Birch Bark - new beginnings, psychic protection, strength, devotion, the Goddess

Blessed Thistle - consecration, protection, healing, and cleansing by fire

Blue Sage - smudging, meditation, relaxation, ancestral wisdom, peace

Blue Vervain - spells of love and advancement, astral travel, initiation

Burdock Root - warding, cleansing, uncrossing, and counter-magick

Calendula - solar rites, divination, remembrance, honoring the dead

Catnip - love-drawing, relaxation, trance work, feline magick

Cedar - ancient wisdom, protection, maturity, strength, and power

Cinnamon - passion, shielding, quick success, spirit evocation, fire magick

Cinquefoil (Five Finger Grass) - for the five blessings: health, money, love, power, and wisdom

Coltsfoot - divination, visions, love magick, healing from within

Comfrey - healing, restoration, lucky herb of travelers and gamblers

Damiana - lust, sex magick, psychic abilities, energy work, spirit quests

Dandelion - wishes, divination, calling spirits, charisma and success

Devil's Claw - protection, exorcism, banishing spells, keeping away evil, confounding enemies

Dill - sexual love, luck, protection against sorcery and disease

Dittany of Crete - a rare herb from Greece, renowned for love magick, manifestation, spirit contact

Elderberry - hidden wisdom, Crone magick, banishing, Faery offerings

Eucalyptus - cleansing, healing, ritual baths, rites of Mercury and Air

Fennel Seed - psychic protection, counter-magick, confidence, and adaptability

Feverfew is a humble flower renowned for its curative properties, a magickal "fix-all."

Galangal - strength and power, victory, luck, hex-breaking, male potency

Ginger - fiery herb of passion, success, and personal power

Hawthorn Berry - fidelity, shielding, clarity, ancestor, and Faery magick

Hibiscus - love and passion, independence, confidence

Horehound - mental clarity, dispelling illusion, quick action, healing

Hyssop - purification, innocence, blessings, sacred baths and washes
Irish Moss - financial luck, folk remedies, safety during travel, sea magick
Jasmine - love, dreams, divination, sensuality, luxury and kindness
Juniper Berry - good luck, prosperity, masculine energy, protection at home
Juniper Leaf — purification, protection, bringing luck, exposing the truth
Lavender - love and attraction, purification, relaxation, restful sleep
Lemon Balm - tranquility, attraction, fidelity, teamwork, harmonious home
Lemon Peel - cleansing, purifying, boosting energy, sweetness and charm
Licorice Root - domination, advantage over others, passion, power, persuasion
Lobelia - spirit communication, love and weather magick, trance, blessings and curses
Mandrake - legendary magickal herb for love magick, protection, and curses
Marjoram - protection, married love, calming the mind, easing grief
Marshmallow Root - love charms, psychic powers, protection, drawing good spirits
Meadowsweet - a sacred flower of Spring, the Maiden, and the Underworld
Mistletoe - good luck, love, and money spells, many traditional charms
Mugwort - scrying, divination, psychic ability, lucid dreaming, lunar magic
Mullein - protection, illumination, courage, hedge-crossing, crone magick
Nettle - courage, consecration, protection, healing, deterring evil
Orange Peel - uplifting and centering Solar herb of joy, blessings, and good luck
Orris Root - charms of love, persuasion, popularity, charisma and success
Patchouli - love and sex magick, attraction, fertility, rites of Earth
Pennyroval - calmness. endurance. patience. dispellina ander.
Peppermint - healing, purification, psychic awareness, love and energy
Pine - persistence, moderation, prosperity, and good health
Raspberry Leaf - love and enjoyment, tempting others, divination
Red Sandalwood - is used in incense for meditation, healing, and trance work
Rose - charms of love and beauty, harmony, divination, goddess rites
Rosemary - cleansing, purification, vitality, wisdom, protection
Rue - warding, exorcism, cleansing, love-drawing, and protective charms
Spearmint - love, psychic ability, cleansing, renewal, house blessing
Star Anise - clairvoyance, good luck, psychic dreams, travel charms
Thyme - beauty, strength, courage, a favorite herb of Faeries
Valerian - warding, enemy spells, transmuting negativity, feline magick
Vervain - Old World herb of wisdom, healing, and second sight
White Sage - cleansing, house blessing, meditation, healing
White Willow Bark - solace, wisdom, long-lasting love, divination, Lunar magick
Wild Lettuce - visions, trance, dream magick, enthrallment and sleep
Witch Hazel - comfort and healing, wisdom, protection, soothing of anger
Wood Betony - herb of St. Bride, used in charms against ill luck, anxiety, and despair
Wormwood - psychic vision, spirit evocation, hexes and curses, reversal magick
Yarrow - ancient medicinal flower used for courage, divination, good fortune

Crocus

Crocus vernus
Folk name: spring crocus, giant crocus, snow crocus

**Most forms of Crocus are
extremely toxic**

Magical Properties
Attracting love
Visions

Draw or Paste your herb here

**Physical Properties & EO
It May:**
Help tumors
Rheumatoid arthritis
Gout

**Essential Oil Properties
It May:**

Use Caution:
Most forms of Crocus are
extremely toxic

Daffodil

Narcissus spp.
Folk name: Asphodel, Goose leek, Lent lily

Magical Properties
Love spells
Fertility increase
Good luck
Attract fairies
Wishes

Draw or Paste your herb here

**Physical Properties & EO
It May:**
Induce sickness
Numbness
Hallucinations
Convulsions
Cardiac effects
Cancer treatments.
Planet - Venus

Use Caution:
Please do not consume or use daffodils in anyway as they are highly toxic

High John the Conqueror

Ipomoea jalapa
Folk name: Bindweed

Magical Properties

Love spells
Sexual Spells
Good luck
Luck at Gambling

Draw or Paste your herb here

Physical Properties
It May: **Use Caution:**

Be a strong laxative
Emetic

Planet -

Rue

Ruta graveolens

Folk Name: Bashoush, Garden rue, Herb of grace, Mother of Herbs

Magical Properties

Healing

Health

Mental powers

Exorcism

Love

Breaks hexes and curses

Physical Properties
It May:

Relieve headaches

Improve thinking

Improve illnesses

Draw or Paste your herb here

Planet - Mars

Use Caution:

Wormwood

Artemisa absinthium

Folk Name: absinthe, green ginger, and old woman

Magical Properties

Love

Protection

Psychic powers

Calling spirits

Immortality

Physical Properties

It May:

Flavor the liqueur absinthe

Repel moths and fleas

Heal the plague

Planet - Mars

Draw or Paste your herb here

Use Caution: Can be lethal if consumed excessively

Peppermint

Mentha piperita

Folk Name: Brandy mint, Lammint

Magical Properties
Healing
Potions
Raises vibrations
Calls good spirits

Draw or Paste your herb here

Physical Properties
It May:
Help headaches
Aid sleep when smelled
Promote dental health
Enhance digestion

Planet - Mercury

Use Caution: Mint can take over your garden

Basil

Ocimum basilicum
Folk Names: Our Herb, Witches Herb, Balanoi, Albahaca

Magical Properties
Sympathy
Soothes tempers
Brings wealth
Good Luck
Protection

Draw or Paste your herb here

Physical Properties
It May:
Reduce stomach spasms
Help loss of appetite
Alleviate intestinal gas
Improve kidney conditions
Help fluid retention
Soothe head colds,
Heal warts

Use Caution:

Planet - Mars

Blackberry

Rubus villosus
Folk Name: Bly, Bramble, Thimbleberry, Dewberry

Magical Properties
Healing
Money
Protection
Water Magic
Sacred to Brigid

Physical Properties
It May:
High in Vitamin C
Heal the skin.
Reduce free radicals in the body.
Help absorb iron.
Shorten the common cold.
Prevent scurvy.

Use Caution:

Planet - Venus

Draw or Paste your herb here

Angelica

Angelica archangelica
Folk Name: Archangel, Masterwort, Root of the Holy Ghost

Magical Properties
Protection from evil
Healing
Exorcism
Ward off the plague
Mental harmony

Physical Properties
It May:
Help Colic
Reduce Gas
Improve Indigestion
Aid Hepatitis
Decrease Heartburn
Improve Nausea
Heal Ulcers

Planet - Sun

Draw or Paste your herb here

Use Caution: This plant can be confused with water hemlock, which is a deadly poison, or hogweed, which causes photodermatitis with just a touch.

It carries a miscarriage risk for pregnant women and should be avoided by them

Imbolc Magical Oils

Imbolc is a magical time of year and these oils can help you to harness that energy. Whether you use them to anoint candles, tools, or your body or simply burn them in an oil burner, these recipes will help you connect with the natural world and create powerful spells and rituals. When making your own magical oil, it is important to choose a carrier oil that suits your needs. If you do not have the herbs or flowers needed for the recipe, it is perfectly acceptable to use essential oils instead.

Blessing Essential Oil Blend
2 drops of Patchouli EO
5 drops of Rosemary EO
3 drops of Lavender EO

Imbolc Magical Oil
3 drops of Jasmine EO
3 drops of Rose EO
3 drops of Lemon EO
1 crushed Chamomile flower
1 crushed Jasmine flower

Imbolc Oil Magical has two other variations
2 drops of Basil EO
2 drops of Bay EO

or 1 crushed Bay leaf
3 drops of Cinnamon EO
1 drop of Rosemary EO
2 drops of Lavender EO

Brigid's Magical Oil
4 drops of Sage EO
4 drops of Dragons Blood EO
1 small crushed garnet
1 crushed white flower
1/4 teaspoon of crushed rosemary

Directions:
Warm over low heat or put in an essential oil burner diffuser or simmer pot

Candle Anointing Oil
3 drops of Juniper EO
2 drops of Eucalyptus EO
1 drop of Pine EO
A few pine needles

Fire Oil
3 drops of Cinnamon EO
6 drops of Orange EO
2 whole Cloves
4 drops of Nutmeg EO

Fire Oil (variation)
1/2 part Ginger EO
1/2 part Rosemary EO
A few drops of Petitgrain EO
A few drops of Clove EO

Purification Oil
3 drops of Orange EO
2 drops of Lemongrass EO
2 drops of Lemon EO
1 drop of Lime EO

Imbolc Incense
3 parts Frankincense Resin
2 parts of Dragons Blood Resin
1/2 part of Red Sandalwood EO
1 part of Cinnamon EO
1 part of Clove EO
3 drops of Red Wine

CHAPTER 28

Correspondance
Crystals

Correspondence Crystals

I have included worksheets to familiarize you with some correspondence associated with this season. Feel free to add others to personalize your unique way of celebrating this sabbat.

Crystal Energy

Each stone has a range of metaphysical properties that can be used for healing emotionally, physically, and spiritually. They can also be carried for protection or to bring luck, boost healing or psychic attunement, or balance emotions.

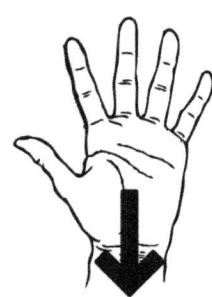

Hold the stone whose properties you want to pull out or force (project) from your life. (Negativity, confusion, being UNgrounded unbalanced emotions, anger, etc.) Right (Projection)

Sit quietly or meditate with these stones and focus on the energy flowing through you.

Creates a continuous flow of energy (a circuit)

Hold the stone whose properties you want to bring to your life. (Luck, self-love, grounding, balanced emotions, mental focus, etc.) Left (Receiving)

Crystal Shapes

Clusters
radiates unity throughout the space and charges other crystals

Pyramids
anchoring crystal and powerful for manifesting desires

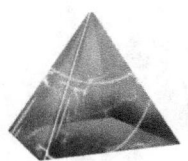

Cubes
consolidates energy, grounding & meditation, and connect to the energy of the Earth

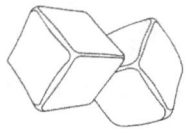

Double Terminated
absorb negative energy, grounding, break down old patterns, and promotes psychic ability

Twin
grounding & harmonizing energies, and balances yin & yang energies

Points
concentrates & directs energy

Crystal Shapes

Wand
healing rituals,
moving &
directing energy

Egg
healing, fertility,
and
balance

Spheres
emits energy
equally
from all direction,
and
ideal for scrying

Druzy
charging, relaxation &
harmony, purify &
amplify body's
natural healing
properties

Geode
amplifies,
conserves &
releases energy,
and
Internal healing

Isis
feminine energy,
healing
emotional
hurt and distress

Choosing the Shape of your Crystal
Look up the energetic properties of your
crystal.

Consider the shape and if it offers benefits such as
enhancing any of the properties you are interested in.

Consider if the crystal shape suits your chosen way to work
with the stone.

Kyanite

Magical Properties
Balance Aura
Calming Emotions
Divine Guidance
Aid Communication with Archangels
Protection
Healing
Telepathy

Classification
Origin
Rarity

Draw or Paste your crystal here

Crystal Pairs With Many
Don't Mix With
Cost
Got it from:
Notes:
Planets - Earth and Uranus
Chakra - Crown, Third Eye, and Throat
Signs - Virgo, Aquarius, Pisces

Identification
Color(s) Blue
Transparency
Lustre
Crystal System - Triclinic
Chemical

Kambaba Jasper

Draw or Paste your crystal here

Magical Properties

Inner peace
Tolerance
Focus during meditation
Intention setting
Release negative thoughts
Increase prosperity
Increase money flow

Classification
Origin
Rarity

Crystal Pairs With Many
Don't Mix With
Cost
Got it from:
Notes:
Planets - Saturn
Chakra - Heart
Signs - Capricorn

Identification
Color(s) Blue and Green
Transparency
Lustre
Crystal System -
Chemical

Mookaite Jasper

Magical Properties
Strength
Stability
Quiets the mind
promote goal reaching
Self Confidence
Inner strength
Removes challenges
Encourage versatility

Classification
Origin
Rarity

Crystal Pairs With
Don't Mix With
Cost
Got it from:
Notes:
Planets - Saturn
Chakra - Root, solar plexus, navel
Signs - Capricorn

Identification
Color(s) Red, yellow, mauve
Transparency
Lustre
Crystal System -
Chemical

Azurite

Magical Properties
Spirit Guides
Angels
Higher Self
Aids the 6 "Clairs"
Mental clarity
Memories
Peace and harmony
Relieves aggravation
Facilitate meditation

Classification
Origin
Rarity

Draw or Paste your crystal here

Crystal Pairs With
Don't Mix With
Cost

Got it from:
Notes:
Planets - Jupiter, Mercury
Chakra - Third eye, Crown
Signs - Sagittarius

Identification
Color(s) Dark blue
Transparency
Lustre
Crystal System -
Chemical

Turquoise

Magical Properties
Connect with the energies of
angel of divine communication
Know and speak your truth
Aids writing
Mood swings
Validation
Courage to do what you need to
Solace

Classification
Origin
Rarity

Draw or Paste your crystal here

Crystal Pairs With
Don't Mix With
Cost

Got it from:
Notes:
Planets - Jupiter, Mercury
Chakra - Throat
Signs - Sagittarius, Gemini

Identification
Color(s) Turquoise
Greenish blue
Transparency
Lustre
Crystal System -
Chemical

Sunstone

Magical Properties
Rest
Self-Healing
Humor
Cheerfulness/positivity
Self-confidence/self-esteem
Temperament
Self-love

Classification
Origin
Rarity

Draw or Paste your crystal here

Crystal Pairs With
Don't Mix With
Cost
Got it from

Notes: Sacral Chakra
Libra and Pisces Signs

Identification
Color(s)
Transparency
Lustre
Crystal System
Chemical

Selenite

Magical Properties

Resolution
Clarity
Enlightenment
Transformation
Clearingaway anger/negativity
Positivity
Past-Life regression
Psychic abilities
Calm & stress relief
Meditation
Healing
Cleanses/charges other crystals

Classification
Origin
Rarity

Draw or Paste your crystal here

Crystal Pairs With
Don't Mix With Salt and water
Cost
Got it from

Identification
Color(s)
Transparency
Lustre
Crystal System
Chemical

Notes: Delicate

Rose Quartz

Draw or Paste your crystal here

Magical Properties
Peace
Harmony
Acceptance
Trust
Love
Healing
Empathy
Intimacy
Romance
Who doesn't need self-love

Classification
Origin
Rarity

Crystal Pairs With
Don't Mix With Sun
Cost
Got it from

Notes: Heart Chakra
Taurus and Leo Sign
Archangel Ariel

Identification
Color(s)
Transparency
Lustre
Crystal System
Chemical

Clear Quartz

Magical Properties

Amplify spells/crystals
Clears away stagnant energy
Cleansing
Healing
Positive vibes
Programmable
Can substitute for any crystal

Classification
Origin
Rarity

Crystal Pairs With
Don't Mix With
Cost
Got it from

Notes: Crown Chakra
Leo Sign
Archangel Raziel

Identification
Color(s)
Transparency
Lustre
Crystal System
Chemical

Lava Rock

Magical Properties
Vitality
Protection
Luck
Love
Calming

Classification
Origin
Rarity

Draw or Paste your crystal here

Crystal Pairs With
Don't Mix With
Cost
Got it from

Notes: Lava beads are porous
and
can absorb essential oils

Identification
Color(s)
Transparency
Lustre
Crystal System
Chemical

Moss Agate

Magical Properties

Growing Love

New beginnings

Trust

Release old fears

New lease on life

Grounding

Drawing strength from nature

Connecting with Fairie

New business/prosperity

Luck

Classification

Origin

Rarity

Draw or Paste your crystal here

Crystal Pairs With

Don't Mix With

Cost

Got it from

Notes:

Cancer and Virgo Signs

Identification

Color(s)

Transparency

Lustre

Crystal System

Chemical

Black Obsidian

Magical Properties
Truth-enhancing
Deep soul healing
Protection
Relieves stress and tension
Absorbs negative energy
Gives clarity of emotions
Blocks psychic attacks
Removes negativity influences
Calming
Compassion
Strength
Prophesy
Helps with shadow self & brings then
to the forefront to be acknolgeked
Breaks through mental barriers
Dissolves mental conditioning

Draw or Paste your crystal here

Classification cooled molten lava
Origin
Rarity

Crystal Pairs With
Don't Mix With   water
Cost
Got it from

Identification
Color(s)
Transparency
Lustre
Crystal System
Chemical

Notes: Base chakra
Scorpio Sign

Put by the bed or under your pillow to draw out mental stress and tension.

Crystal Name

Magical Properties

_____
_____
_____
_____
_____
_____
_____

Draw or Paste your crystal here

Classification _____
Origin _____
Rarity _____
_____
_____

Crystal Pairs With _____
Don't Mix With _____
Cost _____
Got it from _____

Notes: _____

Identification _____
Color(s) _____
Transparency _____
Lustre _____
Crystal System _____
Chemical _____

_____
_____
_____
_____
_____
_____
_____
_____

Crystal Name

Magical Properties

_____

_____

_____

_____

_____

_____

_____

_____

Classification _____

Origin _____

Rarity _____

_____

_____

Draw or Paste your crystal here

Crystal Pairs With _____

Don't Mix With _____

Cost _____

Got it from _____

_____

Notes: _____

Identification _____

Color(s) _____

Transparency _____

Lustre _____

Crystal System _____

Chemical _____

_____

_____

_____

_____

_____

_____

_____

_____

If you're looking for a way to add some beauty and tranquility to your home, are in the "broom closet" and need something that doesn't scream; "Look At Me, I Am A Witch", then consider making crystal bowls. They're pretty to look at and can also be used for spells and other magical purposes.

Grab and Go Combos

Insight
rosemary, lemongrass, nutmeg, orange, aquamarine, howlite, or clear citrine.

Wisdom
parsley, thyme, chamomile, cumin, yellow quartz, and, lapis lazuli

Money
ginger, patchouly, dill, spearmint, gold, malachite, moss agate, and pearl

Peace
cumin, lavender, violet, marjoram, amazonite, blue lace agate, and silver

Relations
pansy, rose, valerian, moss agate, peridot, and sapphire

Love
vanilla, apple, clove, lavender, rose, amber, calcite, moonstone, and rose quartz

Banishing
clove, dragon's blood, garlic, hot pepper, obsidian, jet, and smoky quartz

Protection
angelica, frankincense, sandalwood, amber, carnelian, citrine, and petrified wood

Travel
dill, caraway, fennel mustard, malachite, moonstone, or tiger's eye

Communication
mint, turquoise, tiger's eye, and sodalite

Success
rosemary, saffron, bay, pyrite, clear quartz, and selenite

Courage
horseradish, basil, chives, nettle, pepper, tigers eye, carnelian, and pyrite

Happiness
cinnamon, mint, thyme, lavender, rose quartz, amethyst, citrine, and clear quartz

Health
cinnamon, coriander, eucalyptus, rosemary, sage, thyme, agate, amethyst, jade, and sunstone.

Binding
spiderwort, witch hazel, knotweed, agrimony, and jet

Grab and Go Crystals

Abundance crystals
citrine
clear quartz
amazonite
pyrite
adventurine
tiger's eye

Breaking Bad Habits crystals
amethyst
carnelian
garnet
hematite
lepidolite
citrine

Productivity crystals
tourmaline
green aventurine
pyrite
amazonite
citrine
smoky quartz

Mindfulness crystals
malachite
citrine
obsidian
turquoises
calcite
carnelian

Healing crystals
clear quartz
lapis lazuli
rose quartz
amethyst
aquamarine
garnet

Motivation crystals
pyrite
carnelian
amethyst
bumblebee
unakite
citrine

Friendship crystals
rose quartz
lapis lazuli
emerald
carnelian
blue lace agate
unakite

Happiness crystals
amazonite
amethyst
tourmaline
citrine
clear quartz
smoky quartz

Protection crystals
labradorite
amethyst
tourmaline
smoky quartz
obsidian
prehnite

Manifestation crystals
rose quartz
green jade
sodalite
citrine
selenite
amethyst

Lucky crystals
pyrite
green jade
tiger's eye
citrine
labradorite
carnelian

Work crystals
tourmaline
amethyst
rose quartz
pyrite
selenite
aventurine

Stress Relief crystals
lepidolite
amethyst
rose quarts
fluorite
sodalite
aquamarine

New Start crystals
aventurine
citrine
kyanite
rutile quartz
moonstone
labradorite

Grab and Go Crystals

New Home crystals
tourmaline
amethyst
rose quartz
clear quartz
sodalite
citrine

Anxiety crystals
moonstone
labradorite
rose quartz
amethyst
clear quartz
aquamarine

Love crystals
rhodonite
garnet
moonstone
sodalite
rose quartz
selenite

Letting Go crystals
Rutilated Quartz
Fire Quartz
smoky quartz
serpentine
black obsidian
rose quartz

Student crystals
amethyst
carnelian
fluorite
howlite
tiger's eye
clear quartz

Confidence crystals
citrine
carnelian
rose quartz
red jasper
orange calcite
tiger's eye

Relaxation crystals
amethyst
celestite
fluorite
tourmaline
angelite
howlite

Spirituality crystals
Fluorite
white howlite
labradorite
aura quartz
blue obsidian
amethyst

Creativity crystals
carnelian
amethyst
smoky quartz
clear quartz
citrine
tiger's eye

Trauma crystals
amazonite
lepidolite
fluorite
black line jasper
rose quartz
mangano calcite

Mental Clarity crystals
amethyst
hematite
apatite
sodalite
fluorite
citrine

Animal crystals
amethyst
smoky quartz
selenite
rose quartz
carnelian
agate

Crystals for breakups
rose quartz
malachite
pyrite
septarian
rhodonite
amethyst

Communication crystals
fluorite
kyanite
amazonite
sodalite
smokey quartz
lapis lazuli

Good Sleep crystals
amethyst
clear quartz
hematite
howlite
agate
moonstone

Grab and Go Crystals

Energy crystals
clear quartz
ruby
orange calcite
amethyst
carnelian
fuorite

Plant crystals
moonstone
tourmaline
aventurine
amethyst
clear quartz
malachite

Driving crystals
amethyst
rose quartz
tourmaline
malachite
carnelian
jasper

Crystals for breakups
rose quartz
malachite
pyrite
septarian
rhodonite
amethyst

Crystals for the bath
rose quartz
carnelian
tiger's eye
citrine
amethyst
clear quartz

Crystals for bedroom
celestite
rose quartz
labradorite
selenite
smoky quartz
howlite

I put them in bowls and up high so the wieners don't get into them. I usually add some salt, lavender, and rose quartz to all of them, but whatever feels right or even gives comfort. So you do you, Boo.

I pair selenite and rosemary for protection and cleansing

I pair rose quartz with (duh) roses for love and forgiveness.

I pair amethyst and chamomile for anxiety and stress relief

I pair garnet and pine for commitment anc longevity

I pair black tourmaline and sage to dissolve negativity

I pair citrine with bay leaf for manifestation magic

I pair green adventure and basil for good fortune

I pair carnelian and cinnamon for sparking creativity

I pair moonstone and jasmine for harnessing confidence

CHAPTER 29

Salt

Types of Salt for Magic

Himalayan/Pink Salt ("purest salt on Earth" because of maturing for 250 million years)
Love, Removes negative blockages and curses and cleansing.
Hawaiian Black Salt (harvested from the evaporated water on Hawaiian Island Molokai) Extra strength.
Table Salt
Purifying, protecting, cleansing, and used in culinary recipes.
Kosher Salt (blessed by a Jewish rabbi)
Draws out negativity or absorbs negativity.
Black Salt (leftover ashes or scrapings from cast iron)
Banishing and protection
Alaea/Hawaiian Red Salt (From iron-rich volcanic clay)
Love and sex, block negative energy, protect aggressively to defend an area that has been set with or encircled with it, and are used in culinary recipes (high in nutrients 80+)
Sel Gris Sea Salt
Blessing
Celtic Sea Salt
Protection and attracts financial abundance.
Sea Salt (carries the power of the sea and water elements)
Purification and cleansing help balance emotions.
Cyprus Black Salt (sea water dried in lav beds mixed with charcoal)
Evokes properties of the pyramids, energy from heaven, used in culinary recipes.
Rock Salt
Return to sender, use to reflect negativity to sender.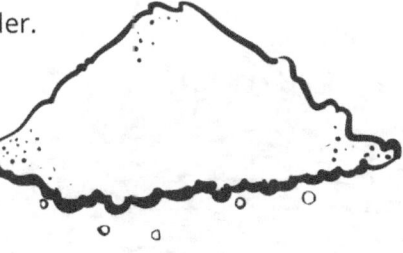
Fleur de Sel Salt (sea salt from France)
Gentler salt, fairies, and elementals.
Gray Salt (developed in clay pools)
Used in liminal workings.
Blue Salt (sea salt mixed with blue flowers)
Protection from the Evil eye, justice, and healing.
That being said, you can make any color salt by mixing colored herbs with it.
Herb infused Salts (salt infused with edible herbs)
Choose an herb that aligns with your intentions.
Epsom Salt
Use in the bath to reduce inflammation and muscle pain, and destress.
Pickling Salt (purest form, no added agents)
Purification, preservation of love, prosperity, etc., and used in culinary recipes.

CHAPTER 30

Disposal of Ritual Offerings

The Power of Fire - Nearly any ritual offering can be disposed of by burning. Sometimes, burning an item can be tied into the working of the spell; if you're trying to get rid of something in your life permanently, burning is a great way to ensure it won't return.

Earth & Water - If your offering is an organic item, such as fruits, vegetables, tobacco, or other plant material, you may want to consider burying it. A garden is an excellent place to do this, particularly if you have a compost bin because the nutrients will go back into the soil as the offering biodegrades, continuing the life cycle. Disposal of organic items into a moving body of water, such as a river or the ocean, is also acceptable in many traditions. Make sure that you're not putting any non-organic materials in the water.

Sharing With Wildlife - As long as they haven't been tainted with anything toxic, you can feel free to scatter them outdoors for the local critters to snack on. They consume it, and the life cycle of the continues on."

Also, please don't discount the science of nature itself. Some offering items can be left out until they go away on their own. For instance, if you make an offering of consecrated water in a bowl, it will eventually evaporate. Likewise, if you do an outdoor ritual and offer herbs and flowers, those will blow away at some point and find their way to a new home.

What About Messy, Gross Things? - Sometimes, let's face it, we do work that involves something negative. In cases like this, you probably want to get the item as far away as possible. In cases like this, simply because of the nature of the ritual, you may want to go ahead and find a place such as a landfill, a port-a-john, or some other foul place to get rid of the items. Just ensure you're not putting anything into the ecosystem that will cause damage down the road.

CHAPTER 31

Self
Reflection

Welcoming the Light

 As the Earth slowly awakens from its slumber, Imbolc invites us to witness the first signs of spring and to connect with the stirring energies of growth and transformation.

This journaling space is an invitation to explore the unique magic that Imbolc holds. Just as the earth begins to quicken with the promise of new life, our spirits can awaken to fresh possibilities, creative inspirations, and gentle nudges of personal growth. Through the pages of this journal, we embark on a reflective and introspective adventure, embracing the themes of purification, light, and the stirring of seeds that lie dormant within.

Imbolc is traditionally associated with the Celtic goddess Brigid, a guardian of the hearth, a muse of inspiration, and a healer. Her energy permeates this season, offering us a guiding light as we delve into our own inner landscapes. This journaling practice encourages you to tap into your intuition, harness the creative fire within, and sow the seeds of your dreams with intention.

As you embark on this Imbolc journey, let the flickering candlelight symbolize the returning sun, and let your words be the seeds planted in the fertile soil of your soul. Embrace the opportunity to release the old, welcome the new, and honor the subtle shifts within and around you. May your journaling experience be a source of insight, healing, and transformation during this season of awakening.

Self-Reflections

Holidays can be chaotic, and we seem to separate from our daily routines. Are there any people in your life that you've lost contact with during the winter months? How about reaching out to them by text or email?

Self-Reflections

What are the projects you have planned for this year? Do you need to order any supplies?

Self-Reflections

What is one thing you dislike about the season changing from cold to hot? What can you do now to alleviate some of that dislike? (ex. Buy bug spray to help combat mosquitos. or stock up on sunscreen to prevent sunburn)

Self-Reflections

Are there any changes in your life that are making you feel off-balanced? Are there any small habits you can start that might make you feel more relaxed?

Self-Reflections

3 reasons you are grateful for Brighid. (Or whichever deity you will honor today!)

Self-Reflections

3 reasons you are grateful for Imbolc.

Self-Reflections

3 things you love about nature at this time of year.

Self-Reflections

3 blessings that have come your way this Winter.

Self-Reflections

3 opportunities that lie before you with the growing days.

Self-Reflections

3 things you are looking forward to in the coming Spring.

Self-Reflections

3 things that have already manifested from your Yule intent!